Allegorising Thought on the Shakespearean Stage

Allegorising Thought on the Shakespearean Stage

The Discovery of the Mind

Claire Guéron

EDINBURGH
University Press

Edinburgh University Press is one of the leading university presses in the UK. We publish academic books and journals in our selected subject areas across the humanities and social sciences, combining cutting-edge scholarship with high editorial and production values to produce academic works of lasting importance. For more information visit our website: edinburghuniversitypress.com

Edinburgh University Press Ltd
The Tun – Holyrood Road
12(2f) Jackson's Entry
Edinburgh EH8 8PJ

Typeset in 11.5/13pt Adobe Sabon by
Cheshire Typesetting Ltd, Cuddington, Cheshire, and
printed and bound in Great Britain

A CIP record for this book is available from the British Library

ISBN 978 1 3995 1065 3 (hardback)
ISBN 978 1 3995 1067 7 (webready PDF)
ISBN 978 1 3995 1068 4 (epub)

Contents

Figures

Acknowledgements

I am grateful for all the help and support I received in the process of writing this book.

Allegorising Thought grew out of a bus ride between Galway and Dublin Airport, on the way back from a conference of the European Society for the Study of English (ESSE). I was lucky to be sitting next to Professor Ladan Niayesh, who was kind enough, as our conversation veered between East Asian martial arts and the Early Modern workshops we had just attended, to take a constructive interest in helping me turn my conference paper into a book project. Her suggestions during that bus ride and her follow-up advice and support over the years have been truly invaluable. My first thanks thus go out to Ladan Niayesh, without whose unstinting help and friendship the book that eventually took shape would never have been written.

Moving from the Emerald Isle to the no less beautiful hills of Scotland, I wish to thank Michelle Houston, my Commissioning Editor at Edinburgh University Press, who believed in my project from the start and guided me through the submission and review processes with a steady and supportive hand. My thanks also to Susannah Butler, Assistant Editor at Edinburgh University Press, for seeing me through the publication process, and to the anonymous reviewers who contributed their time, expertise and constructive comments. My gratitude naturally also goes out to Professor Bridget Escolme, whom I first met on the occasion of the wonderfully named 'Bloody Passions' symposium held at the University of Portsmouth, and whose helpful and encouraging feedback carried me over the finish line.

I thank the University of Burgundy for granting me the sabbatical I needed to write up the final chapters, and my colleague Sophie Aymes-Stokes for patiently letting me bounce ideas off her over coffee and chocolates. I also wish to thank the conference organisers, workshop conveners and book editors who hosted my earlier efforts, thus allowing me to work my way towards this book, including François Laroque, Pascale Drouet, Yan Brailowsky, Sophie Chiari, Attila Kiss, Jessica Dyson, Stephen Curtis, Michele Marrapodi and many others.

I am grateful to my parents, Jacqueline and Maurice Guéron, for introducing me to Shakespeare at an early age and encouraging me ever since, to my sister Sophie Guéron and her family for their unflagging support, and to my husband, Philippe, for believing in me.

Introduction

And departing from hir, he went by and by to signifie what answer he had received; but before he came to where the king lay, his mind was altered.[1]

In their search for novelty with which to sustain the interest of audiences in the new commercial playhouses, Shakespeare and his fellow playwrights found a treasure trove of inspiration in the narrative works of Plutarch, Holinshed, Cinthio, Bandello, Lodge, and others. With this treasure came problems. Dramatising a narrative source meant devising ways of theatrically rendering an omniscient narrative voice, one with a God's eye view of extensive landscapes, hidden locations and the inside of a character's mind. The three appear in combination in the above quotation from Raphael Holinshed's *Chronicles*, Shakespeare's principal source for *Macbeth*, when a gentleman is described as changing his mind about committing regicide as he rides from a witch's den to the king's castle. Leaving aside the gentleman's progression inside the castle, the two remaining difficulties combined in this line, namely how to show a character travelling over wide expanses of land and how to show a character's inner thoughts, might be rendered mimetically, with a player walking back and forth across the stage and speaking aloud to himself. This is indeed how some of Macbeth's soliloquies might be staged, such as in 1.7.1–28,[2] when the would-be murderer voices his misgivings. However, the line quoted above does not specify how the change of mind occurred or whether travelling contributed to the gentleman's thoughts in any way. The ensuing depiction of thought as a mysterious process could not be easily conveyed by a soliloquy. Neither could it be conveyed by making no mention whatsoever of the character's inner debate, for his change of disposition would then appear absurd and unmotivated.

What appears in the above example is that Shakespeare was confronted with the problem not only of representing thought content but of representing thought as mysterious or hidden. This need can be related to the themes of the narratives he adapted, most of which involved betrayal, suspicion and deception. It can also be related to a growing interest in the workings of the mind in the early modern period, as attested by treatises such as Thomas Wright's *Passions of the Minde in Generall* (1601) and Timothy Bright's *Treatise of Melancholy* (1586). What was needed was a way to represent thought with pithy *energeia*, yet also as an object of wonder and enquiry.

The argument of this book is that Shakespeare drew on the human and material components of theatrical performance – the players' bodies and gestures, playhouse architecture, stage properties and costumes, performance style and audience – to make characters' thoughts visible. I will also argue that such indirect encoding strategies produced an excess of meaning, whereby a character's thoughts transcended the dramatic situation and took on broader philosophical relevance. Deriving as it did from the parameters of theatrical production, this excess of meaning was only partly under the playwright's control. For Shakespeare, the problem of staging thought was coupled with other staging problems: how to contract space, how to show the inside of a building or the inside of the body, how to show a crowd tearing through the streets of a city, how to show a blushing character, how to make a distant player's facial expression visible, how to control a restive audience. It was by juggling these practical constraints that Shakespeare gave his allegories of thought the ring of authenticity and inscribed them within the Renaissance mind–body debate. I have chosen to explore this link between theatricality and Renaissance mind theory through the lens of allegory, in order to connect stage semiotics, textual poetics, and the pedagogical imagery of early modern Galenic treatises.

The Material Turn

My performance-centred approach is inspired by the material turn in Shakespeare studies, allied with audience-response theory and phenomenology, both of which posit the playgoer's experience as a primary source of meaning. These approaches are roughly contemporary with the 1997 building of Shakespeare's Globe, a replica of the 1599 Globe theatre that hosted the original performances of most of the plays discussed in this book. For scholars affiliated with Shakespeare's Globe, such as Farah Karim-Cooper, its Head of Higher Education and Research, the venue, later extended by the Sam Wanamaker Playhouse,[3] offers a fruitful testing ground for hypotheses about early modern performance styles and audience reception. Even beyond its immediate reach, the building has contributed to a revived interest in the pragmatics of performance and reception, in the play as experience rather than text. These approaches have given us Jennifer Low and Nova Myhill's *Imagining the Audience in Early Modern Drama, 1558–1642* (2011), Farah Karim-Cooper and Tiffany Stern's *Shakespeare's Theatres and the Effects of Performance* (2013), Farah Karim-Cooper's *The Hand on the Shakespearean Stage* (2016) and Miranda Fay Thomas's *Shakespeare's Body Language* (2020).

Implied in this phenomenological recentring of scholarship is an interest in the way the non-verbal components of a theatrical production generate meaning in excess of the play-text. This issue is semiotically codified in Robert Weimann and Douglas Bruster's theory of 'contrariety', whereby the 'presentational' component of performance (typically the actor) vies with its 'representational' one (the character).[4] Weimann and Bruster's trademark concept – later taken up by Erika T. Lin[5] – is the *locus/platea* binary, introduced as a means of distinguishing degrees of geographical, ontological and epistemological proximity (the term 'levels of awareness' is sometimes used) between character and audience. In recent years, semiotic approaches to the early modern stage have also taken a turn towards object-oriented materialism. This angle too is useful, as early modern playwrights – Shakespeare in particular – often played on the interchangeability of actors and stage properties, as when Snout the tinker 'presents' (3.1.67) a wall in *A Midsummer Night's Dream* or when Lear takes his daughter for a joint stool in the *King Lear* Quarto, or even when the assembled court takes Hermione for a statue in *The Winter's Tale*. Pamela Bickley and Jenny Stevens have convincingly drawn on 'thing theory' to foreground the duality of stage props as both objects in their own right and signifying components of the drama.[6] Though these authors do not refer to the parameters of theatrical production as allegories, the term will be useful in identifying common ground between early modern stage practices and early modern culture's poetic, medical and theological discourses on the mind.

Allegory: Early Modern Terminology

Given my emphasis on spectacle rather than playscript, my use of the term 'allegory' requires some theoretical contextualising. In the conceptual toolbox of our own time, justification for referring to non-verbal theatrical structures as 'allegories' can be found in the concept of 'scenic' figures of speech developed in the 1930s and 40s by the Prague School of structuralist and semiotic criticism. In this theatrical co-optation of rhetoric, a prop, costume or piece of scenery is given the status of 'metaphor' or 'metonymy' when it stands for something related to it by analogy or proximity. For example, in Jiří Veltruský's concept of 'scenic metonymy', 'a prop stands for its user'.[7] I propose to extend this principle to what could be referred to as 'scenic allegory' or 'stage allegory', whereby props and other parts of the spectacle stand for unseen thoughts and emotions, or for images of the mind. Yet my interest in enlisting allegory as a working concept is also rooted in early modern usage.

Renaissance rhetoricians followed classical precedent in defining allegory as a rhetorical trope, as when George Puttenham glosses it as 'when we speak one thing and think another'.[8] Though overly broad, this definition is useful in its flexibility, and in its foregrounding of thought. It nevertheless requires narrowing down, which Puttenham does by comparing allegory to metaphor:

> Allegory is when we do speak in sense translative [...] as before we said of the metaphor. As for example, if we should call the commonwealth a ship, the prince a pilot, the councillors mariners, the storms wars, the calm and haven peace, this is spoken all in allegory. (247)

Here, Puttenham is illustrating Quintilian's definition of allegory as an 'extended metaphor', which we also find in John Hoskyns's description of allegory as 'the continual following of a metaphor' (401). In his letter to Raleigh, Edmund Spenser doubles down on this notion of extension by describing his epic as a 'continued allegory' (299). This idea of allegory as an 'extended' system of correspondences is naturally of interest for analysing plot-based forms like drama. In several of this book's chapters, I will be identifying master metaphors that run through and undergird the plays, including the Hydra metaphor in Chapter 5.

Contrasting with this proximity to metaphor is the Renaissance emphasis on allegory as a 'dark and covert' mode of expression (232). Thus, Puttenham compares allegory to the figure of 'enigma' (249), and Spenser calls it a 'dark conceit' (296) in which meaning is 'cloudily enwrapped' (299). Mystery vies with openness in George Gascoigne's statement that he may 'discover [his] disquiet in shadows *per allegoriam*' (163). The oxymoronic juxtaposition of 'discovery' and 'shadows' cuts to the heart of allegory's paradox: how it simultaneously discovers and conceals, obscures and clarifies. The 'dark side' of allegory is relevant to my claim about Shakespeare's interest in representing thinking as a mysterious process, and I will be building on it in Chapters 2, 3 and 6.

Also of interest to theatrical analysis is the early modern habit of defining allegory – of allegorising it, in fact – in theatrical terms. Thus, Puttenham describes allegory as 'the courtier' and 'dissembler', who wears a 'disguise' or 'cloak' (292) and whose words 'bear a contrary countenance to their intent' (247). As for Spenser, he describes allegory as 'a shady vele'.[9] Intriguing though they are, these theatrical echoes are not quite the same thing as granting allegorical status to theatrical performance itself. This will require a more up-to-date definition of allegory, yet one that does not sever all ties with early modern rhetoric.

Despite their rich semantics, the definitions discussed above are not sufficient, for they leave out what we now call 'personification', the practice of humanising an object, animal or abstract notion. In poetry, this was *prosopopoeia*, which Puttenham defines as follows:

> if ye will feign any person with such features, qualities and conditions, or if ye will attribute any human quality, as reason or speech, to dumb creatures or other insensible things, and do study (as one may say) to give them human person, it is [...] *prosopopoeia*. (275)

Puttenham goes on to adduce the characters 'avarice, envy and old age' in Chaucer's translation of the *Roman de la Rose*. As the word 'feign' suggests, there is theatrical potential in the *prosopopoeia*. This potential is foregrounded in Hoskyns's definition of *prosopopoeia* as 'feigning the [...] discourse of some such persons as either are not at all, or, if there be, speak not but in imagination' (426). *Prosopopoeia*, as Lynn Enterline has discussed, was one of the principal means of instruction in the humanist curriculum, with grammar school boys set to deliver emotional speeches in the manner of mythological characters such as Hecuba.[10] *Prosopopoeia*, as both a figure of speech and an oratorial practice, thus suggests a kinship between personification and stage performance in the minds of playwrights, players, and audiences with a grammar school education. In the wider culture, personification and performance also came together in the humanised vices and virtues of the late medieval morality plays, Tudor civic pageants and Jacobean masques. These figures were not referred to as *prosopopoeia* (or by any other generic designation as far as I have been able to establish) but were conceptually related to it as embodiments of abstract notions.

'Emblem' is another term we have come to use interchangeably with 'allegory'. Early modern rhetoricians, however, observed a distinction between allegory and emblem. For Hoskyns, the difference lies in the fact that in the emblem, allegorical meaning is distributed between a picture, a motto and an explanatory 'application' (also called 'subscription'). The issue is not the pictorial component *per se*, but Hoskyns's understanding of 'emblem' as referring only to the picture and motto. Without the application, the emblem does not make sense and therefore does not constitute a full allegory. Thus, Hoskyns writes, 'an emblem is but the one part of a similitude, the other part expressed [...] in one sentence' (402). This implies that if 'emblem' is taken to mean all three components, it becomes an allegory.

In what follows, I will claim personification and emblem as representatives of the allegorical mode – in keeping with present-day use – in order to include performing bodies and iconic stage sets or properties within the scope of my 'allegories of thought'. Nor should this presentist expansion be taken as too forceful an annexation, as early modern rhetoricians were quite willing to acknowledge the proximity of allegory, *prosopopoeia* and emblem. Puttenham's nicknames for allegory ('the dissembler') and for *prosopopoeia* ('the counterfeit impersonation') testify to this proximity. Concerning emblem and allegory, as seen above, the difference Hoskyns establishes is only a matter of which parts of the emblem are being considered.

Claiming the full range of rhetorical and iconic forms discussed above for my study of Shakespeare's 'allegories of mind' will allow me to address the contribution of cultural practices built around those forms to early modern theatrical allegory. These practices include morality plays, civic pageants, classroom impersonations and the emblem tradition. Because they were so central to early modern visual, humanist and festive cultures, these practices were naturally incorporated in the drama of the second half of the sixteenth century, along with their attendant dynamics of mystery and revelation. Beyond the direct source material they may have provided, these forms offered templates for iconic constructions of meaning. For example, the emblem offered intriguing ways of combining visual and verbal input in an initially puzzling but ultimately edifying way. The effort of decrypting the puzzle was key to both enjoyment and edification, in keeping with the Horatian principle of teaching by pleasing. Yet even as they incorporated extra-theatrical allegorical forms, early modern dramatists were putting them to new uses, because both the poetics of allegory and ideas about allegory's purpose were undergoing profound changes. In short, allegory was becoming less about concepts and more about experience.

Early Modern Practice: 'Grounded' Allegory and Experience

An illustration of how the deployment of allegory was mutating in Shakespeare's day appears in his late Romance *Cymbeline*. Steeped in Roman and Celtic folklore, *Cymbeline* is rich in classical resonances, thanks in part to a style marked by apostrophes, such as invocations to personified virtues and Greco-Roman deities. An arresting instance is Imogen's reaction to finding out that peasants can be kinder than their social betters, which is expressed in the following rhyming couplet:

> Our courtiers say all's savage but at court:
> Experience, O, thou disprov'st report.
>
> (4.2.33–4)

The contrast between personified 'Experience' and 'report' indicates that the line involves a psychomachic reduction of Imogen's thoughts, with the struggle between the personified figures of report and Experience functioning as a counterpart to the character's cognitive bewilderment. Personified Experience was in fact a commonplace of sermons and philosophical treatises, as in Jean Calvin's comment that 'Experience is the schoolmistress of fools.'[11] In *Cymbeline*, however, the personified figure of Experience is deployed in such a way as to convey the character's lived experience, as opposed to the concept of Experience. For one thing, Imogen's use of an invocation reflects her heightened emotional state, coupled with a developing spirit of inquiry. Next, given that 'experience' could also mean 'experiment', personified Experience is tied to the evil Queen's pharmaceutical experimentation, which results in Imogen going through altered states of consciousness. Finally, in showing a character apostrophising Experience, Shakespeare is destabilising the opposition between abstract and concrete inherent to the concept of allegory. If allegory is a concrete figuration of an abstract notion,[12] how is the difficult-to-picture figure of Experience more concrete than 'hands-on' experience, especially on a stage where the suffering figure of Imogen is so much more vivid than the vague personification she invokes? Here, Shakespeare seems to be subtly transferring the job of personifying Experience from the verbal figure of speech to the physical body on the stage. The embodied figure of Imogen becomes the personification of experience in an immediate and sustained, or 'extended' way.

The issue of experience is at the heart of twentieth- and twenty-first-century research into early modern allegory. Walter Benjamin, Angus Fletcher and Judith Anderson see the late sixteenth and early seventeenth centuries as marking a shift away from the Platonic abstraction of classical and medieval allegory, in an effort to enlist allegorical form for the depiction of reality. Art philosopher and critic Walter Benjamin might have been taking his cue from *Cymbeline*'s Imogen when he insisted that allegory could truly express experience, which was rooted in awareness of the world's impermanence and of the unbridgeable divide between reality and the ideal. In his discussion of baroque 'mourning' drama (*Trauerspiele*), Benjamin elaborates on the way seventeenth-century drama turns the dead body into an emblem of the historical experience of loss,[13] with no redeeming suggestion of Platonic or Christian transcendence.[14] This aspect will be in evidence in my discussion of *Cymbeline* in Chapter 3.

For Angus Fletcher and Judith Anderson, Spenser's *Faerie Queene* marked the turning-point from Platonic to experience-bound allegory. In an essay provocatively entitled 'Allegory Without Ideas',[15] Fletcher points out that, perhaps as an effect of the sixteenth-century flowering of historical chronicle, Spenser's *Faerie Queene* is replete with references to current events and courtly characters (including, of course, Queen Elizabeth herself). Fletcher sees the same trend at work in the seventeenth-century masque, where 'the burlesque [...] antimasque undermines the eternal perfection that the allegorical idea had been imagined, since Plato, to possess'.[16] For Anderson, *The Faerie Queene* marks a shift towards psychological realism, thanks to its sustained reliance on what Fletcher refers to as a 'projection',[17] that is, when a minor character represents a facet of a major character. Though one could argue that medieval moralities are such projections, they lack the fluidity of Spenser's allegories, whereby a given character may drift in and out of allegorical status. For example, in the first book of Spenser's *Faerie Queene*, Redcrosse Knight's despair is first projected as Sans Joy, then as Despair. Given that Sans Joy is convincing as a character in his own right, he can be detached from his allegorical function, which is then taken over by Despair, allowing for Redcrosse's desperation to be depicted as an idiosyncratic psychological '*process*',[18] rather than as a timeless abstraction. To account for this turn towards process and realism, Anderson coined the term 'grounded' allegory. By 'grounded', she refers to a use of allegory that 'combines mind with matter, emblem with narrative, abstraction with history'.[19] I will be building on this definition throughout the book.

About two decades before *Cymbeline*, drama underwent a similar shift towards realism. Anthony S. Brennan has noted a dissatisfaction with dramatised allegorical pageantry around the late 1580s, leading playwrights to experiment with more integrated forms: 'Drama became a complete form when the various tatters of older forms – allegorical figures, prologues, inductions, choruses, and so forth were digested by the play proper.'[20] With the concept of 'digesting' allegorical figures, Brennan seems to be referring to the process of projection discussed above, whereby a character functions as both an autonomous *persona* and a hypostasis of another character's mind. In toggling from one to the other, the plays construct a representation of the mind as a complex, layered and heterogeneous entity. In Shakespeare scholarship, this technique has been identified by the psychoanalytical school of criticism, as when Sigmund Freud and Ernest Jones, later followed by Jacques Lacan, suggested that Claudius functioned as a repressed double to Hamlet (hence the latter's inability to carry out his revenge).[21] Though psychoanalytical readings can be enlightening, they leave out much of the context that gives Shakespeare's allegories their 'grounded' character, including the overlapping semiotic practices of theatrical performance and Galenic treatises on the mind.

Staging Early Modern Allegories of Mind

Shakespeare's characters use the term 'mind' in roughly the same way that we use it now, that is, as the locus of thought. When *Macbeth*'s King Duncan muses that 'there's no art / To find the mind's construction in the face' (1.4.11–12), we know he means that one cannot tell what people are thinking or feeling by looking at them. Yet however unproblematic its use may seem, defining the 'mind' was a thorny subject for early modern natural philosophers delving into the causes of 'melancholy', with 'melancholy' often functioning as a catch-all term for all disturbances affecting mood and cognition. The underlying issue was the mind's relation to the body, or in other words, the degree to which physiological phenomena affect the quality of one's thoughts and emotional well-being. For authors like Timothy Bright, Thomas Wright and Robert Burton, the issue was how to reconcile the materialist Galenic model of the mind with the spiritual Christian one. The difficulty of this approach is illustrated in Bright's 1586 *Treatise of Melancholy*. Though Bright mostly aligns the mind with the immortal and all-powerful soul, he sometimes makes it synonymous with the material brain. For example, Bright's statement that the mind 'discerneth, [...] remembereth, [...] foreseeth, [...] determineth' recalls his earlier statement ascribing the same faculties to the inner brain, which 'thinketh, imagineth and remembereth'.[22] This ambivalence, part of what present-day scholars refer to as 'the mind–body problem', was sometimes camouflaged by the recourse to allegory.

Unsurprisingly, given the difficulty of the subject and invisibility of the processes involved, early modern authors writing about thought, emotions and the structure of the mind often relied on allegory, including theatrical allegory, to convey their meaning. Examples appear in Bright, in Wright's *Passions of the Minde in Generall* (1601) and in Burton's *Anatomy of Melancholy* (1621), where the mind is in turns likened to a fortress or castle, the sun, a hand, an eye, a father, a judge weighing evidence, a god or, more originally, a hydraulic pump.[23] Some of these representations had a long history; for example, the allegory of the mind as a castle or citadel protecting reason from the emotions, as discussed by Christiana Whitehead and David Wiles, harked back to Stoicism[24] and early Christianity. What is remarkable about many of these allegories is how stage compatible they are. The allegory of the mind as a castle or citadel, for example, had already become invested in the symbolism of the stage by the late medieval period.[25] In Bright, images of the spirit as the 'hand' of the soul,[26] of the body as the mind's 'axe or flail',[27] and of the mind as an engine[28] hint at the rich allegorical potential of theatrical gesture, stage properties and stage machinery. Also relevant was the 'memory theatre', a widely recognised mnemonic method and metaphor, implying that it was no great imaginative leap for an audience to take stage space as an image of a character's mind.[29]

It might seem, then, that the images contained in the medical and theological treatises of Shakespeare's time are harnessed by the plays for the purpose of characterisation and thought representation. Though this is partly the case I wish to make, such harnessing is never straightforward, as the proto-scientific clarity purported by these didactic allegories tends to break down when transposed to the stage, given that theatrical allegories are inherently unstable and reversible. Dramatisation also exposes the shakiness of the allegories used in Galenic and philosophical treatises. The question of whether the mind is material or immaterial comes no nearer to resolution when Bright compares it to a judge, or when Marcus Aurelius compares it to a citadel. For if the mind is to be understood as a citadel, are the walls of the citadel to be taken as some ineffable operation of grace (as in Calvinist theology) or as actual tissue, such as the membranes of the brain or spirit-carrying sinews of the body (as in Galenic humoral theory)? The fuzziness of such images is brought out on the stage by the double semiotics of the staged allegory, whereby the object functions both mimetically and allegorically. If we take the example of Hamlet's 'distracted globe' (1.5.97), the commonplace of the mind as theatre is complicated by the containing presence of the actual Globe theatre, which undercuts the sense of closure and withdrawal otherwise associated with the image of an inner theatre. The resulting indeterminacy and its relation to the plays' *agon* is what this book is about.

Choice of Corpus

Throughout this book, I will be relating the 'grounded' quality of Shakespeare's staged allegories to the depth of his characterisation. By 'grounded', in an extension of Anderson's definition, I am referring to allegories that emerge from the process of adaptation, are rooted in the material givens of theatrical production, and illustrate concrete mental processes. A 'grounded allegory' occurs when body, gesture, movement, stage space or interaction with the audience can be constructed as a non-mimetic (or only partially mimetic) representation of a character's thoughts, emotions or state of mind.

Many if not most of Shakespeare's plays lend themselves to this kind of exploration, as mind-reading and theatricality are concerns that cut through the canon. Yet several plays stand out as exhibiting particular interest in modes of concealing, exposing or conveying inner thoughts and emotions. These naturally include the great tragedies and Histories, with their focus on treason and betrayal. Of these I have chosen *Macbeth*, because it combines the *topos* of concealment with an often-noted allegorical use of stage space[30] and Galen-inspired discourses on the mind.

Betrayal can also encompass self-betrayal, suggesting that characters at odds with themselves offer fertile ground for allegorical investigation. Though the Prince of Denmark comes to mind, *Hamlet*'s choice of soliloquy as the main vehicle for the character's thoughts keeps its allegories of mind (such as the above-mentioned 'globe') on a mostly discursive level. Instead, I will focus on the Roman tragedies, where alienation, rooted in the conflicted models of self which are implied by the Stoic ethics of self-control and self-negating *pietà*, is embedded in the plays' performative dimension. In this category I have chosen *Julius Caesar* and *Coriolanus* because of their respective reliance on projection allegory and the master metaphor of the Hydra, or water monster.

Though the emphasis on inner division rules out the Romantic comedies, in which the characters' sense of alienation is superficial enough to be overcome by the plot's ultimate resolution of conflicts, the darker 'problem' comedies withhold such resolution, even staging a struggle for self-control as one of the mainsprings of laughter. I will explore this dynamic in *The Merchant of Venice*, which turns the theatrical problem of staging emotional suppression into an exploration of the expressive potential of the static body on the stage.

Betrayal and alienation come together in the phenomenon of blushing, which raises specific problems of performance. Though blushing comes up remarkably often in early modern drama, perhaps most famously in *Much Ado About Nothing*, *Troilus and Cressida* will be the object of my study because the play's sustained juxtaposition of blushing and masks raises the question of whether the blush is a manifestation of deep-rooted otherness within the self.

Romance offers a particularly rich ground for the exploration of otherness as it often involves transformation and disguise. *Cymbeline* stands out because its master metaphor of poison is tied to an allegorising of gesture as the visual counterpart of forbidden thoughts. Furthermore, *Cymbeline*'s insistent recourse to apostrophe, as seen above, offers a hint as to the importance of allegory for the play. This use of rhetorical personification as a gateway to spectacle-based allegory was in fact another criterion of choice for this corpus, in which allegory-laden speeches work in tandem with allegorical characters, settings and props. An example of such proximity appears in *Julius Caesar*, when Brutus addresses a personification of 'slumber' while contemplating the sleeping figure of his young servant, Lucius:

> O murd'rous slumber!
> Layest thou thy leaden mace upon my boy,
> That plays thee music?
>
> (4.3.267–9)

In these lines, to which I will return in Chapter 1, the rhetorical allegory of 'slumber' as an arresting sergeant overlaps with the character Lucius's own allegorical function as a projection of Brutus's mind. More than a tip-off for the spectator/reader, this conflation of rhetorical and projection allegories reveals the layered quality of theatrical allegory.

This book looks at how the plays use rhetorical allegory and conventional morality play figures as springboards towards forms of allegory more deeply embedded in the various parameters – or Aristotelian 'parts'[31] – of theatrical production. With a view to demonstrating the specificity of such theatrical forms of signification, I will proceed along a spectrum, from the most conventional or text-based allegories to those that are most tightly bound to the here-and-now of performance. I will argue that the more performative the allegory is, the more complex and layered is the image of the mind that emerges.

Outline

Julius Caesar is an apt play to start off this series as its protagonist's mental struggle is filtered through Brutus's young servant, Lucius, who evokes a long textual tradition of allegorical servants, including *The Faerie Queene*'s *Anamnestes*. In Spenser's epic poem, *Anamnestes* is a young page who assists a librarian in the allegorical Castle of Alma by bringing him old books and records. As the personification of his master's recollective faculty, *Anamnestes* offers a pithy picture of how memory works. In Chapter 1, I argue that *Julius Caesar*'s Lucius, like *Anamnestes*, stands for his master's power of recollection. As he moves back and forth between the inner sanctum of Brutus's house and Rome's streets and Forum, Lucius allows Shakespeare to stage the hypostasis of Brutus's memory, splitting it into a historical, public component and a private one. Ultimately, Lucius's comings and goings identify the play's tragic outcome as the result of Brutus's inability to acknowledge and reconcile the contending claims on his memory. Lucius's proximity to his prototype in Spenser's narrative may suggest that his allegorical function is not particularly linked to the parameters of theatrical performance; a description of his actions might have conveyed his function as well as their staged performance. Yet I will argue that the play adds complexity to Lucius's allegorical function by playing on the versatility of theatrical space and by drawing attention to the flesh-and-blood presence of the player performing Lucius's part, thus highlighting the embodied dimension of memory and affect.

The versatility of theatrical space is a more sustained feature in *Macbeth*, with the castle of the mind functioning as a master metaphor, in conjunction with other patterns. Chapter 2 uses T. S. Eliot's definition of the 'objective correlative', which he famously applied to Lady Macbeth's hand-rubbing scene, in order to connect the play's two signifiers of irreversibility, doorways and oaths. Beginning with the Holinshed source's insistent correlation of emotional states and motion through space (including multiple instances of thresholds being crossed and doors broken down), I build on Tim Fitzpatrick's work on the semiotics of the two-door Globe stage,[32] combined with the pervasive doorway imagery of early modern affect literature, to argue that the play's stage movements double as allegorical representations of a mind committing to evil. This correspondence is charged with a vibrant sense of mystery thanks to a string of ritual oaths and promises that are somehow always a bit 'off', or in speech act terms, 'infelicitous'. In such 'threshold' allegory, the mystical dimension of the device is stronger than its explanatory dimension, in keeping with the play's supernatural bent.

The equation between spatial and mental movement is more organically rooted in the performing body in *Cymbeline*, where gestures come to express hidden and forbidden thoughts, in a manner redolent of – or rather anticipating – the Freudian unconscious. The paradoxical link between thought and gesture is implicit in Imogen's pun on 'tender' in the line 'Why tender'st thou that paper to me with / A look untender?' (3.4.11–12). This sense of an 'Other' expressing itself through the body is tightly bound up with the Ovidian transformation theme common to many of Shakespeare's Romances and, more specifically, with the 'poison' motif that runs through Shakespeare's Celtic/Roman play. In discussing gesture as an allegory of hidden or unconscious thought in Chapter 3, I will come close to a psychoanalytical reading of *Cymbeline*. However, I will also argue that the pre-Cartesian belief in the body's cognitive faculties may moot the need for Freudian theories. In *Cymbeline*, the expressive potential of gesture is grounded in its supposedly voluntary nature. Yet on the early modern stage, the allegorical potential of involuntary motions offers a perhaps even more baffling representation of selfhood.

Staging a blushing character was both a problem and a matter of endless fascination for early modern companies, based on the sheer number of references to onstage blushing in the plays. My fourth chapter focuses on *Troilus & Cressida*, where blushing is caught up in a network of meta-theatrical signifiers of concealment such as masks, veils, tents and curtains. Though these may come up as verbal metaphors, my interest is in their material manifestations as stage properties. What gives concealing props allegorical resonance is the fact than in contemporary medical treatises by the likes of Annibale Pocaterra, Lodowick Bryskett and Robert Burton, blushing was commonly likened to drawing a mask, veil or handkerchief over the face. Given the physical near impossibility of performing a blush on demand, the mask over a player's face can be taken as what it is, namely a mask, or as a theatrical stand-in for the blush itself. In a play very much focused on issues of personal responsibility and blame, the allegory of the veil constructs blushing either as a completely involuntary action (if the mask is a mask, designed to conceal) or as a deliberate gesture (if the donned mask is the blush itself). Because blushing was widely seen as stemming from a virtuous sense of shame, the allegory of the mask/veil/kerchief raises the question of whether moral sense dwells in the body, in the mind, or in that curious intermediary entity sometimes referred to as 'nature' in early modern affect literature. In *Troilus and Cressida*, the question of embodied moral agency bears on issues both of manly valour (or *virtus*) and feminine modesty.

The fourth chapter's discussion of blushing, a phenomenon that most agree requires an audience, is a reminder of the audience's central role in generating meaning. For plays involving crowd scenes, the Roman plays and Histories in particular, the play's occasional mirroring of audience movement opens up intriguing perspectives. Chapter 5, taking *Coriolanus* as its case study, explores the way the audience (implied in the text, actual in production) is woven into a network of allegorical signifiers of liquidity that includes the city, the crowd, the city's rivers, and the veins and sinews of the human body. In Shakespeare's *Coriolanus*, the river Tiber functions both as synecdoche for the city and metaphor for its crowds. Networks of analogies between the river, the city's crowds and infrastructures, and the audience's movements in and out of the playhouse allow the river to also function as an allegory of characters' minds in motion. In *Coriolanus*, the multiple symbolic valences of Rome's water-works, allied with the mythological figure of the Hydra (this chapter's master metaphor), become a way of contrasting embodied and abstract models of thought. While the animality of the Hydra offers a sense-bound model of mental phenomena, its neat mathematical growth pattern offers a more coolly rational image of mental activity.

The sixth chapter also looks to the audience for allegorical meaning, but in a way that incorporates both the ritualistic dimension of the theatre and the issue of early modern performative style. The problem of whether a 'formalist' acting style is more conducive to allegory than a 'naturalistic' one is broached, with an emphasis on the phenomenology of reception. Because of its sustained intertwining of religion and performance, *The*

Merchant of Venice is this chapter's case study. Building on Paul Menzer's essay on the early modern performance of emotional repression,[33] I discuss Shakespeare's use of the tension between motion and stasis to represent powerful, pent-up affects and establish a subtle link between suppressed emotion, empathy and grace. In *The Merchant of Venice*, the audience's imaginative response to the player's static body turns it into a double allegory, signifying both emotional frailty and the contemplative mind's receptiveness to grace. This double association makes the static body a locus of ethical choice, in a manner reminiscent of the medieval morality play, but with a more pointed evocation of man's simultaneously earthly and divine nature.

The concluding chapter briefly looks at the way staged allegories of mind juggle the particular and the universal. On the one hand, I argue that 'grounded' allegory anchors representation in the particularities of a given performance. This implies that the images of the mind generated by performance may vary from production to production, depending on venue, directorial choices and historical/cultural context. On the other hand, there is also a universalising effect of staged allegories, especially those that integrate collective audience response in the production of meaning. The Conclusion briefly touches on several facets of the particular/universal opposition, including class, religion, gender and culture.

Notes

1 Raphael Holinshed, *The Chronicles of England, Scotland and Ireland*, vol. 2, 'Chronicles of Scotland', extracted in Geoffrey Bullough (ed.), *Narrative and Dramatic Sources of Shakespeare. Volume VII, Major Tragedies: Hamlet, Othello, King Lear, Macbeth*, London: Routledge and Kegan Paul, 1975, p. 478.

2 *Macbeth*, in *The Riverside Shakespeare*, 2nd edn, Houghton Mifflin, 1997. Unless stated otherwise, all further references to Shakespeare's plays will be to this edition.

3 The Sam Wanamaker Playhouse, a replica of Shakespeare's indoor Blackfriars theatre, was inaugurated in 2014.

4 Robert Weimann and Douglas Bruster, *Shakespeare and the Power of Performance: Stage and Page in the Elizabethan Theatre*, Cambridge: Cambridge University Press, 2008.

5 Erika T. Lin, *Shakespeare and the Materiality of Performance*, New York: Palgrave Macmillan, 2012.

6   Pamela Bickley and Jenny Stevens, *Shakespeare and Early Modern Drama: Text and Performance*, The Arden Shakespeare, London: Bloomsbury, 2016, pp. 191–2.

7   Jiří Veltruský, quoted in Keir Elam, *The Semiotics of Theatre and Drama*, London and New York: Routledge, 2002, p. 25.

8   George Puttenham, quoted in Brian Vickers (ed.), *English Renaissance Literary Criticism* (1999), Oxford: Clarendon Press, 2003, p. 247. In the rest of this section, quotes from this anthology will be referenced by page number.

9   Edmund Spenser, Dedicatory Sonnet 3 to the Earl of Oxford, in *The Faerie Queene*, ed. A. C. Hamilton, London and New York: Longman, 1977, p. 741.

10   Lynn Enterline, *Shakespeare's Schoolroom: Rhetoric, Discipline, Emotion*, Philadelphia: University of Pennsylvania Press, 2012, pp. 33–61.

11   Jean Calvin, *A commentarie of Iohn Caluine, vpon the first booke of Moses called Genesis*, trans. Thomas Tymme, 1578, The Huntington Library, p. 249. See also Roger Ascham, who, quoting Erasmus, described experience as 'the common schoolhouse of fools and ill men'. *The Scholemaster* (1570), in *English Works*, ed. William Aldis Wright, Cambridge: Cambridge University Press, 1904, p. 215.

12   A. D. Nuttal describes allegorical thought as 'the practice of thinking of universals as if they were concrete things' in his introduction to *Two Concepts of Allegory*, London: Routledge and Kegan Paul, 1967, p. xi.

13   Although Benjamin centred his argument on German drama, his theories are routinely discussed in conjunction with late Shakespearean and Jacobean drama.

14   See Angus J. S. Fletcher, 'Allegory Without Ideas', in Brenda Machowsky (ed.), *Thinking Allegory Otherwise*, Stanford, CA: Stanford University Press, 2010, pp. 9–33 (p. 22).

15   Ibid. Though Fletcher (following Benjamin) does not capitalise 'ideas' in the body of his chapter, he is referring to Platonic Ideas, or universals.

16   Ibid.

17   See Angus J. S. Fletcher, *Allegory: The Theory of a Symbolic Mode*, Ithaca, NY, and London: Cornell University Press, 1964, p. 35.

18   Judith Anderson, *Reading the Allegorical Intertext: Chaucer, Spenser, Shakespeare, Milton*, New York: Fordham University Press, 2008, p. 65.

19   Ibid. p. 5.

20   Anthony S. Brennan, '"That Within Which Passes Show": The Function of the Chorus in *Henry V*', *Philological Quarterly*, vol. 58, no. 1 (Winter 1979), pp. 40–52 (p. 42).

21 Discussed in William Kerrigan, *Hamlet's Perfection*, Baltimore, MD, and London: Johns Hopkins University Press, 1994, p. 75.

22 Timothy Bright, *A Treatise of Melancholy*, London, 1586, EEBO, The Huntington Library, pp. 68, 65.

23 Ibid. p. 66.

24 '[T]he mind which is free from passions is a citadel.' Marcus Aurelius, *Meditations* (AD 167), trans. Meric Casaubon, London, 1634, p. 44.

25 See Christiania Whitehead, *Castles of the Mind: A Study of Medieval Architectural Allegory*, Cardiff: University of Wales Press, 2003; and David Wiles, 'Place et espace du mal dans *Macbeth*', trans. François Laroque, in Gisèle Venet (ed.), *Le Mal et ses masques: théâtre, imaginaire, société*, Lyons: ENS Éditions, 1998, pp. 347–62, http://books.openedition.org/enseditions/7228, last accessed 24 April 2022.

26 Bright, *Treatise of Melancholy*, p. 63.

27 Ibid.

28 Ibid. p. 65.

29 On the Renaissance memory theatre, see Frances Yates, *The Art of Memory* (1966), London: Pimlico, 1992; and Lina Perkins Wilder, *Shakespeare's Memory Theatre: Recollection, Properties, and Character*, Cambridge: Cambridge University Press, 2010, pp. 24–58.

30 See, for example, Donald C. Freeman, '"Catching the nearest way": *Macbeth* and Cognitive Metaphor', in Jonathan Culpeper, Mick Short and Peter Verdonk (eds), *Exploring the Language of Drama: From Text to Context*, The Interface Series, Abingdon and New York: Routledge, 1998, pp. 96–111.

31 The six Aristotelian 'parts' include plot, character, diction (language), thought (theme), spectacle and lyric poetry (rhythm). See Aristotle, *Poetics*, trans. Stephen Halliwell, in *Aristotle: Poetics, Longinus: On the Sublime. Demetrius: On Style*, Loeb Classical Library, Cambridge, MA: Harvard University Press, 1995, pp. 27–141 (pp. 49–55). For the purpose of this book, 'character' and 'spectacle' are foremost.

32 Tim Fitzpatrick, 'Shakespeare's Exploitation of a Two-door Stage: *Macbeth*', *Theatre Research International*, vol. 20, no. 3 (1995), pp. 207–30.

33 Paul Menzer, 'The Actor's Inhibition: Early Modern Acting and the Rhetoric of Restraint', in Mary Floyd-Wilson and Garrett A. Sullivan, Jr (eds), *Renaissance Drama 35: Embodiment and Environment in Early Modern Drama and Performance*, Evanston, IL: Northwestern University Press, 2006, pp. 83–111.

Chapter 1

Lucius in *Julius Caesar*

Since Cassius did whet me against Caesar,
I have not slept.
Between the acting of a dreadful thing
And the first motion, all the interim is
Like a phantasma, or a hideous dream:
The genius and the mortal instruments
Are then in council, and the state of man,
Like to a little kingdom, suffers then
The nature of an insurrection.

(*Julius Caesar*, 2.1.61–9)

These words are spoken by Brutus in his garden on the eve of the assassination, as he awaits a visit from his co-conspirators. In an attempt to make sense of the inner turmoil caused by the fateful decision to kill 'his best lover' (3.2.45), Brutus resorts to a body politic metaphor, whereby the 'mortal instruments' overthrow 'the genius'. It is also, of course, a *mise en abyme* of the play's main action, involving Caesar's overthrow by a group of senators, Rome's political 'instruments'. Brutus's internalisation of the events being played out in the main action establishes the link between thought and political action as both causal and analogical, signalling that an allegorical reading of the play's action may offer insights into the main character's psyche. This is supported by the polysemy of 'acting', which could mean either 'doing' or 'deciding'.[1] Yet if polysemy tends to reinforce allegorical connections, it also breeds indeterminacy, as appears in editorial footnotes relating to 'genius' and 'mortal instruments'. In the 1998 Arden edition, David Daniell glosses 'genius' as 'guardian spirit', and the 'mortal instruments', as 'the human functions of mind and body'.[2] These definitions are broad enough to blur the line between material and immaterial agents, consistent with the openness of 'acting'. Is Brutus, then, referring to the brain and the hand? The soul and the brain? The heart and the will?

Though the exact referents of Brutus's metaphor may be elusive, the speech showcases allegory as a cognitive tool for exploring states of mind and the mechanics of decision-making. While the opacity of Brutus's speech, in keeping with the darkness of the night, suggests that the tool is an imperfect one, it is perhaps no accident that his musings at this juncture are repeatedly interrupted by a young servant with the evocative name of 'Lucius', who runs around performing errands for him, lets in characters from the outside, and jogs his flagging memory. Lucius, as it turns out, offers an alternative to poetic, speech-based allegory, in such a way as to shine a light into Brutus's mind.

Julius Caesar's Allegorical Texture

Understanding Lucius's allegorical function in *Julius Caesar* requires that we first look at the allegorical 'texture' of the play, meaning the various forms of allegory present in it. *Julius Caesar*, in fact, runs the gamut from personification, which involves speaking of an abstract notion as if it were a human being, to incarnation, whereby the actor's body is the vehicle of meaning.

Personification is widespread in the play, often appearing in the form of an apostrophe, as when Brutus, looking upon a sleeping Lucius, addresses 'slumber' as a particularly vicious sergeant:

> O murd'rous slumber!
> Layest thou thy leaden mace upon my boy,
> That plays thee music?
>
> (4.3.267–9)

In the above apostrophe to 'slumber', personification adds vividness by giving soliloquy the form of a dialogue. Vividness is also rooted in the mundane image of the sergeant and the tactile implications of his 'leaden mace'. Personifications can also be found in Caesar's speeches, as when, scoffing at his wife Calpurnia's warning that there is danger for him at the Capitol, he images 'danger' as a lion. Yet Caesar's personification of 'danger' rings hollow, due to a strained association of vehicle and tenor:

> Danger knows full well
> That Caesar is more dangerous than he.
> We are two lions littered in one day,
> And I the elder and more terrible,
> And Caesar shall go forth.
>
> (2.2.44–8)

The concept of 'danger' is rather too diffuse to be neatly packed into the heraldic/allegorical vehicle of a lion, lending the speech a fabricated quality that betrays both the speaker's lack of conviction and, fatefully, his unwillingness to address concrete security threats in a practical manner. The strangeness of the allegory is also due to its belatedness, with the image of the twinned lions coming after the oddly abstract 'Danger knows', as if Caesar were groping around for the appropriate metaphorical vehicle.

A more heroic note is struck in Mark Antony's appeal to Ate, the Greek personification of revenge:

> Caesar's spirit, ranging for revenge
> With Ate by his side come hot from hell,
> Shall in these confines with a monarch's voice
> Cry havoc and let slip the dogs of war.
>
> (3.1.270–3)

Classical divinities were typically personifications of concepts and emotions. Ate is identified as the goddess of revenge in the nineteenth book of Homer's *Iliad*, which Shakespeare could have read in either Latin or French translations or discussed with his fellow poet and playwright George Chapman.[3] Ate is also the first speaker in the anonymous *Locrine* (1595), which, like *Julius Caesar*, has a Roman revenge theme.[4] Antony's evocation of Ate is rhetorically powerful not only because of its metaphysical and mythological dimensions, but also because it functions as a self-description: as he speaks, Antony is the only character 'by [Caesar's] side', both physically and in spirit. In the above speech, Antony can thus be said to lend his body to the figure of Ate, through his words and possibly also a vengeful physical stance. In *Locrine*, Ate enters 'with a burning torch in one hande and a bloodie swoord in the other'.[5] Antony, who is probably unarmed but covered in blood from shaking hands with the conspirators earlier in the scene, could cut an equally vengeful figure by shaking a bloody fist, as does Marlon Brando in his 1953 portrayal of Mark Antony.[6]

Grounding personification in actual bodies is in fact a political strategy throughout the play. Thus, Cinna's cry of 'Tyranny is dead' (3.1.78) is an attempt to draw attention away from Caesar the man by turning him into a personification of tyranny. In a sense, this process is a de-personification,[7] as the flesh-and-blood Caesar is distilled into an abstract notion. More broadly, the question of who personifies Rome drives the plot, up to the moment when Antony acknowledges that Brutus, 'the noblest Roman of them all' (5.5.68), personified a – presumably now defunct – Roman ideal.

Politicisation is only one of the many ways in which abstract personifications tend to reach out for actual bodies throughout the play. A more contemplative example of this tendency appears in Brutus's address to 'conspiracy':

> O conspiracy,
> Sham'st thou to show thy dangerous brow by night,
> When evils are most free? O, then by day
> When wilt thou find a cavern dark enough
> To mask thy monstrous visage? Seek none, conspiracy;
> Hide it in smiles and affability
>
> (2.1.77–82)

Brutus's personified figure of 'conspiracy' emerges from Lucius's report that the visitors at the gate have covered their faces. In Brutus's speech, 'conspiracy' is spoken of as a single abstract figure addressed as 'thou', but the plural 'smiles', though ostensibly referring to one face, briefly conjures up the several faces of the conspirators waiting to see him. In Brutus's personification of the conspirators as 'conspiracy', then, unlike his appeal to 'slumber', the personification hovers close to the physical reality it describes.

The issue of the semiotic connection between physical body and allegorical thought reaches a climax in the episode of Calpurnia's dream. In the pivotal scene before Caesar is led to the Capitol, disagreement centres on Calpurnia's dream vision of Caesar's statue as a fountain spouting blood which the people of Rome greedily drink up. While Caesar's wife (rightly) interprets the dream as an evil omen, Decius, a conspirator who has come to lead Caesar to his death on the Senate floor, quickly improvises an alternative reading, whereby the 'lusty Romans' are not relishing the spoils of their kill, but 'suck[ing] reviving blood' (2.2.88) from Caesar's wounds. About this second interpretation, John Dover Wilson points out that 'Caesar, taken with the notion of his blood being sacred, doesn't notice that it implies his death no less than Calpurnia's interpretation.'[8] Another way of explaining Caesar's obliviousness involves reading the semiotics of 'sacred blood' along Protestant rather than Catholic lines, and taking the image of Romans frolicking in Caesar's blood as a metaphor for their drawing strength from the power of his spirit. This interpretation is all the more reassuring as it mingles the Christian iconography of 'sacred blood' with the pagan imagery of Rome's emblematic nursing she-wolf, thus turning Caesar's statue into an allegory of Rome. The problem of whether Caesar personifies Rome through the martyrdom of his body (in the manner of a patron saint) or through the force of his spirit is at the heart of the scene.

There is yet another level to the scene's exploration of allegory. In disagreeing about whether to read the statue as Caesar's reviving spirit or as his dead body, Decius and Calpurnia act out a medieval psychomachia, with Decius personifying Caesar's pride, and Calpurnia, his fear.[9] Decius and Calpurnia share with medieval psychomachia the function of embodying facets of the main character's mind, but on a more 'grounded' level. Beyond the fact that they are based on actual historical figures and performed by flesh-and-blood actors, Decius and Calpurnia each enjoy a mimetic (realistic) relationship with Caesar involving emotional bonds, respectively of envy and love. The scene then foregrounds the polymorphism and reversibility of allegory by juxtaposing allegorical statuary, emblematic animals, dream-visions and psychomachia.

This psychomachic episode connects with a broader pattern of projection allegory, whereby various characters appear as facets of Brutus's character. This dynamic functions on several levels, as establishing oneself as 'a part of' Brutus belongs to the rhetorical toolbox of manipulative characters such as Cassius as much as it belongs to the play's own array of poetic devices. Cassius's offer to be Brutus's 'glass' (1.2.68), meaning looking glass, suggests that he is attempting to position himself as his friend's conscience, or 'genius'. Something of the kind can also be detected in Portia's appeal to Brutus's love, especially when she insists on their unity. Portia's one dialogue with her husband, on the eve of the assassination, is very much focused on the nature of their relationship. Upset at Brutus's failure to share his troubles with her, Portia reminds him of her role as a wife, pointing out that the marriage vows have made the spouses 'one', and that she is Brutus's 'self' and his 'half' (2.1.274–5). This speech, emphasising the mystical power of the marriage bond, is remarkable in simultaneously expressing Portia's love for her husband and suggesting an allegorical dimension to the character. Portia seems to embody some reluctance, some moral qualm in Brutus's mind, in the same way that Calpurnia embodies Caesar's fear. For both wives, allegorical function is wrapped up in the mimetic character's emotional life.

These variations around allegorical representation, in which abstract figures tend to be displaced by fully realised characters and their embodied incarnations on the stage, form the backdrop for Lucius, Brutus's 'genius' in the orchard scene, but also a character in his own right. Making sense of Lucius, I will argue, involves confronting his status as a character, his relation to a number of extra-textual models of mind, and the physical presence of the actor playing him on the stage.

Lucius, Allegory and Renaissance Memory Models

That Lucius bears an allegorical relationship to Brutus is signalled in several ways, including his name (whose significance is emphasised by the fact that he mostly appears at night and is in charge of lighting candles), his effectively exclusive relationship with his master (he shares the stage only with Brutus and, briefly, with Brutus's wife), the nature of that relationship (the young servant is a staple of biblical allegory), and his highly symbolical actions, such as lighting a lamp and fetching books. Books feature prominently in medieval and Renaissance symbology. Among the many Shakespearean uses of the trope discussed by Ernst Curtius, the book of memory and the accounting book may be the most relevant to *Julius Caesar*.[10] Though the name 'Lucius' suggests nothing other than moral clarity, the character's actions align him more specifically with memory.

Many of Lucius's actions have to do with time. He is often seen sleeping, in a reminder (to both Brutus and the audience) of natural time running alongside the political calendar of the events unfolding in Rome. Lucius also fetches a calendar for Brutus, reminding him that the next day is the fateful Ides of March (2.1.59). At times, Lucius interestingly has perfect recall: he knows when the letter purportedly from the 'people of Rome' (actually written by Cassius) was deposited in Brutus's house, and he also remembers quite well that Brutus did not give him the mislaid book (4.3.254). Yet in other instances he is a bit hazy on dates and, like Brutus, needs a calendar to remind him of what day of the month it is (2.1.41). He also has trouble placing the conspirators, whose faces he does not recognise. This combination of perfect recall and confusion pertains to Lucius's double status as embodiment of Brutus's recollection and character in his own right, a duality that structures the play's representation of Brutus's troubled memory.

Lucius's allegorical figuration of Brutus's mind relies on a number of contemporary memory models. One of these is the memory theatre. The many ways in which memory and theatre were linked in early modern culture is the subject of Lina Perkins Wilder's *Shakespeare's Memory Theatre*. Not only was the Elizabethan stage a place where valuable lessons could be impressed on the spectator's mind, but theatrical practice was a standard pedagogical method in grammar schools and at the Inns of Court.[11] Lucius's knowledge of where things are at all times aligns him more particularly with the classical rhetorical technique of memory places, whereby the rhetor could store parts of a speech, or other types of data, in an imagined or remembered building, to be mentally visited for retrieval at a later date. The practice went back to the antiquity and, according to Frances Yates, came to Renaissance culture by way of Cicero's *De Oratore*, the anonymous *Ad C. Herennium* and Quintilian's *Institutio Oratoria*. Quintilian, in particular, outlined the method, encouraging the rhetor to think of his speech as a leisurely walk through a mnemonic building;[12] any building sufficiently provided with rooms and ornaments was suitable. Yates argues that the emergence of the theatre as the memory building of choice may have originated with Giulio Camillo, an early sixteenth-century Christian Neoplatonist, who built a model theatre furnished with nooks, doors and zodiacal images conducive to mnemonic recording and recalling.[13] As pointed out by Wilder, awareness of this method could endow actual theatrical space with a mnemonic function.[14] In the scene set in Brutus's orchard, where the action is distributed between the orchard (the stage), the house (the tiring house or discovery space) and the gate (one of the doors or exits), Lucius's movements contribute to turning theatrical space into a recognisable place of memory and a spatial figuration of Brutus's brain.

Another way in which memory was commonly spatialised in the literature of the Elizabethan period was through various modellings of the brain's structure and processes. Following Aristotle, most Renaissance authors agreed that the mental faculties (Imagination, Reason and Memory) were located in the brain, though there was some disagreement as to where in the brain each faculty dwelt. While Jesuit priest and natural philosopher Thomas Wright admitted puzzlement, Spanish physician Juan Huarte, French theologian Pierre Charron, and Jacobean court physician Helkiah Crooke believed the faculties were distributed over the entire area of the brain.[15] Yet another model held that each faculty occupied a separate 'ventricle' or 'cell' in the brain, memory having the hindmost one.[16] Deriving from late classical Alexandrian commentaries of Galen,[17] this compartmentalised model survived in medieval and early sixteenth-century works such as Hieronymus Brunschwig's treatise on surgery.[18] In this model, cognitive input collected by the senses travels from the Imagination, located in the foremost ventricle of the brain, to Reason, in the central ventricle, where, after being processed, it is sent to the back of the brain, where it is stored in the Memory, ready to be called up again when needed. The process lent itself easily to allegorising, with the cells corresponding to rooms in a building and Imagination, Reason and Memory to homunculi working for the soul. Though distancing himself from the compartmentalised model, Crooke fell in with the allegorical mode by describing memory as 'a Faithfull recorder or Maister of the Rolls that doth preserue, and store vp and dispose in due order all [...] notions or abstracted forms'.[19] In *The Faerie Queene*, Edmund Spenser introduced a similar allegory, while giving Memory, depicted as an old man, a young assistant with a key role to play.

One of *The Faerie Queene*'s most remarkable passages, when it comes to depicting the mechanics of memory, occurs in Book 2 when Guyon, the knight of temperance, and his companion, Arthur, are taken on a tour of the Castle of Alma (the soul), an architectural rendition of the human body, and shown into the turret, where the rational faculties dwell. The two knights are led through a room occupied by a young man named *Phantastes* (the imagination) to a chamber belonging to a middle-aged sage who stands for reason, and finally shown into the library of an old man named *Eumnestes* (memory) who is attended by a young boy, *Anamnestes* (recollection):

That chamber seemed ruinous and old,
And therefore was removed farre behind
Yet were the wals, that did the same uphold,
Right firm and strong, though somewhat they declined;
And therin sat an old old man, half blinde,
And all decrepit in his feeble corse [...]

His chamber was all hangd about with rolles,
And old records from ancient times deriu'd
Some made in books, some in old parchment scrolles,
That were all worme-eaten, and full of canker holes.

Amidst them all he in a chaire was set,
Tossing and turning them withouten end;
But for he was unable them to fet[ch],
A little boy did on him attend
To reach, when euer he for aught did send;
And oft, when things were lost, or laid amiss,
That boy them sought, and unto him did lend.
Therefore he *Anamnestes* cleped is,
And that old man *Eumnestes*, by their propertis.
(Book 2, Canto 9, stanzas 55–8)

There are clear parallels between this description, which Evelyn B. Tribble has referred to as 'a *locus classicus* of [...] Medieval and Renaissance faculty psychology',[20] and the scene that takes place in Brutus's orchard on the eve of the assassination. Like *Anamnestes*, Lucius runs to and fro fetching items for his master, supplementing Brutus's impeded, half-blinded and sleepless senses with his sprightliness and mental acuity. More specifically, Shakespeare comes close to Spenser's model by making Lucius a retriever of artefacts having to do with national history. Christopher Ivic, pointing out that the books *Anamnestes* fetches for *Eumnestes* are mainly chronicles of England, has emphasised the historical component of individual memory in Spenser's design, suggesting that '[i]n *The Faerie Queene*, memory is crucial to the nation-building projects to which such exemplary figures as *Eumnestes* and Guyon are committed.'[21] The letters Lucius brings Brutus, with their reminders of the feats of his glorious forefathers, are the counterparts of *Eumnestes*'s history books, one of which tellingly refers to another Brutus's 'fattal error'.[22] Just as *Anamnestes* embodies *Eumnestes*'s recollection of England's past, Lucius embodies Brutus's recollection of the endangered greatness of Rome.

Of course, the intertextual reference to Brutus's 'fattal error' implies a moral gap between Spenser's *Anamnestes* and Shakespeare's Lucius. If Brutus's decision to take part in the assassination is read as an error – which the play's tragic pattern seems to establish – the implication is that Brutus's memory has been playing tricks on him. This glitch in the system may be explained by a weakness Tribble detected in the Spenserian model. Though the operations of *Eumnestes*'s memory chamber may appear to hum along quite nicely, Tribble suggests that the model implies a vulnerability to deterioration:

> If memory is figured as a trusted holding space, a 'treasury' owned and ordered by an individual agent, it must be defended both against its own tendencies to slide into disorder and against the onslaughts of other minds and competing memories.[23]

Those 'other minds' and 'competing memories' are precisely what Lucius fails to keep out in act 2, scene 4 of *Julius Caesar*, when he opens the door to the conspirators waiting at the gate of Brutus's house. Sticking to the Spenserian blueprint, the conspirators appear as counterparts of the monstrous passions laying siege to Spenser's Castle of Alma.[24] In letting in the conspirators, Lucius is allowing a historical narrative distorted by jealousy, envy and frustration to take hold of his master's mind. There is some indeterminacy, however, because of simultaneously possible mimetic and allegorical readings of Lucius. If Lucius is understood as an autonomous character, the passions originate in the conspirators, and Brutus is duped into taking an adulterated narrative for a truthful one. If Lucius is read as an allegory of Brutus's recollection, however, the emotions originate in Brutus himself. In both cases, a parallel with Spenser's model designates the emotions as negative, distorting forces.

This reading runs counter to recent anti-Stoic interpretations of *Julius Caesar* inspired by the cognitive turn in Shakespeare studies. For example, Donald Wehrs interprets Brutus's misguided decision to murder Caesar as the consequence of a Stoic overreliance on abstract thought and ideals for guidance, at the expense of the mollifying effect of the body's affects and emotions. Arguing from the twinned perspectives of Renaissance humanism and late twentieth-century neuroscience, Wehrs contends that the play involves 'a dramatization of how embodiment works against dissociation'.[25]

The crux here is that the moral value of the emotions (or passions, or affects as they were also called) was the object of much debate in Shakespeare's day, a debate here reflected by the double semiotics of Lucius's status as Brutus's 'genius' or 'spirit'. While Lucius is never explicitly referred to as Brutus's spirit, the psychomachic pattern of the ghost sequence, in which Brutus's 'evil spirit' (4.3.282) appears in the semblance of Caesar's ghost as soon as Lucius falls asleep, suggests that Lucius occupies the structural position of his 'good spirit'. Though the ghost scene draws on a moral acceptation of 'spirit', the physiological meaning may be just as relevant to the play's figuration of Lucius.

Aristotle- and Galen-inspired Renaissance physiology distinguished three types of spirits, all functioning as messengers, or conveyors of data (Crooke tellingly refers to the 'services' performed by the spirits and Wright speaks of how 'the spirites and humours wait upon the Passions, as their Lords and Maisters'[26]). While the natural spirits are associated with the liver, the vital spirits work for the heart, and the animal spirits, for the brain.[27] In *Shakespeare's Memory Theatre*, Wilder sums up what is sometimes taken as the early modern consensus on the action of the animal spirits in the brain:

> To be placed in the memory, sensory impressions flow with the animal spirits from the front to the back of the brain; to be remembered, 'images' stored in the memory are carried forward from the ventricle of memory to the imagination, where they can be scanned by 'the eye of the mind'.[28]

It is this second process that seems to be at stake in Lucius's encounter with Brutus's wife, Portia, who, we have seen, is a projection allegory in her own capacity. Given that one aspect of Lucius's 'groundedness' is his continued involvement in the plot, his interaction with another allegorical character contributes to his overall significance. Let us therefore turn to the scene of Portia's bungled attempt to deliver a last-minute message to Brutus before he commits his fateful act. Standing before Brutus's house, Portia and Lucius engage in this curious little dialogue:

> *Por.* I prithee boy, run to the Senate House.
>   Stay not to answer me, but get thee gone.
>   Why dost thou stay?
> *Luc.* To know my errand, madam.
> *Por.* I would have had thee there and here again
>   Ere I can tell thee what thou should do there.
>   (*Aside*) O constancy, be strong upon my side;
>   Set a huge mountain 'tween my heart and tongue!

> I have a man's mind, but a woman's might.
> How hard it is for women to keep counsel!
> Art thou here yet?
> *Luc.* Madam, what should I do?
> Run to the Capitol, and nothing else?
> And so return to you, and nothing else?
>
> (2.4.1–12)

The exchange is Shakespeare's adaptation of Plutarch's *Lives*, where Portia frantically sends 'messenger after messenger' to inquire about her husband's doings.[29] Shakespeare reduces 'messenger after messenger' to Lucius and adds to the request for news an errand Portia struggles to remember. The scene invites us to speculate as to what message Portia originally wished to deliver to her husband, and what caused her to forget, or recoil from speaking. If, as Arthur Humphreys supposes,[30] we assume that Portia is now privy to her husband's plan, it is not unreasonable to think that what she means to tell him is simply not to do it – to hold his murderous hand. This would square with her previously expressed suspicion of the conspirators and with the fact that she is Cato's daughter. Plutarch's 'Life of Cato the Younger' emphasises the Roman senator's hatred of conspiracy, as evidenced by his ruthless prosecution of the Catiline conspirators.[31] As the proud daughter of Cato (2.1.295), Shakespeare's Portia seems to share that distaste. As for her failure to effectively deliver the message, it can be explained by her vow to keep Brutus's secret, by her suspicion of Lucius (2.4.42) and by her reluctance to step out of her subservient marital role. This is the literal interpretation of the scene, taken as mimetic action. However, the scene's uselessness to the plot, the oddity of Portia's behaviour, the previously established allegorical functions of both characters, and the vaguely stichomythic pattern suggested by Portia's reluctance and Lucius's urging, invite a reading whereby both Portia and Lucius are hypostatic projections of Brutus's mind. Portia's confusion and hesitation jibe well with her previous characterisation as Brutus's reluctance. Lucius's repeated prompting of a forgetful Portia associates him once again with memory.[32] But what is the nature of this reluctance, and what prevents it from being effectively activated? Though Portia describes her attempt to intervene as a characteristically womanish failure to 'keep council' (2.4.9), that is, to keep a secret, envisioning Lucius as an animal spirit allows for a different interpretation.

Animal spirits feature prominently in classical and early modern physiological explanations of *akrasia*, or weakness of will, something Renaissance authors sometimes characterised as self-forgetfulness.[33] In his *Treatise of Melancholy*, Timothy Bright explains errors of the mind/soul as failures of the animal spirits to carry data from the heart to the brain, then from the inward brain (the realm of thought, imagination and memory) to the outward brain (which controls motion and bodily functions). In this Galen-inspired theory, failure of animal spirits is attributed to humoral imbalance, mainly to melancholy, which can close up the 'pores'[34] of the body and make it difficult for the animal spirits to get through. Humoral imbalance, in turn, can be put down to several causes, including bad nutrition, climate, illness or violent emotions. Bright explains how melancholy 'locketh up the gates of the heart whereout the spirits should break forth upon just occasion to the comfort of all the family of their fellow members'.[35] In the mechanistic Galenic model of human action, bad transmission is at the root of moral failure.

Transmission is clearly at stake in the dialogue between Portia and Lucius, as is underscored by the caesuras introduced by the shared lines, prosodic counterparts of the broken connections between memory and acting mind, or alternatively between brain and body. It seems, then, that the Portia–Lucius scene shows us Brutus's memory attempting to send his will (or imagination, depending on the model) a message to desist. Lucius's inability to deliver the message could be the allegorical counterpart of the animal spirits being rendered sluggish or blocked in the heart by melancholy. In this reading, Brutus's action is the result of melancholy caused by worry, sleeplessness or too much reading.[36] And yet Bright's choice of metaphor allows for another interpretation. In describing the closed heart and the comfortless 'family' of the locked-out members, Bright is using allegory to depict the physical progress of the spirits from the heart to the brain and body as an emotional process. This indeterminacy as to whether the spirits are hindered by the emotions or help carry the emotions reflects the period's ambivalence as to the value of the emotions. While a Stoic tradition was suspicious of the affects, an Augustinian and Thomistic one considered them necessary to virtuous action. Most authors, including Bright, Burton and Wright, attempted some level of synthesis of the two, at the cost of the occasional contradiction.

This leads to several possible understandings of how the emotions are represented in the Portia–Lucius episode. In one reading, the dialogue shows emotions preventing the contents of memory from reaching the will, or outward brain. In another, the scene shows the emotions being kept locked in the heart (or inward brain) and unable to get to the brain (or outward brain), via animal spirits.[37] On the macro scale, these models allow us to interpret Brutus's decision as due either to a blocking of fellow-feeling or to an emotional involvement in the conspiracy – whether it be rooted in pride, melancholy or friendship – which prevents him from telling right from wrong. Though in both cases, Lucius's prompting of Portia indicates that he represents the tug of Brutus's 'true self' recalling itself to his memory, it is not entirely clear whether that true self is of an emotional or a rational nature.

The difficulty in ascribing a definite allegorical role to Lucius stems from the fact that, unlike morality play characters and some early modern stage personifications,[38] his name, though carrying allegorical potential, does not entirely define him. Lucius is no 'Fellowship' or 'Good Deeds' whose relationship to the protagonist is established with mathematical precision from the outset. Instead, Lucius's allegorical function must be pieced together thanks to intertextual models and mimetic characterisation. Having established, based on Spenserian and Galenic models of the brain, that Lucius is associated with both public and private memory, both with the emotions and the repression thereof, we must now look to Lucius's embodied stage presence for a more decisive – if not clinching – piece of the puzzle, which I will introduce by way of a curious directorial choice in the recent history of the play's production.

Lucius and the Senses

In his 2008–11 world-touring production of *Julius Caesar*, Paris-born Bostonian director Arthur Nauzyciel chose to make his Lucius deaf. The textual rationale for this may have been Lucius's claim not to hear the noise Portia mentions in 2.4.16, and his apparent failure to overhear her speaking aloud to herself (2.4.42). Though this choice is consistent with the play's construction of Lucius as a locus of pathos, it tends to obscure the extent to which Lucius is associated with the senses throughout the play. Far from being deaf, Lucius is a fine musician, with a keen ear for harmony. His name and actions also associate him with vision, while his young body's need for sleep counterpoints the repeated calls from the conspirators for Brutus to 'awake'. It can also be noted that Lucius's relationship with his master is mediated by touch, as when Brutus gently removes the harp from the sleeping boy's hands (4.3.272). Music is perhaps the strongest indicator of Lucius's flesh-and-blood presence, for its effect would extend to the audience, possibly drawing such physiological responses as goose bumps or shivers down the spine. The Pythagorean model of music as a reflection of cosmic order makes Lucius a conduit between the senses and reason. This connection is played out in act 4, scene 2, where Lucius's role as an agent of Brutus's awareness of human frailty is developed.

Act 4, scene 3 is an intimate scene set in Brutus's tent on the eve of the Battle of Philippi, throughout which Lucius reminds Brutus of his past errors. This begins when Brutus finds the book he previously mislaid and apologises for wrongfully accusing Lucius of losing it. In his apology, Brutus mentions his 'forgetful[ness]' (255), drawing an implicit contrast with Lucius's perfect recall ('I was sure your lordship did not give it me'; 254). A brief glimpse of an unscene,[39] in which Brutus reproaches his servant with the loss of the book and Lucius (tearfully?) denies it, hovers behind the dialogue, creating echoes of the episode of the quarrel with Cassius, and perhaps also of the unfairness of Brutus's 'unkindest cut' (3.2.183). Later in the scene, Lucius's function as an agent of Brutus's self-awareness is paradoxically enhanced by the boy's hero-worship of his master and attempt to imitate his Stoic abnegation of self. When Brutus tells Lucius to get some sleep, the boy insists on fighting his drowsiness in order to play music, despite Brutus's statement that he does not wish to urge the boy's 'duty' beyond his 'might' (4.3.260). This rather un-Stoic acknowledgement of human frailty, albeit that of a young slave, seems to amount to a questioning of some of Brutus's previous choices. In this episode, Lucius functions allegorically in at least two different ways. We have seen that Lucius's eventually falling asleep in mid-song, leaving Brutus alone with a vision of his 'evil spirit', places him in the stichomythic position of Brutus's 'good spirit', or angel. More interestingly, though, the boy's attempt to imitate his master's stalwartness, and his failure to do so, reveals another facet to Lucius's allegorical function, one which is bound up in parody.

By the late sixteenth century, using a character's servant as a grotesque parodic representation of his master's tragic hubris or comic bluster had become a standard feature of drama.

A sustained exercise in such grotesque mirroring appears in Christopher Marlowe's *Doctor Faustus*,[40] where the magician's conjuring is imitated by his bungling servant, whose bringing forth of monstrous creatures is a comic send-up of his master's overweening belief in his God-like status. Though parody and allegory are two distinct figures, they are related by the process of caricature and by their opposition of the material and the spiritual. Parody involves the grotesque amplification of a defect, while allegory is the perceptible and readable representation of an intangible or hidden feature. In Lucius's falling asleep, parody takes on an allegorical dimension because Lucius's unnatural resistance to his body's needs externalises Brutus's struggle against the pull of natural feeling as well as transposing it to a lesser character. Here, body, emotions and nature form a virtuous triangle, in an implied critique of Stoic abnegation.

Lucius's character, then, is related to Brutus's in at least four ways, including mimetic interaction, moral allegory, physiological allegory and parody. Bringing these layers together can lead to a reading of Brutus's error not dissimilar to that of Wehrs, whereby neglect of the emotions is the root cause of the tragedy. However, the variety of models discussed in this chapter has shown that the emotions – rather than their rejection – may be part of the problem. Was Brutus wrong to reject the emotions, or did he give in too easily to the emotional pull of friendship? Did his Stoic spurning of the body's needs lead him to a cold-blooded, abstract analysis of the situation, or did his sleeplessness impede his ability to reason properly? Or perhaps his dilemma can be schematised as a conflict between positive and negative emotions. This indeterminacy, as we have seen, derives both from the inherent reversibility of the grounded allegorical form, in which the mimetic and figurative modes are both present, and from the ambiguities of early modern models of thought. Though such indeterminacies are frustrating, the layering of thought they involve suggests that Shakespeare, like Spenser before him, is intent on evoking a buried substratum to his protagonist's mind, thus contributing to the complexity of his characterisation.

In this chapter, we have seen that Lucius's ability to project the deep layers of Brutus's memory is vested in the more grounded aspects of the character, including the bodily presence of the player, to which attention is drawn through his music-playing and various other references to the senses. Theatrical space is also enlisted, with the house, garden and city (materialised by the stage and two offstage spaces) standing for the 'ventricles' of the brain. The careful parcelling out of stage space, in a way that recalls early modern models of the brain, is in fact central to establishing Lucius's allegorical status. While the allegorical use of stage space concerns a limited number of scenes in *Julius Caesar*, it is structural in *Macbeth*, where the castle of the mind functions as a master metaphor, and stage doors stand for thresholds of the mind.

Notes

1 *OED*, 2a and 1a, respectively.
2 David Daniell, in William Shakespeare, *Julius Caesar*, ed. David Daniell, The Arden Shakespeare, Walton-on-Thames: Thomas Nelson and Sons, 1998, p. 201n.
3 Chapman was in the process of translating the *Iliad* into English when Shakespeare was writing *Julius Caesar*.
4 *Locrine* has sometimes been attributed to Shakespeare, due to the title page's statement that the play was 'Newly set forth, overseene and corrected by W.S.'
5 Anon., *The lamentable tragedie of Locrine*, London, 1595, EEBO, The Huntington Library.
6 In Joseph Mankiewicz's 1953 film adaptation of Shakespeare's *Julius Caesar* for MGM.
7 I am indebted to Ladan Niayesh for this insight.
8 John Dover Wilson, in *Julius Caesar*, ed. John Dover Wilson, The Cambridge Dover Wilson Shakespeare, Cambridge: Cambridge University Press, 1949, p. 140n.
9 The term 'psychomachia', Greek for 'battle of spirits', derives from Christian Latin poet Prudentius's fifth-century poem depicting a battle of virtues and vices vying for possession of a human soul. The pattern became a staple of medieval allegory, as in *The Castle of Perseverance* (c. 1405), where Mankind is torn between the advice of his good and bad angels. Christopher Marlowe took up the Good Angel/Bad Angel device in *Doctor Faustus* (c. 1594).
10 See Ernst Robert Curtius, *European Literature and the Latin Middle Ages*, trans. Willard R. Trask, Princeton, NJ: Princeton University Press, 1953, pp. 332–40.
11 See Lina Perkins Wilder, *Shakespeare's Memory Theatre: Recollection, Properties, and Character*, Cambridge: Cambridge University Press, 2010, p. 32.
12 See Frances Yates, *The Art of Memory* (1966), London: Pimlico, 1992, p. 18.

13 Ibid. p. 136.

14 Wilder, *Shakespeare's Memory Theatre*, p. 15.

15 Discussed in D. R. Kelley and R. H. Popkin (eds), *The Shapes of Knowledge from the Renaissance to the Enlightenment*, Dordrecht, Boston and London: Kluwer Academic Publishers, 1991, p. 79.

16 See, for example, Daniel C. Boughner, 'The Psychology of Memory in Spenser's *Faerie Queene*', *PMLA*, vol. 47, no. 1 (March 1932), pp. 89–96 (pp. 92–4).

17 Mainly by Agnellus of Ravenna and John of Alexandria. See Michael Frampton, *Embodiments of Will: Anatomical and Physiological Theories of Voluntary Animal Motion from Greek Antiquity to the Latin Middle Ages, 400 B.C.–A.D. 1300*, Saarbrücken: VDM Verlag Dr. Müller, 2008, p. 278.

18 Hieronymus Brunschwig, *The noble experyence of the handie warke of surgeri* (1525), London, 1561, Proquest. See, in particular, image 5 (unnumbered page), with its compartmentalised map of the brain's faculties.

19 Helkiah Crooke, *Mikrokosmographia*, London, 1615, EEBO, The Huntington Library, p. 502.

20 Evelyn B. Tribble, '"The Dark Backward Abysm of Time": *The Tempest* and Memory', *College Literature*, vol. 33, no. 1 (Winter 2006), pp. 151–68 (p. 152).

21 Christopher Ivic, 'Spenser and Interpellative Memory', in Donald Beecher and Grant Williams (eds), *Ars Reminiscendi: Mind and Memory in Renaissance Culture*, Toronto: Center for Reformation and Renaissance Studies, 2009, pp. 289–310 (pp. 290–1).

22 Edmund Spenser, *The Faerie Queene*, ed. A. C. Hamilton, London and New York: Longman, 1977, Book 2, Canto 10, stanza 9, line 8, p. 260. One of London's medieval origin myths involved a legendary descendent of Aeneas, Brutus of Troy, who was banished from Italy after accidentally killing his father and wandered over to Britain, eventually becoming its first king.

23 Tribble, '"Dark Backward Abysm of Time"', p. 153

24 Spenser, *Faerie Queene*, Book 2, Canto 9, stanzas 12–16. The passions are described as 'a thousand villeins' (stanza 13, line 2, p. 249) swarming around the castle, trying to gain admittance.

25 Donald Wehrs, 'Moral Physiology, Ethical Prototypes and the Denaturing of Sense in Shakespearean Tragedy', *College Literature*, vol. 33, no. 1 (2006), pp. 67–92 (pp. 76–7).

26 Crooke, *Mikrokosmographia*, p. 472; and Thomas Wright, *The Passions of the Minde in Generall* (1601), London, 1604, EEBO, Yale University Library, p. 4.

27 The distinction between natural, vital and animal spirits goes back to the Alexandrian physicians of the third century BC, mainly Erasistratus. It was popularised by Galen in the second century

AD. The system is explained in the pseudo-Aristotelian *Problems of Aristotle*, 1595, EEBO, Bodleian Library, However, the distinction was not always emphasised in sixteenth- and early seventeenth-century treatises, where the term 'spirit' was often used on its own. The compartmentalisation of the spirits was to be more systematically set out in the works of Descartes and his contemporaries.

28   Wilder, *Shakespeare's Memory Theatre*, p. 48. As discussed above, this Alexandrian-derived model was in fact only one among several, but its appealing imagery seems to have made it a favourite for early modern poets and dramatists.

29   See Plutarch's 'Life of Marcus Brutus', extracted in Geoffrey Bullough (ed.), *Narrative and Dramatic Sources of Shakespeare. Volume V, The Roman Plays: Julius Caesar, Antony and Cleopatra, Coriolanus*, London: Routledge and Kegan Paul, 1964, p. 100.

30   Arthur Humphreys, in William Shakespeare, *Julius Caesar*, ed. Arthur Humphreys (1984), The Oxford Shakespeare, Oxford and New York: Oxford University Press, 2008, p. 155n.

31   See Plutarch, *The Parallel Lives*, 'Life of Cato the Younger', extracted in Bullough, *Narrative and Dramatic Sources, Vol. V*, pp. 289–91. The 'Life of Cato the Younger' was first translated into English by John Dryden in 1683 and is not included in Sir Thomas North's sixteenth-century translation of Plutarch's *Lives of the Noble Grecians and Romans*, commonly referred to as *The Parallel Lives*, which was the edition used by Shakespeare and his contemporaries. Shakespeare would therefore not have been able to read it in English but could have read it in Latin or known about it from other sources.

32   The meta-dramatic implications of such prompting might have contributed to conveying the impression that Portia's 'blockage' was of a mnemonic nature.

33   On *akrasia* as self-forgetfulness in Spenser's *Faerie Queene* and *View of the Present State of Ireland*, see Ivic, 'Spenser and Interpellative Memory', pp. 292–300.

34   Timothy Bright, *A Treatise of Melancholy*, London, 1586, EEBO, The Huntington Library, pp. 65, 123.

35   Ibid. p. 98.

36   Melancholy was something of a catch-all ailment in Renaissance culture, being associated with all forms of discomfort and dissatisfaction. For a comic run-down of melancholy types, see Jaques's speech in *As You Like It* (4.1.10–20). See also Douglas Trevor's discussion of 'the reinvention of sadness' in early modern culture, in *The Poetics of Melancholy in Early Modern England*, Cambridge: Cambridge University Press, 2004, pp. 1–24.

37   In the first reading, Portia might stand for Brutus's melancholy, blocking transmission of memory data to the animal spirits; in the

second, she might stand for his heart or inward brain, repressing the emotions that would facilitate the animal spirits' journey. The emotions would thus be rendered allegorically in the first reading and mimetically in the second. At any rate, the dialogue's allegorical attributions remain somewhat open, as literal and metaphorical signification overlap. Portia can be read as the allegorical embodiment of Brutus's heart or emotions, but also as a full-blown character with a heart and mind of her own, involving internal transmission issues (''tween my heart and my tongue').

38   Frederick Kiefer points out that personified abstractions lingered well into the 1580s on the early modern stage. *Shakespeare's Visual Theatre*, Cambridge: Cambridge University Press, 2003, p. 13.

39   The term 'unscene', coined by Margery Garber, now has full currency in Shakespearean criticism.

40   Christopher Marlowe, *Dr Faustus* (A-text, 1594), ed. Roma Gill, London: A&C Black; New York: Norton, 1989, scenes 4 and 8.

Chapter 2

A Mind Made Up:
Macbeth's Doorways

Just as Brutus's house stood for his memory, Macbeth's castle stands for his conscience. The play's foregrounding of fateful entrances and doorways, as in Lady Macbeth's 'hoarse raven' speech and in the porter scene, has led critics such as David Wiles and Jennifer C. Vaught to point out parallels between Shakespeare's Scottish play and such medieval morality plays as *The Castle of Perseverance*, where the castle stands for the soul's protection against the temptation of evil, its gates functioning both as vulnerable points of entry and strategic bulwarks.[1] The parallels lie in great part in a moralised use of stage space, which allows characters' movements to be read as spiritual progresses. On the medieval stage, for example, 'the movement from left to right [...] leads to hell'.[2] Yet it does not lead there irrevocably, because of the pre-Reformation assumption that the soul is free. *Macbeth*, however, is a tragedy. Its movements, both physical and mental, are one-directional. In this chapter, I will argue that the play constitutes the murderous thane's castle as a tragic allegory of his mind through a poetics of thresholds. In *Macbeth*, doorways are powerful signifiers of irreversibility, the allegorical counterparts of a mind committed to evil. Though *Macbeth* can work in all kinds of venues, the following discussion will assume a seventeenth-century Globe performance, as the allegorical model I will be developing is rooted in the Globe theatre's architecture, in classical, medieval and Renaissance castle metaphors, and in the cultural moment defined by the 1605 Gunpowder Plot. These contextual elements come together in one thick knot, resulting in a vibrant 'objective correlative'[3] of Macbeth's mind surrendering to evil. This chapter thus explores the 'grounded' dimension of

Macbeth's castle allegory, arguing that its sinister vitality derives from the process of adaptation, the epistemological context, and the ritual power of the staged oath. I will begin, as Shakespeare did, with the Holinshed source.

Staging Holinshed: Vanishing, Tracking and Blending

It can safely be assumed that sometime in the early years of the seventeenth century, Shakespeare could be found poring over Raphael Holinshed's 'Chronicles of Scotland',[4] with a view to adapting the story of Macbeth, the treacherous thane, for the stage. Allowing ourselves a glimpse into the bard's mind, we can imagine a slight reflective pause when, coming to the end of the episode of Macbeth and Banquo's first encounter with the witches ('women in strange and wild apparel'), he read: 'the foresaid women vanished immediatelie out of their sight'.[5] The practical difficulty of staging disappearing women would have been immediately apparent to the actor/playwright/director, and possibly appealed to him as a challenging puzzle. Obviously, the players portraying the weird sisters could not simply vanish into thin air; they would have to use one of the Globe's stage doors or a possible trap door leading to the space usually referred to as 'hell' located under the thrust stage. In the 1623 Folio *Macbeth*, the only extant text of the play, the supernatural disappearance is cued for in the stage direction, '*Witches vanish*', and commented on in the characters' dialogue:

> *Ban.* [...] wither are they vanished?
> *Macb.* Into the air; and what seemed corporal melted
> As breath into the wind.
>
> (1.3.80–2)

In a footnote to the Oxford World's Classics edition, Nicholas Brooke calls the stage direction 'disappointingly vague' and notes that '[t]he resources of the Globe theatre included smoke, trap-doors and at least one winch', adding, however, that 'it is unlikely that three actors could have been flown fast enough'.[6] Possibly, smoke might have been used to cover the actors' exits through one or several doors, but the effect would still have fallen short of the witches simply 'vanish[ing]'.

The above example is only one of the many challenges to dramatic adaptation posed by Holinshed's *Chronicles*. Indeed, the 'Macbeth' narrative sometimes reads as if it were purposely designed to be unstageable, given its predilection for tracking characters over wide expanses of land and in and out of enclosed spaces, for describing simultaneously unfolding events, and for reporting characters' unvoiced thoughts at length. One obvious solution to such problems involves a narrative rendition of the material, as in messenger speeches and soliloquies. These are the default settings of Senecan tragedy, and Shakespeare makes use of them in several places, as in the bleeding Sergeant's report of Macbeth's battlefield heroics (1.2.7–42). More relevant to my interest in staged allegory, however, is Shakespeare's use of staged entrances and exits as a means of contracting space, and thus overcoming the problems of tracking and simultaneity. The strategy begins with the murder of Duncan.

Holinshed's *Chronicles* make short shrift of Duncan's murder ('he slew the king at Enverns, or as some say, at Botgosuane'[7]), but Geoffrey Bullough, considering that Shakespeare consolidated several of Holinshed's king-killing episodes, included the following passage, telling of a prior regicide, as a source for *Macbeth*:

> Donwald, though he abhorred the act greatlie in his heart, yet through the instigation of his wife, hee called foure of his servants unto him (whome he had made privie to his wicked intent before, and framed to his purpose with large gifts) and now declaring unto them, after what sort they should worke the feat, they gladlie obeied the instructions, & speedilie going about the murther, they enter the chamber (in which the king laie) a little before cocks crow, where they secretlie cut his throte as he lay sleeping, without anie buskling at all: and immediatlie by a posterne gate they carried foorth the dead bodie into the fields, and throwing it upon an horsse there provided readie for that purpose, they convey it unto a place, about two miles distant from the castell.[8]

The Holinshed passage tracks the murderers as they make their way into the king's chamber, then out again after the murder and onto open ground. At the Globe, due to the restricted and mostly undivided space of the stage, the tracking cannot be continuous. Instead, the murder occurs offstage and is signalled to the audience by Macbeth's 'I have done the deed' (2.2.15). However, the tracking effect is not completely lost, being supplied by the alternating appearances of Macbeth and Lady Macbeth between 2.1 and 2.2, each of which supplies a little piece of the narrative. The alternation allows Lady Macbeth's description of the layout of the king's chamber and position of the murder weapons

(2.2.1–14) to take up and extend Macbeth's earlier proleptic reference to Tarquin's steps (2.1.34–65), in a not quite fluid but nevertheless continuous movement. Continuity is thus established through the substitutive presence of an accomplice onstage – Lady Macbeth – who functions as a kind of double, having previously trodden over the ground her husband is covering, in a failed attempt to commit the murder herself. Her reference to open doors (2.2.5) reinforces the scene's in-and-out dynamic and thematises thresholds.

Doorways feature even more prominently in Shakespeare's adaptation of the Holinshed passage in which the king's servants, after knocking insistently, batter down 'doore after doore' to reach his murdered body:

> first they knocked at the doore softlie, then they rapped hard thereat: lastlie, doubting that which had happened, they brake open doore after doore, till at length they came into the chamber where the king lay cold dead upon the floor.[9]

In Shakespeare's *Macbeth*, this becomes the porter episode, involving just one door. The insistent knocking is heard by Macbeth, who at first takes it for the call of his conscience, then by the porter, who facetiously takes it for the knocking of the damned at the gates of hell. The knocking is thus drawn out over several scenes, replicating the sense of duration conveyed by Holinshed's 'lastlie', 'doore after doore' and 'at length'. What in Holinshed was a gradual process of attrition becomes a sudden yielding under sustained pressure. This reduction of many doors to one very resistant door results in a foregrounding of thresholds as places of radical change. Also significant is the shift in point of view. As practical considerations preclude the tracking of characters from outside to inside, the knocking is heard from within the castle, which gives it a haunting, otherworldly dimension, justifying Macbeth's and the porter's allegorising flights of fancy. Collapsing the two characters' perspectives, we have an image of either remorse or damnation gaining entry into Macbeth's mind. A similar shift in perspective operates in Shakespeare's adaptation of Lady Macduff's murder, which Holinshed describes with the following 'tracking shot':

> [Macbeth] came hastily with a big power into Fife, and foorthwith besieged the castell where Makduffe dwelled, trusting to have found him therein. They that kept the house, without anie resistance opened the gates, and suffered him to enter, mistrusting

none evill. But neverthelesse Makbeth most cruellie caused the wife and children of Makduffe, with all other whom he found in that castell, to be slaine.[10]

In Shakespeare, Holinshed's tracking of the murderers as they advance on Macduff's castle, lay siege to it and are eventually admitted is replaced by Lady Macduff's point of view, as her quiet domesticity is shattered by Ross's report of Macduff's flight, then by a messenger's warning of the advancing 'danger' and finally by the intrusion of the killers (4.2). These repeated entrances and exits give the space of the stage the qualities of privacy and interiority associated with the inner self, with the shift in perspective emphasising that inner space's vulnerability to penetration from without.

Simultaneity is the other challenge I mentioned. The source includes frequent references to actions happening in different places at the same time, as when Holinshed's narrator describes a gathering of witches, then 'cuts' to the ailing king with the words: 'the king, at the very same time that these things were a dooing within the castle of Flores, was delivered of his languor'.[11] Though this incident does not make its way into *Macbeth*, the episode of Banquo's murder illustrates Shakespeare's handling of the problem. In the *Chronicles*, Holinshed makes it clear that Macbeth has ordered for the murder to take place during the feast in order to provide himself with an alibi.[12] In the play, the simultaneity of the murder and the feast is signified by having the murderers report back to Macbeth when the banquet is already under way, right before the entrance of Banquo's ghost. The problem that arises here is that the murderers share the stage with the guests, who presumably do not see them. In a footnote, Brooke suggests that the guests would have been seated in the Globe's 'discovery space' (a recess or opening within the tiring house wall), while Macbeth conferred with the murderers off to the side.[13] This might have provided dramatic justification for the guests' inability to notice Macbeth speaking to the murderers, but it does involve a loss of topographical verisimilitude, as the open stage becomes imaginatively split into sealed-off compartments. This loss of verisimilitude would have been compounded by the multiple entrances of Banquo's ghost, so that the stage progressively doubled as a representation of Macbeth's mind, juggling between the requirements of kingship (his guests), dissembling (the murderers) and a guilty conscience (Banquo). The

ghost's allegorising effect, first encountered with the disappearing witches, is of course heightened by his supernatural status.
Returning to the opening scene of the vanishing witches, we can
see how the probable use of trap doors (Brooke's point about
the impracticality of the winch seems valid) would contribute to
allegorising the stage's various passageways. Banquo's statement
about the witches' incorporeal quality suggests that the opening
and closing of a stage door might stand for a less tangible
process, such as the fleeting intrusion of a wicked thought. As
the witches become conflated with Macbeth's desiring thoughts,
their entrances and exits establish a correspondence between
liminal stage spaces and the passages into and out of Macbeth's
mind.

In adapting Holinshed, Shakespeare was naturally con-
strained by the specific architectural features of the Globe theatre,
Macbeth's original venue. Most significantly, there has been much
debate about whether the Globe had two or three stage doors.
Though there is no surviving blueprint of the floorplan of the
Globe's stage, Jean Wilson has argued that 'internal evidence'[14]
from the plays suggests that there were two stage entrances. If we
assume that most Elizabethan playhouses shared a basic design,
the sketch of the Swan theatre made by visiting Dutch student
Johan de Witt in 1596, which is the only surviving contemporary image of an Elizabethan theatre in the archive, confirms this
and further indicates that those stage entrances were fitted with
actual doors. Andrew Gurr, however, has argued for a three-door
plan, with two 'flanking doors' and a 'central opening' or 'discovery space', the latter being used for 'special entrances'.[15] Tim
Fitzpatrick, though acknowledging the possibility of a central
opening, argues for an almost exclusive use of the flanking doors
in production.[16]

Fitzpatrick's case study of *Macbeth*, in which he works out
how entrances and exits would have been orchestrated in this two-
door system, is particularly enlightening. In his central argument,
Fitzpatrick notes the frequent occurrence of situations that can
be staged thanks to 'triangulation'. Triangulation, he explains,
occurs 'in cases when the stage can be seen as an intermediate
place between an offstage place which is "further inwards" and
another offstage place which is "further outwards"'.[17] After a
close analysis of episodes in which characters move from 'outside'
to an in-between space, then proceed 'inside',[18] Fitzpatrick con-
cludes that there is evidence for 'a regularity or default setting, a

"bias" to the stage, a repeated and non-reversible use of one particular door for "inwards" and the other door for "outwards"'.[19]
This 'default setting', as Fitzpatrick explains, was a matter of
practicality, as it helped actors remember which door they were
supposed to use for a given entrance or exit. For example, the
actors playing Lady Macduff's murderers knew they must enter
Stage Left because that was the 'further outward' door and pursue
their victim out Stage Right because that was the 'further inward'
door. If Fitzpatrick is correct in his surmise, these instances of
triangulation contributed to turning the stage into a tragic space
by investing characters' movements with a sense of inevitable
directionality. What is more, this triangulation turned the stage
itself into a passageway, thus foregrounding the play's concern
with liminality. In a carefully comparative discussion of this
issue, Evelyn B. Tribble agrees with Fitzpatrick's analysis, pointing out that '[t]he binary structure Fitzpatrick proposes [...] has
the virtue of reducing complexity – or simplifying perception
and choice.'[20] Reduction, simplicity and choice are indeed of the
essence, and it seems clear that the virtual railroading of stage
movement implied by the inward/outward scheme contributes to
the allegorical effects discussed above by building an assumption
of irreversibility into the play's stage dynamics.

The practical constraints of adapting Holinshed for the stage
thus imply a contraction and unidirectionality conducive to
turning the stage into a tragic mindscape. This process, however,
also relies on verbal imagery, including Lady Macbeth's doorway
metaphors, which are rich with Galenic echoes.

The Tragic Doorways of the Mind

Lady Macbeth's agenda is all about turning the inside of the castle
into a tragic space, or in other words, a trap. This is clear in her
statement about 'the fatal entrance of Duncan under my battlements' (1.5.39–40) and in her expressed wish that Duncan, once
he has entered, should 'never [...] go [...] hence' (1.5.59–60).
What is remarkable about Lady Macbeth's speeches is that tragic
physical space is almost systematically allegorised as tragic mental
space, as the castle's doorways double as irreversible transforma-
tions of the mind. Thus, Lady Macbeth's imagined transformation
of the castle into a trap is immediately followed by the imagined
compartmentalisation of her own body and mind:

The raven himself is hoarse
That croaks the fatal entrance of Duncan
Under my battlements. Come, you spirits
That tend on mortal thoughts, unsex me here,
And fill me from the crown to the toe, top-full
Of direst cruelty. Make thick my blood,
Stop up th'access and passage to remorse,
That no compunctious visitings of nature
Shall fell my purpose

(1.5.38–46)

Trapping Duncan in the castle thus goes hand in hand with Lady Macbeth trapping her own evil thoughts in some inner recess of the mind, after blocking the 'passage' or doorway that connects it to mercy. The reference to blood indicates a Galenic model of the body, in which thought is carried from the heart to the brain by blood-borne spirits.[21] Further along in the first act, Lady Macbeth conflates spatial and mental penetrability when she exposes her plan to drug the chamberlains guarding the doors to Duncan's chamber:

his two chamberlains
Will I with wine and wassail so convince
That memory, the warder of the brain,
Shall be a fume, and the receipt of reason
A limbeck only; when in swinish sleep
Their drenchèd natures lie as in a death,
What cannot you and I perform upon
Th'unguarded Duncan? What not put upon
His spongy officers who shall bear the guilt
Of our great quell?

(1.7.63–72)

This time, the speech establishes a connection between the doors of the king's chamber and those of the chamberlains' brains. Duncan will be 'unguarded' because his guards' own brains are unguarded, having lost their 'warder[s]' to wine. What could strike one as the scene's inordinate interest in the brains of lowly grooms makes dramatic sense only if the guards' neglect of their charge under the influence of wine and drugs functions as a projected allegory of what is happening in the minds of the actual murderers. Here projection feeds on scapegoating, as the guards will be made to shoulder the castle holders' burden of guilt. Thus, the defeat of reason taking place in the chamberlains' minds can be read as a mirror of what is taking place in the Macbeths' own minds, as their 'drenchèd natures' give in to the lure of ambition. The connection is reinforced in the next scene, in which Lady Macbeth describes the state of the guards she has now plied with wine and drugs, while in the next room Macbeth is committing the murder:

> That which hath made them drunk, hath made me bold;
> What hath quenched them, hath given me fire [...]
> The doors are open, and the surfeited grooms
> Do mock their charges with snores. I have drugged their possets,
> That death and nature do contend about them
> Whether they live or die.
>
> (2.2.1–8)

Lady Macbeth does not specify which doors she is referring to. This indeterminacy contributes to the doors' allegorical function as images of the Macbeths' minds, an effect that would have been reinforced if the stage doors had been left open. Here, open doors may stand either for indecision or for the surrender of the will. Though the open door may sound like an image of free will and possibility, the accumulation of verbs in the present perfect indicates that the die is cast, in an anticipation of Macbeth's 'I have done the deed' (2.2.14).

These allegorising speeches of Lady Macbeth's, one should note, are grounded in early modern philosophical discourses, in which the mind is represented as a citadel, castle or stronghold. In these discourses, the doorways of the mind may sometimes appear as traps: what goes in never 'goes hence' again.

The Citadel of the Soul

The castle as an allegory of the soul fighting sin, as we have seen, belongs to the medieval tradition. The recognition of this tradition, however, may obscure how widespread the image of the 'citadel of the mind' was in Shakespeare's theological and philosophical environment. Citadel of mind imagery appears in the works of Roman Emperor Marcus Aurelius, in the writings of the fathers of the church, including Augustine and Saint Thomas Aquinas, in the works of Renaissance Aristotelians Nicolas Coeffeteau and Jean Fernel and in those of Protestant reformer Jean Calvin. This surface agreement, however, conceals very different perspectives on how thought is processed, on the relationship between mind and soul, and ultimately on the existence of free will.

In Stoic and patristic writings, the citadel is a place of safety, affording protection from the outside world and the passions. Thus, Marcus Aurelius enjoined his reader to 'let thy chiefe fort and place of defence be, a minde free from passions. A stronger place, (whereunto to make his refuge, and so to become impregnable), and better fortified than this, hath no man.'[22] The citadel of the soul takes on a mystical dimension in Christian Neoplatonism, where it is characterised as the place within the soul that holds the image of God. Medieval theologian Meister Eckhart and Renaissance hermetic philosopher Marsilio Ficino both invoked the 'citadel' in this sense,[23] and traces of this idea can be found in Calvin's model of the mind as a citadel around the soul, penetrable only by God's grace. In Calvin's view, derived from Augustine, conversion occurs when the mind is touched by grace and frees the bound will within, allowing it to contemplate the *imago dei*.[24] However, Augustine and Calvin also use the image of the entrance into the citadel to indicate the soul's complete surrender to evil. In his *Institutes*, Calvin writes that 'wicked impiety possessed the very castell of [Adam's] minde, and pride pierced to the innermost part of his heart'.[25] In this model, once corruption has entered the soul, its effect is complete and devastating. In his sermon on the ten commandments, Calvin warns that 'once the minde, that is, the understanding of men, is so defiled, the rest is easilie corrupted'.[26]

This darker construction of the citadel of the mind as a deadly trap is not limited to Calvinist pessimism; it is also expressed in the medical/theological writings of Jesuit priest Thomas Wright, which come very close to the language of Lady Macbeth's fateful speeches. Like Lady Macbeth, Wright describes conscience as the 'guardian of the soul' and likens the passions to wine:

> [As] wine maketh men drunke, and robbeth the use of reason, so inordinate love and affection make drunken the soule, and deprive it of judgement; this, in fine, robbeth soules from God, and carrieth them to the Diuell. [...] A wicked will commanding the wit, to find out reasons to pleade for passions; for this corrupteth, yea wholly destroyeth the remorce of conscience, the careful guardian of the soul: this maketh men obstinate in all enormious vices; for when the wit is once perswaded, and no further appellation can be administered, then the soule is confirmed almost in malice.[27]

The sense that evil is irreversible once it has made it past a guarded door connects this passage with several of Lady Macbeth's speeches. However, Wright's imagery of robbery, drunkenness and corruption, though close to the play's own, hints at a form of violation, depicting the soul as a passive victim rather than an active participant. In *Macbeth*, on the contrary, the irreversible dimension of evil is given the force of a commitment, thanks to a systematic triangulation of doorways, thought and promising.

Closed Doors and Solemn Vows

In Cognitive Metaphor Theory, which posits that categories of thought derive from early childhood spatial exploration, the closed door is cognitively related to the concept of finality. This is the point Donald C. Freeman makes in his analysis of the play, in which he argues that *Macbeth*'s action is underpinned by the twinned metaphors of PATH and CONTAINER (capitalised in his discussion), two patterns identified by cognitive linguist George Lakoff as structuring the early stages of embodied experience.[28] While Freeman focuses on imagery, Mary Thomas Crane applies Cognitive Metaphor Theory by way of wordplay. Drawing on Patricia Parker's practice of unlocking key themes of a play through a close study of polysemy,[29] Crane argues that 'Shakespeare's wordplay, in exploring the spatial structuration of polysemic words, can sometimes also expose the ways in which spatial relationships work to create meaning.'[30] In *Macbeth*, this approach is well suited to Banquo's statement that the king (Duncan) is 'shut up / In measureless content' (2.1.16–17). In a footnote to the Oxford edition, Brooke points out that the term 'shut up' was used 'for concluding affairs as well as for withdrawing to the confinement of a chamber'.[31] Indeed, the image subsists to this day in the idiom of 'closing a deal'. The closed door thus comes to stand for a decision, for commitment to a course of action. The double meaning of 'shut up', as I will argue, helps align *Macbeth* with a dramatic tradition whereby what John Kerrigan calls 'binding language',[32] meaning pacts, oaths and promises, stands for a mind made up, a door closed against further deliberation.

If the wordplay discussed above is a bit too subtle to produce a strong dramatic impact, the comic porter scene presents a visually compelling association of doors and oaths. In act 2, scene 3, the drunk porter entertains himself by imagining that he is the 'porter of hell-gate', and that the knocking at the castle door comes from (among others), '[a]n equivocator, that could swear in both the scales against either scale, who committed treason enough for God's sake, yet could not equivocate to Heaven: O, come in, equivocator' (2.3.8–11). This, as Garry Wills has shown, is a reference to the Jesuitic practice of equivocation, used by Father Garnett to avoid self-incrimination at his Gunpowder Plot trial in 1605.[33] In the porter's little fantasy, the equivocator mistakenly believes that swearing falsely does not commit him to anything – the porter will show him otherwise by ushering him through the gates of hell. Though there may be an allegorical dimension to this story, with the doors of hell standing for the soul's fall into damnation, the equivocator's swearing appears as a freely chosen speech act rather than an irrepressible act of the mind. The porter's allegory is a moral fable, not a psychological tragedy. Elsewhere, however, doors and promises come together as tragic signifiers of inner resolution, thanks to the ritual resonances of dramatised – or even reported – oaths.

John Kerrigan, Frances A. Shirley and William Kerrigan have all emphasised the dramatic potency of staged swearing. As any playgoer can testify, oath-taking scenes rank among the most striking in Shakespeare's plays, as when Hamlet swears his companions to secrecy after seeing the ghost, Iago swears to devote his efforts to avenging Othello's supposedly besmirched honour, or, on a tragicomic note, when Claudio pledges to marry Hero ('I am yours'; 2.1.308) in *Much Ado About Nothing*. One of the reasons such scenes stand out is because of their ritual quality. Oath-taking involves prescribed gestures and formulae, implies a transcendent observer (one swears 'before God') and results in the speaker's irreversible transformation as he or she achieves a new ontological state. The intrinsic theatricality of the ritual contributes to blurring the boundary between mystical and theatrical performance. Though, like all dramatised speech acts, the promise is 'in a peculiar way hollow or void if spoken by an actor on the stage',[34] it remains loaded with a numinous energy that calls to be redirected and absorbed in the dramatic economy of the play. In the theatre, the sense of mystical awe associated with oath-taking, and to a lesser extent promising, becomes attached to the quasi-magical process of displaying the oath-taker's mind to the audience. Thus, John Kerrigan points out that 'oaths and vows are used, sometimes rather externally, to mark changes in motive and attachment'.[35] This means that oaths and vows are not only mimetic counterparts to real-life speech acts (or in Peircean terms, 'icons') but also perceptible traces of something not seen ('indexes') as well as conventional counterparts ('symbols').[36] This semiotic function is also implied by Cynthia Marshall's observation that Shakespearian statements of commitment or resolve often seem 'to commemorate, rather than express, the process of making a choice'.[37] Promising then becomes the outward sign of a mind made up.

The idea of the promise as an external sign of psychological commitment may have entered early modern drama by way of Christopher Marlowe's *Doctor Faustus*, where the protagonist signs away his soul in exchange for infinite knowledge and power. In Marlowe's play, binding language functions not only in a denotative or even connotative way but quasi-allegorically, as the verbal counterpart of a state of mental frailty. The idea of the promise as a sign is articulated in the third scene of the A-text, when Mephistophilis, appearing in response to the magician's conjuring, nevertheless denies any performative power to Faustus's words:

FAUSTUS
Did not my conjuring speeches raise thee? Speak!
MEPHISTOPHILIS
That was the cause, but yet *per accidens*,
For when we hear one rack the name of God,
Abjure the Scriptures, and his saviour Christ,
We fly in hope to get his glorious soul,
Nor will we come, unless he use such means
Whereby he is in danger to be damned.[38]

Referring to J. L. Austin's distinction between words that perform and words that refer,[39] we can note that Mephistophilis demotes Faustus's incantations to a referential status. A hint of the Calvinist belief in willed human acts as no more than signs of a pre-ordained eschatological status is perceptible here. Though conjuring is a different speech act from promising, Mephistophilis's scepticism about the performative power of human words carries over to the demonic pact itself, which is repeatedly referred to as a promise, as when Lucifer reminds Faustus that he has spoken of Christ 'contrary to [his] promise' (scene 5, line 265). Though the issue of whether Faustus damns himself by signing the pact or whether the pact is but a manifestation of an irretrievably hardened heart is never entirely resolved, Mephistophilis's previous speech about the inefficacy of Faustus's words hints at the second explanation.

There is something of the Faustian pact in Lady Macbeth's appeal to 'spirits', discussed above. Just as Faustus 'abjures the Scriptures', Lady Macbeth abjures her femininity and the gentle thoughts conventionally associated with it. As she disavows the tender allegorical connotations of the female form, Lady Macbeth plays on the ambiguity of the word 'spirit', with its Galenic and demonic denotations, thereby conflating the physical blockage of the brain's passageways and the finality of the satanic pact. In this speech as in others, the metaphorical status of promises is foregrounded by a blurring of boundaries: promises tend to merge with slightly different speech and thought acts such as invocations, prophecies and imagination. Thus, when Banquo refers to the weird sisters' prophecy as a 'promise' (3.1.2), their swift crossings of stage thresholds become allegorical substitutes for psychological commitment. Another instance of a slightly 'off' mention of swearing is Lady Macbeth's reproof of her husband's weakness, when he balks at committing murder:

> I have given suck, and know
> How tender 'tis to love the babe that milks me;
> I would, while it was smiling in my face,
> Have plucked my nipple from its boneless gums
> And dashed the brains out, had I so sworn
> As you have done to this.

> (1.7.54–9)

The passage, which famously inspired L. C. Knight's tongue-in-cheek 'How many children had Lady Macbeth?' is startling in many ways. In addition to the horror of the description, the post-positioned reference to swearing raises several questions. The first, perhaps, is why Lady Macbeth would have sworn to something so evil and unnatural in the first place. The second is whether Macbeth has really sworn to kill the king, and in what circumstances. As far as the Folio text – the only one available – can tell us, Macbeth never actually swore to kill Duncan. Critics have puzzled over the inconsistency, speculating about the possibility of a lost scene or implied offstage events.[40] Dismissing these explanations, Brooke insists that these lines should be taken as acknowledgement of a tacit understanding between the conspiring spouses: 'The same information provoked the same thought in both their minds, as they knew it would.'[41] This reduction of a formal vow to a shared, unvoiced thought is intriguing, and shifts the act of vowing from the outer plane of explicit agreement to the inner plane of psychological conviction. Here again, the in/out opposition contributes to the promise's semiotic charge, as swearing appears on the same line as the image of brains exiting the skull, which Freeman has identified as a variation on the PATH/CONTAINER motif.[42]

Promising, then, appears as the audible counterpart of a state of psychological commitment. In Peircean terms, it is both index and symbol. Throughout the play, the symbolisms of stage doors and of performed or unperformed promises reinforce each other, while standing apart in their modes of signification. Because stage doors are material and promises immaterial, their juxtaposition raises the question of the ontological nature of the process by which thought ceases to flow freely and becomes mired in evil.

The Nature of Thought and the Issue of Materiality

What happens when the mind commits to evil? Or rather, how does it happen? Does signifying a closed mind thanks to a closed door or thanks to a promise involve different understandings of what the mind is? On the basis of similarity, one might think the first would point towards a more material conception, and the second, towards a more immaterial, purely rational one. This interpretation, however, makes light of the inherently figurative dimension of the allegorical symbol, whereby the material stands for the immaterial. The question is whether theatrical signs should be seen mostly as iconic, based on similarity with the referent, or as mostly symbolic, based on convention. Rather than offering an analysis of the nature of thought, the coexistence of these two modes of signification serves to foreground the mysteriousness of the process whereby the mind falls victim to evil. Metaphysical anxiety as to the inner mechanics of the mind is clearly expressed in Macbeth's question to the doctor about his ability to cure his wife's mental anguish:

> *Macb*. Canst thou not minister to a mind diseased?
>   Pluck from the memory a rooted sorrow,
>   Raze out the written troubles of the brain,
>   And with some sweet oblivious antidote

> Cleanse the stuffed bosom of that perilous stuff
> Which weighs upon the heart?
> *Doct.* Therein the patient
>   Must minister to himself.
> *Macb.* Throw physic to the dogs, I'll none of it.
>
> (5.3.40–6)

Macbeth's hope that diseases of the mind are reversible leads him to emphasise the physicality of the mind, which he identifies with the brain. The doctor's answer implies that diseases of the mind are of a spiritual rather than a physical nature. However, Macbeth's reference to 'written troubles', which is clearly metaphorical, breaks down that dichotomy by suggesting that the rest of the description may be metaphorical as well. In particular, the polyptotonic variation on 'stuff' draws attention to the indeterminacy of the word and leaves open whether the 'stuff' in question is a material or a spiritual blockage barring the heart's access to physical or spiritual health. The same vagueness applies to the other images. For example, are memories material objects that can be 'rooted out' by mechanical means? This ambiguity resonates with the scene of the disappearing witches. Granted that the weird sisters' 'promise' can be read as a sign of Macbeth's commitment to evil, is the process made of 'earth' or 'bubbles' (1.3.79)? Meaning, is it material or spiritual?

Macbeth's dialogue with the doctor dramatises the link between the play's semiotic versatility and the ambiguities of Galenic affect literature. For example, Wright's statement that 'whatsoever we understand passes by the gates of our imagination'[43] does not necessarily imply the humoral framework found in other parts of the treatise. The gates may be allegorical, or not. Wright's treatise, as has been noted by Erin Sullivan,[44] is written from the double perspective of the natural philosopher and the Jesuit theologian, so that the mind is described as both a material and a spiritual entity. *Macbeth*'s allegorical structure thus draws attention to the unknowable – or unknown – relation between the material brain, the rational mind and the immortal soul.

Macbeth's allegorical design, then, tends to corroborate T. S. Eliot's choice of the play as the textbook illustration of his concept of the 'objective correlative', which he defined as 'a set of objects, a situation, a chain of events which shall be the formula of that particular emotion'.[45] Macbeth's powerful evocation of a mind's tragic commitment to evil is achieved thanks to several markers of irreversibility, including stage doors, metaphors and solemn oaths, in association with other signifiers of closure and finality, such as cauldrons, death and the grammatical present perfect. Beyond its tragic function, however, the play's composite allegory of mental commitment evokes the black box of the mind, the mysterious dimension of the process that takes Macbeth from 'We will proceed no further in this business' (1.7.31) to 'I am settled' (1.7.80) in a mere fifty lines. Unlike *Julius Caesar's* embodied memory images, which highlighted process, allegory in *Macbeth* shows us a result. Here, the architectural framework of the stage is enlisted for the purpose of picturing the mind as a trap, in a way that is corroborated by the play's figurative language and ritualised speech acts. The stark binaries (in/out, past/present) implied by this poetic design, however, avoid the pitfall of caricature by playing architectural and verbal signifying modes against each other, in such a way as to represent human thought as both a physical and a metaphysical mystery, carrying the whiff of damnation and disease.

Though *Macbeth's* use of 'castle of the mind' imagery draws much of its signifying force from Stoic and medieval citadel models, the time-worn allegory of the citadel of the mind is rejuvenated by its equation with the Globe stage, the rhetoric of promising and Galenic medicine. This rejuvenation, one should note, is dependent on movement. The use of the body's movements as a vehicle for allegorical thought representation is a powerful theatrical tool, which grounds the allegory in what is the very essence of theatricality: a speaking body's motion in space. In *Macbeth*, however, the emphasis on doorways limits the meaning of stage movement to changes of state, as defined by the in/out binary. Elsewhere, the body may signify more freely, in a way more intimately rooted in theatrical performance. For this greater sense of denotative freedom, let us move away from the creaky doors of tragedy and turn to the pastoral spaces of *Cymbeline*, a play that tends to equate the body's movements with forbidden thoughts and desires.

Notes

1   David Wiles, 'Place et espace du mal dans *Macbeth*', trans. François Laroque, in Gisèle Venet (ed.), *Le Mal et ses masques: théâtre, imaginaire, société*, Lyons: ENS Éditions, 1998, pp. 347–62,

http://books.openedition.org/enseditions/7228, last accessed 24 April 2022, § 8; and Jennifer C. Vaught, *Architectural Rhetoric in Shakespeare and Spenser*, Berlin and Boston: Walter de Gruyter, 2019, p. 132.

2   Wiles, 'Place et espace du mal', § 8 (my translation).

3   The term, coined by T. S. Eliot, will be discussed at the end of this chapter.

4   Raphael Holinshed, *The Chronicles of England, Scotland and Ireland*, vol. 2, 'Chronicles of Scotland', extracted in Geoffrey Bullough (ed.), *Narrative and Dramatic Sources of Shakespeare. Volume VII, Major Tragedies: Hamlet, Othello, King Lear, Macbeth*, London: Routledge and Kegan Paul, 1975.

5   Ibid. pp. 494, 495.

6   William Shakespeare, *Macbeth*, ed. Nicholas Brooke (1990), The Oxford Shakespeare, Oxford World's Classics, Oxford and New York: Oxford University Press, 1998, p. 104n.

7   Bullough, *Narrative and Dramatic Sources, Vol. VII*, p. 496.

8   Ibid. p. 482.

9   Ibid. p. 487.

10 Ibid. p. 501.

11 Ibid. p. 480.

12 Ibid. p. 498.

13 Brooke, in Shakespeare, *Macbeth*, p. 153n.

14 Jean Wilson, *The Shakespeare Legacy: The Material Legacy of Shakespeare's Theatre*, London: Bramley Books, 1995, p. 74.

15 Andrew Gurr and Mariko Ichikawa, *Staging in Shakespeare's Theatres* (2000), Oxford: Oxford University Press, 2013, pp. 6–7.

16 Tim Fitzpatrick, 'Shakespeare's Exploitation of a Two-door Stage: *Macbeth*', *Theatre Research International*, vol. 20, no. 3 (1995), pp. 207–30.

17 Ibid. p. 214.

18 Fitzpatrick mentions 'Act III when Macbeth, now King, is at Forres planning and executing Banquo's death; [...] Act IV, with the killing of Lady Macduff at Fife; and [...] the final act, where Macbeth is holed up in Dunsinane'. Ibid.

19 Ibid. p. 215.

20 Evelyn B. Tribble, *Cognition in the Globe: Attention and Memory in Shakespeare's Theatre*, New York: Palgrave Macmillan, 2011, p. 41.

21 See Chapter 1, p. 32.

22 Marcus Aurelius, *Meditations* (AD 167), trans. Meric Casaubon, London, 1634, p. 135. Though the first English translation of *Meditations* was published in 1634, Shakespeare would have been able to read it in Latin. A Latin translation (from the original

Greek) by W. Xylander Holzmann appeared in 1558, with a second edition in 1568.

23   '[T]he people who have discovered something important in any of the noble arts have principally done so when they have abandoned the body and taken refuge in the citadel of the soul.' Marsilio Ficino, in *Platonic Theology, Volume 4: Books XII–XIV*, trans. James Hankins and William R. Bowen, Cambridge, MA: Harvard University Press, 2001, p. 123.

24   For Calvin's view of the human mind as a case for God's image, see, for example, Obbie Tyler Todd, 'The Preeminence of Knowledge in John Calvin's Doctrine of Conversion and Its Influence Upon His Ministry in Geneva', *Thelemios*, vol. 42, no. 2 (2017), pp. 306–20.

25   Jean Calvin, *The Institution of Christian Religion*, trans. Thomas Norton (from the 1536 Latin edn), London, 1634, EEBO, Harvard University Library, pp. 108–9. Shakespeare would have had access to this in the original Latin.

26   Jean Calvin, Sermon 4, in *Sermons of M. Iohn Calvin, upon the X Commandementes of the Lawe*, trans. John Harison, London, 1579, EEBO, The Huntington Library, p. 28.

27   Thomas Wright, *The Passions of the Minde in Generall* (1601), London, 1604, EEBO, Yale University Library, p. 97.

28   Donald C. Freeman, '"Catching the nearest way": *Macbeth* and Cognitive Metaphor', in Jonathan Culpeper, Mick Short and Peter Verdonk (eds), *Exploring the Language of Drama: From Text to Context*, The Interface Series, Abingdon and New York: Routledge, 1998, pp. 96–111.

29   See Patricia Parker, *Shakespeare from the Margins: Language, Culture, Context*, Chicago and London: University of Chicago Press, 1996.

30   Mary Thomas Crane, *Shakespeare's Brain: Reading with Cognitive Theory*, Princeton, NJ, and Oxford: Princeton University Press, 2001, p. 33.

31   William Shakespeare, *Macbeth*, ed. Nicholas Brooke (1990), The Oxford Shakespeare, Oxford World's Classics, Oxford and New York: Oxford University Press, 1998, p. 123n. Also *OED*, 7.

32   John Kerrigan, *Shakespeare's Binding Language*, Oxford: Oxford University Press, 2016.

33   Garry Wills, *Witches and Jesuits: Shakespeare's* Macbeth, New York and Oxford: Oxford University Press, 1995, pp. 93–105.

34   J. L. Austin, *How to Do Things with Words*, The William James Lectures, Cambridge, MA: Harvard University Press, 1962, p. 22.

35   John Kerrigan, 'Shakespeare, Oaths and Vows', *Proceeding of the British Academy*, vol. 167 (2010), pp. 61–89 (p. 66).

36   Charles Sanders Peirce distinguishes three types of signs. An 'icon' is based on resemblance (a portrait is an icon of the sitter); an 'index',

on cause and effect (smoke is an index of fire); and a 'symbol', on convention (a green light symbolises 'go'). For a clear discussion of Peircean semiotics, see Keir Elam, *The Semiotics of Theatre and Drama*, London and New York: Routledge, 2002, pp. 18–22.

37 Cynthia Marshall, 'Shakespeare, Crossing the Rubicon', in Peter Holland (ed.), *Shakespeare Survey: An Annual Survey of Shakespeare Studies and Production. Volume 53: Shakespeare and Narrative*, Cambridge: Cambridge University Press, 2000, pp. 73–88 (p. 87).

38 Christopher Marlowe, *Dr Faustus* (A-text, 1594), ed. Roma Gill, London: A&C Black; New York: Norton, 1989, scene 3, lines 46–52.

39 Austin, *How to Do Things with Words*, pp. 1–13.

40 In an address to the French Shakespeare Society (Société Française Shakespeare) on 18 March 2022, Rory Loughnane argued for missing scenes, given that *Macbeth* is about a third shorter than the other great tragedies.

41 Brooke, in Shakespeare, *Macbeth*, p. 120n.

42 Freeman, '"Catching the nearest way"', p. 99.

43 Wright, *Passions of the Minde*, p. 51.

44 Erin Sullivan, 'The Passions of Thomas Wright: Renaissance Emotion across Body And Soul', in R. Meek and E. Sullivan (eds), *The Renaissance of Emotion: Understanding Affect in Shakespeare and His Contemporaries*, Manchester: Manchester University Press, 2015, pp. 25–44.

45 T. S. Eliot, 'Hamlet and His Problems' (1920), reprinted as 'Hamlet', in *Selected Essays*, 3rd edn, London: Faber and Faber, 1951, pp. 141–6 (p. 145).

Chapter 3

Tender Motions: Gesture in *Cymbeline*

In the programme for her 2006 Kneehigh/Royal Shakespeare Company (RSC) production of *Cymbeline*, Emma Rice wrote, 'I want this production to celebrate the child in all of us.'[1] *Cymbeline*'s affinity with children's stories has long been recognised by theatre professionals and scholars alike. Peter Hall's 1957 RSC production adopted a fairy-tale aesthetic which Kennan Tynan praised as 'a Grimm fable transmuted by the Cocteau of *La Belle et la Bête*'.[2] This is consistent with Catherine Belsey's recognition of the play's Snow White motif, involving a wicked stepmother (the Queen), a reluctant hit man (Pisanio), and the poison-induced, death-like sleep of the heroine (Imogen).[3] In addition to the fairy-tale pattern, the plot is rooted in a number of incidents going back to the protagonists' childhoods. Imogen is heiress to the throne of Britain because her brothers, Guiderius and Arviragus, were kidnapped as toddlers. Her status as heiress is the main reason why her stepbrother, Cloten, covets her and will eventually be killed in pursuit of her. Also part of the backstory is the idyllic childhood friendship of Imogen and Posthumus, a court-raised orphan, which has blossomed into love, leading to a clandestine marriage. Posthumus's low birth is responsible for his banishment, and for the insecurity that leads him to lend his ear to slanderous accusations of his wife, and eventually to order her murder at the hands of his servant, Pisanio. Underscoring these plot features, the play has a pantomime quality, with an emphasis on gestures of approaching, giving and taking away, combined with a curious stylistic reliance on the rhetorical figure of apostrophe, involving addresses to absent people or abstract notions that are reminiscent of a child chatting with an imaginary friend.

It is partly through apostrophe that *Cymbeline*'s fairy-tale aesthetic dovetails with more properly allegorical modes of storytelling. With their vocative addresses to 'sleep', 'boldness' or 'Nature', characters are shown grappling with forces unseen, giving verbal shape to numinous experience. Symbolic objects such as rings, bracelets and handkerchiefs may find themselves on the receiving end of such apostrophes, in a way that connects the magic objects of fairy tale to the symbolic signifiers of allegory. The line between fairy tale and allegory is also straddled by the play's dream sequence (5.4.29–92), which includes a mythological masque featuring Jupiter swooping down on an eagle and delivering an allegorical prophecy involving lions, trees and eagles. As befits prophecies, this one is obscure, becoming fully intelligible only after its realisation.

The obscurity of the prophecy suggests that the coexistence of fairy-tale and allegorical modes involves a tension – or perhaps an overlap – between the simplicity of children's stories and the obscurity long associated with allegory. Long before Bruno Bettelheim started applying psychoanalysis to fairy tales,[4] Neoplatonic philosophers of the late antiquity and Middle Ages described allegory as a secret language thanks to which the mysteries of religion could be both encoded and revealed.[5] As mentioned in the Introduction, sixteenth-century rhetorician George Puttenham also emphasised allegory's affinity with secrecy, calling it 'a duplicitie of meaning or dissimulation under couert and darke intendments'.[6] This darkness, however, is not to be found in *Cymbeline*'s apostrophes, which are based on straightforward personifications. Instead, I will argue that it resides in the play's stylised gestures, both performed and described. Though the play's gestures do make for narrative clarity, as befitting a tale told to a child, they also contribute to complex and sometimes disturbing allegorical depictions of the protagonists' minds.

Foregrounding Gesture in *Cymbeline*

Cymbeline's pantomime quality is hinted at as early as the first line, with the first gentleman's reference to the courtier's frowning (1.1.1).[7] As facial expression segues into emphatic gesture, this quality becomes more pronounced. Though there is a paucity of stage directions, the Folio play-text clearly cues for salient, often emphatic gestures at key moments of the plot. An early

example is the handshake and transfer of the ring that seal the
wager between Posthumus and Iachimo (1.4.145–73), cued by
'here's my ring' (145–6), 'Your hand' (164) and 'Agreed' (169).
Gesturing is also prominent in the second act, when the two
men bandy back and forth the bracelet and ring that now stand
as debased tokens of Imogen's chastity (2.4.106–30). In such
scenes, repetition gives gestures a sometimes comically over-the-
top quality, an effect also encountered in the farcical device of
Iachimo emerging from the trunk in order to spy on the sleeping
Imogen. Even Posthumus's striking of Imogen in the final scene,
before he recognises her, can be played for laughs, as being simply
'too much'.[8] Beyond such occasional comic effects, gestures are
often salient enough to carry the storytelling. A quick thought
experiment with the text is enough to establish that the 'Snow
White and the huntsman' sequence, in which Pisanio reveals
Posthumus's murderous instructions to Imogen, refuses to carry
them out and puts himself at her service, could be played in
dumb show and remain perfectly clear (3.4.10–82). The sequence
of Pisanio handing Imogen the letter (10), Imogen reading it
(21–31), then grabbing Pisanio's sword and pointing it at herself
(67), followed by Pisanio taking up and casting away the sword
(73) and Imogen pulling out and throwing away all Posthumus's
letters to her (82) speaks for itself.

It is notable, however, that the scene is not a dumb show, at
a time when dumb shows were gaining in popularity.[9] Even in
Cymbeline's most physical scenes, gesture is both foregrounded
and thematised by speech. Act 2, scene 4 is a good example of
this dual dynamic. Not only are the characters' gestures underscored verbally (as when as when Posthumus says, 'Here, take
this too' (106) while handing Iachimo the ring in acknowledgement of his lost wager), but they are also commented on, in
terms that draw attention to the expressive power of physical
motions. For example, when Iachimo falsely claims to have
obtained Imogen's bracelet from her, he states that her gesture of
removing the bracelet was more precious than the bracelet itself:
'Her pretty action did outsell her gift, and yet enriched it, too'
(102–3). Iachimo's tribute to the dazzling power of gesture ironi-
cally comes right after he himself has used it to gull Posthumus.
It is indeed Iachimo's 'Hey presto!' action of producing Imogen's
bracelet (cued by 'See!'; 96) that convinces Posthumus of his
wife's infidelity, rather than the bracelet itself, which he does not
recognise (98–9). The play's elevation of gesture over object can

in fact be noticed as early as Pisanio's report of Posthumus waving a 'glove or hat or handkerchief' (1.3.11) as he sails away. While the waving is clearly correlated with the 'fits and stirs of's mind' (12), the object being waved does not really matter. Similarly, Guiderius's imitation of crushing an enemy's neck with his foot (3.3.92) does not require the presence of an actual enemy in order to prove his valour; the gesture is enough. Through their cumulative effect, these instances of privileging gesture over object invite the audience to pay attention to gesture and ponder its dramatic function.

The Dramatic Function of Gesture: Intelligibility, Naturalism and Rhetorical Efficacy

One of the functions of gesture in *Cymbeline* is no doubt to add clarity. As Andrew Gurr has observed, there were a number of obstacles to both vision and hearing at the Globe and Blackfriars theatres, two possible venues for *Cymbeline*'s early performances. Distance from the stage, bulky hats, audience rowdiness, and a stage crowded by players and gentlefolk (at the second venue) made it difficult to catch every word or facial expression performed onstage, or to see every prop. For Gurr,

> [w]riters always expected their audience to have impeded views at times, whether from the large posts holding up the front of the galleries, from the headgear of other audience-members, or (mostly with the groundlings) the crowd of players on stage.[10]

Thus, Pisanio's refusal to murder his mistress is conveyed in words, gestures and no doubt facial expression, with each mode of figuration potentially filling in whatever may have been missed in the others. Similarly, the kidnapped princes' bravery is conveyed by their own words, by Belarius's description of their heroic gestures, by his imitation of said gestures as he describes them, and so on (3.3.86–95). This redundancy of signifying systems is of course a general feature of early modern drama, but in *Cymbeline*, performed gestures may also have helped blaze a notoriously complex plot by signalling changes in the characters' relationships and states of mind. Thus, Posthumus's new-found love for his wife in act 5, scene 1 can be symbolised by his clutching and possibly kissing the bloodied handkerchief before putting it away close to his heart.

In addition to providing clarity, the coupling of word and action might have been seen as a naturalistic feature. The idea that gesture naturally accompanied thought and intention was commonplace, deriving in part from the rhetorical treatises of Cicero and Quintilian. According to Cicero,

> nature has assigned to every emotion a particular look and tone of voice and bearing of its own; and the whole of a person's frame and every look on his face and utterance of his voice are like the strings of the harp, and sound according as they are struck by each successive emotion.[11]

Similarly, Quintilian insisted that the orator's eloquence required a harmonious balance of speech, facial expression and gesture: 'all emotional appeals will inevitably fall flat, unless they are given the fire that voice, look, and the whole carriage of the body can give them'.[12]

Early modern rhetoricians and playwrights carried over these principles of oratory to the stage, recommending hand–speech harmony for the sake of naturalism and decorum. Thus, Thomas Heywood stressed the similarity between oratory and acting by pointing out that '[rhetoric] instructs [the scholar] to fit his phrases to his action, and his action to his phrase, and his pronunciation to them both.'[13] The same idea is famously articulated by Hamlet in his advice to the players: 'Suit the action to the word, the word to the action, with this special observance, that you o'erstep not the modesty of nature' (*Hamlet*, 3.2.16–18). These appeals to the harmony of voice and gesture are premised on the idea that gesture naturally and spontaneously expresses the mind, a connection that has been made much of in recent cognitive and stage-centred scholarship.

The Correlation of Gesture and Thought

The correlation between gesture and thought was both a given and a source of fascination in early modern rhetoric. Not only did gesture reflect and illustrate a speaker's thoughts, but it conveyed them in such a way as to strike the interlocutor's eye and affect his or her own thoughts. In *The Hand on the Shakespearean Stage*, Farah Karim-Cooper emphasises the way early modern medical and rhetorical treatises established 'semantic links between the hand and thought' and made the hand 'synonymous with the brain'.[14] Nor was this sympathy of gesture and body restricted to the hand. In his courtesy manual *Boke Named the Governour*, Thomas Elyot wrote that dancing expressed 'the motions of the minde'.[15] Still, the hand was the privileged vehicle of gesture, being both the main instrument of action in the world and 'a symbol of the self'.[16] In *Cymbeline*, this correlation between hand and thought is captured in the sequence of Iachimo persuading Posthumus of Imogen's infidelity (2.4.95–123), with Posthumus alternating between handing over the ring Iachimo has 'won' from him and taking it back, as he wavers between belief and disbelief. In the sequence, words and gesture work together as parallel expressions of inner doubt.

Yet the acknowledgement of a triangular relationship between words, gestures and mind does not imply an absolute equivalence of verbal and kinetic signifying systems. Unlike speech, gestures were believed to involve both a spontaneous and a deliberate dimension. This dichotomy, as Karim-Cooper, Evelyn Tribble and John Wesley have argued, is reflected in John Bulwer's *Chironomia/Chirologia*,[17] an illustrated compendium of gestures in two parts, the first of which is devoted to gestures naturally expressing a speaker's meaning, the second, to gestures deliberately performed by an orator as an illustration of his words. Referring to the first category, Bulwer stressed the un-mediated expressivity of spontaneous gesture, and its organic link to the mind:

> [The hand has a] natural competency to express the motives and affections of the Minde [and] takes oftentimes the thoughts from the forestalled Tongue, making a more quick dispatch by gesture [...] For the gesture of the Hand many times gives a hint of our intention and speakes out a good part of our meaning, before our words, which accompany or follow it, can put themselves in a vocal posture to be understood.[18]

This dichotomy between the unprocessed, pre-linguistic gesture and the artificial oratorial one suggests a layered quality to gesture, reflecting the gap between instinctive and expressed thought. Awareness of these two components may be at work in the way *Cymbeline*'s polysemic gestures reveal characters' divided states of mind.

The Ambiguity of Gesture

There is a production of *Macbeth* I remember from my own childhood which did away with all props. Instead, the body's postures, movements and gestures shaped the empty space where the prop (sword, letter, cup) should have been. A similar staging of *Cymbeline* would bring out some of the play's gestural ambiguities. For example, playing the 'Snow White' scene without props would underscore the similarity of the gesture with which Pisanio hands Imogen her husband's cruel letter to that which he would have performed had he followed the murderous instructions contained in that letter. In this instance, what John Wesley refers to as gesture's 'inherent equivocality'[19] is mobilised, with one gesture conflating two opposite intentions: helping and stabbing Imogen.

The Janus-like ambiguity of gesture, or, in Bulwer's words, the 'contrariety of pathetical expression',[20] is a structural feature of the play, beginning with the comic confusion over which of Cloten or Posthumus won the offstage swordfight in act 1, scene 2. The problem of interpreting gesture is stated explicitly when Iachimo, back in Italy, produces Imogen's bracelet as evidence of his successful wooing of her, saying, 'she stripped it from her arm' (2.4.101). Not immediately convinced, Posthumus objects, 'Maybe she plucked it off / To send it me' (104–5). Posthumus's doubts about Imogen's intention are part of the play's broader pattern of probing the relation between gesture and thought. This pattern is also in evidence in the way verbs referring to gesture – such as 'tender', 'strike' and 'wave' – may reflect diametrically opposite intentions. For example, 'waving' expresses friendship in (1.3.12) and (5.5.478), respectively when Posthumus waves goodbye to Pisanio and when the Roman and British ensign wave together, but mortal enmity when Cloten 'wave[s] [his sword] against [Guiderius's] throat' (4.2.149). These ambiguities crystallise in the gesture of the extended hand. If the handfast mentioned in 1.5.78 is an unequivocal symbol of love and commitment, the handshake between Lucius, the Roman general, and Cloten is much more ambiguous, expressing both personal friendship and political enmity (3.5.12–14). Comic effects may even be drawn from this interplay of meanings, as when Cloten secures Pisanio's services with the words 'give me thy hand, here's my purse' (3.5.123). Within just one line, the meaning of an extended hand shifts from honourable oath of fealty to mercenary pact.

Among the polysemic words relating to gesture, the word 'tender' holds a special place. Variations on 'tender' and its cognates run through the play, beginning when Posthumus worries about displaying more 'tenderness' than befits a man (1.1.95). To this meaning, which is immediately understandable by a present-day readership or audience, are added more archaic meanings. As part of his attempt to corrupt Imogen, Iachimo 'tender[s]', or 'offers' his 'services' (1.6.139). 'Tender' could also refer more specifically to payment, as when Lucius complains that the British tribute to Rome is still 'untendered' (3.1.9). For the purpose of this chapter, the most relevant meaning of 'tender' is to 'hold out', 'hand out' or 'reach out', a meaning corresponding to the French verb *tendre*. Imogen puns on this meaning and the first one mentioned above when she asks Pisanio, who is holding out Posthumus's letter to her, 'Why tender'st thou that paper to me with / A look untender?' (3.4.11–12). The question fills several functions in performance. On the level of the play's intelligibility for a Globe or Blackfriars audience, it is a neat way of indicating to those with reduced visibility, who may not be able to make out what is in Pisanio's hand or the look on his face, that Pisanio is giving Imogen a letter and that he looks unhappy about it. On the level of the play's semiotics of gesture, however, this is a hint that gestures may not unequivocally reflect inner thoughts or feelings.

Yet if we are to move beyond simply registering ambiguity, some form of productive signifying system is necessary. In the next two sections I will argue that textual and extra-textual allegories, allied with mythological and psychoanalytical critical approaches, offer insights into a deeper layer of characters' minds, a layer not yet referred to as the unconscious but already intuited as a mysterious recess of the self.

Gesture and Allegory

Cymbeline is indebted to a rich array of allegorical traditions. The mythological dream vision (5.4.29–92), for example, is a staple of such medieval allegories as *Le Roman de la Rose* and *The Divine Comedy*, or, closer to Shakespeare, Chaucer's *House of Fame* and John Lydgate's *Temple of Glass*. Another traditional element is the ornamented room that reflects its owner's mind, a convention derived from medieval French patronage allegory.[21] For the purpose of working out how gesture takes on allegorical meaning, however, Ovidian apostrophe, involving addresses to gods or abstract notions, offers a useful point of entry.

One of the ways in which gesture takes on allegorical status is by absorbing an apostrophe and the personification it contains. Though Iachimo's invocation of personified 'boldness' and 'audacity' (1.6.18–19) may or may not be accompanied by physical movement, Belarius's later account of Giderius's (aka Polydore's) enactment of the heroic tales he has been feeding him clearly involves gestures denoting boldness:

> I'th'cave where they bow, their thoughts do hit
> The roofs of palaces, and nature prompts them
> In simple and low things to prince it much
> Beyond the trick of others. This Polydore,
> The heir of Cymbeline and Britain, who
> The King his father called Guiderius – Jove!
> When on my three-foot stool I sit and tell
> The warlike feats I have done, his spirits fly out
> Into my story; say 'Thus mine enemy fell,
> And thus I set my foot on's neck', even then
> The princely blood flows in his cheek, he sweats,
> Strains his young nerves, and puts himself in posture
> That acts my words.
>
> (3.3.83–95)

As Guiderius acts out Belarius's words, he becomes a personification of 'boldness', which Iachimo never was. More than this, Belarius's speech confers an emblematic quality to Guiderius's bold stance. Belarius's vignette is structurally similar to an emblem, with a motto ('boldness'), a *pictura* (Guiderius's action) and an application (Belarius's speech). As in an emblem, the application reveals the full meaning of the *pictura*: Guiderius is a prince. Unlike the bowing, which is at odds with the princes' high thoughts (83–4), the bold gesture (possibly performed by Belarius as he speaks) stands allegorically for the royal courage that shapes the princes' every thought. Gesture and apostrophe are also connected in Imogen's address to 'Experience' (4.2.34), which I briefly discussed in the Introduction. Experience, as illustrated by Imogen's travails in Wales, is mediated by feeling ('felt'; 4.2.306), in the sense of both emotion and tactile sensation. Though her address to Experience is framed as a socio-political observation, Imogen's adventures in Wales involve deeply somatic experiences, such as hunger, fatigue, sickness and sleep. This discovery of the body's frailty is possibly meant to be accompanied (and signified) by staged gestures, such as Imogen holding a hand to her stomach when she tells her brothers that she is sick (4.2.5). Clutching her belly, Imogen becomes a personification of (bitter) experience.

At this stage, it may be useful to pause and ponder the difference between a gesture that is allegorical and one that is simply expressive. When Bulwer, in the above quote, writes that the hand 'speaks', he is metaphorically making the point that gesture is expressive, but not necessarily implying that it is allegorical. Karim-Cooper acknowledges a difference between expression and allegory when she says of 'the lady' in Lyly's *Endymion* that her handwringing, performed in a dumb show, '*allegorizes* rather than *reflects* the emotion beneath it; it has a graphic quality'.[22] The idea is that a gesture is allegorical when it is so stylised as to become a conventional sign of a state of mind, that is, a symbol rather than an icon or index. It is easy to see where such allegorical gestures might appear in *Cymbeline*: Imogen kissing the bracelet her husband gave her (2.3.146), Imogen throwing away Posthumus's letters (3.4.82), the Roman and Briton ensigns waving together (5.5.479), and so on. This type of allegory can be defined as rhetorical, for it posits that gestures work like a language, relying on a conventional system of correspondences. Yet coexisting with this rhetorical model was a philosophical one. In this second model, gesture does not so much express the mind as evoke its hidden mechanisms.

In *De Anima* ('On the Soul'), Aristotle claimed that 'the soul is analogous to the hand: for as the hand is the tool of tools, so thought is the form of forms and sense the form of sensible things'.[23] Timothy Bright took up this analogy, offering the working hand as a metaphor of the thinking mind: 'I place the spirit and body close to the mind, as the saw or axe in the workman's hand.'[24] In this explanatory allegory, the moving hand is no longer the expression of a specific thought or emotion but an image of the mind in action – an allegory of thinking. When transposed to the stage, this implies that a hand gesture may function as a signal that the audience is being offered a sudden glimpse into the inner workings of a character's mind. This level of representation is not available to pantomime or dumb shows, whose expressive value relies on an unequivocal relation between gesture and meaning. However, it is available to a play like *Cymbeline*, which ties gestures like waving to the 'fits and stirs of [the] mind' (1.3.12) in a less than self-explanatory way. This allegorical mode, whereby stage gesture is a metaphor for a mind at work, requires an interpretative key. How can an audience make sense of a gesture whose link to thought is not mimetic or conventional? Given what has been said about this play's relation to childhood forms and motifs, I will now argue that a foray into that special sympathy between allegory and psychoanalysis is in order.

Cymbeline, Allegory and Psychoanalytical Theory

Much of *Cymbeline*'s rich allegorical content – apostrophe, the dream vision, Wales as a *locus amoenus*, the fairy-tale characters and mythological references – also made it a favourite among psychoanalytically inclined Shakespeare scholars in the last three decades of the twentieth century, when such Freudian concepts as repressed desire, transference and the Oedipal complex were gaining new leverage.

Freudian interpretations (of both dreams and fiction) are comparable to allegorical readings in that they are based on recognising processes of displacement, whereby one character stands for another, and condensation, whereby apparently different dream sequences are tied to a common desire.[25] These processes are seen as strategies of evasion and repression, thanks to which the dreamer expresses deep-rooted traumas and unconscious desires through coded visual and verbal language. When literature is read in this manner, as a dream, displacement becomes projection allegory, and discovering the text's hidden meaning involves working out how secondary characters function as projections of central ones.

Cymbeline, as has often been noted, offers ample scope for such readings, with its games of disguise and substitution. A commonplace of psychoanalytical *Cymbeline* scholarship involves seeing the play's two male villains, Cloten and Iachimo, both of whom unsuccessfully attempt to bed Imogen – respectively through violence and deceit – as demonic projections of the heroine's much-loved banished husband, Posthumus. Posthumus's easy acceptance of Iachimo's lies about Imogen's chastity and ensuing murderous rage against her are seen as symptoms of something ugly and Cloten-like in his feelings for his wife, something that must be processed and purged before their eventual reunion. For Meredith Skura, 'Cloten is a parody of Posthumus.'[26] In the same spirit, Arthur Kirsch and D. E. Landry use Freudian dream theory to argue that the Wales episodes sketch out the landscape of Posthumus's unconscious at work. In this reading, the mishaps of such stand-ins as Pisanio, Cloten and Iachimo function as symbolic stages in Posthumus's psychic recovery.[27] In her introduction to the Arden edition, Valerie Wayne points out that this composite view of Posthumus is supported in production by the frequent doubling of Posthumus and Cloten.[28] Fixing her lens on the play's heroine, Ruth Nevo connects Posthumus's complaint about Imogen's frequent sexual unavailability to him to a number of signifiers of virginity scattered throughout the play, including the Queen's desire to keep the British isle intact, concluding that Imogen is struggling with 'the ambivalence of untried sexuality'.[29]

Given the tendency for psychoanalytical readings to paint characters and relationships as wildly antithetical to their surface representations, it is not surprising that pushback against this approach should have emerged among the less theoretically inclined Shakespeare scholars. Brian Vickers is among the most dismissive of psychoanalytical criticism, deploring its tendency to 'relate a surprising number of [characters] to the main figure [...] by a process known as "splitting"'.[30] In his discussion of *Cymbeline*'s psychoanalytical commentators, Vickers directs most of his exasperation at Nevo, characterising her depiction of Cloten as Posthumus's 'repressed libido' as 'a typical Freudian fragmentation of character into abstractions and allegory' and scoffing at what he sees as her evidence-defying characterisation of Imogen as a squeamish prude.[31]

Vickers's objections to Freudian readings may stem from a sense of anachronism, or lack of textual evidence ('psychocritics may "substitute" or "replace" any character *ad libitum*', he grumbles[32]). However, Vickers's flat-out rejection of psychocriticism glosses over the fact that some of its hermeneutic tools, far from being strange and newfangled, hark back to methods of characterisation that pre-date Elizabethan drama. The practice of projection allegory, in particular, goes back to the medieval morality play and, as we have seen, was amply made use of in Spenser's *Faerie Queene*. Vickers was of course well aware of this, which suggests that his objection may have been motivated by a sense that 'psychocritics' were blithely mapping the Freudian categories of Id, Ego and Superego onto early modern subjectivities. This is a valid concern, and one that is shared by historically minded critics close to the schools of New Historicism and Cultural Materialism.[33] In order to walk the fine line between the insights of Freudian theory and the pitfalls of anachronism, I propose to follow Skura in replacing the 'conscious/unconscious' polarity with the more nuanced belief that *Cymbeline* exhibits 'different ways of being aware' or 'different modes of consciousness'.[34] This belief in the play's articulation of 'different modes of consciousness' dovetails well with the above-discussed early modern understanding of gesture as stemming from – and thus displaying – hidden recesses of the mind. Acknowledging the allegorical dimension of gesture may thus allow us to develop a Freud-inspired reading of the play that is nonetheless anchored both in early modern mind theory and in the kinetics of the theatrical performance.

Allegorical Gesture and Levels of Consciousness

Cymbeline's most emotionally powerful moments often involve a nexus in which apostrophe, metaphor and gesture are woven together in such a way as to offer two possible interpretations of the gesture, one overt, the other indicating a substratum of meaning. One such nexus is what I have termed the 'Snow White' episode, in which Pisanio hands over Posthumus's letter to Imogen, then casts away the sword with which he was meant to stab her. In addition to an apostrophe to the sword ('Hence, vile instrument. / Thou shalt not damn my hand'; 3.4.73–4), Pisanio uses a metaphor when he compares the harm inflicted by the letter to a deadly sword thrust ('What shall I need to draw my sword? The paper / Hath cut her throat already'; 3.4.32–3). The remark suggests that Pisanio's 'tendering' of the letter can be read allegorically as a visual figuration of the emotional blow Imogen receives upon learning that her husband wants her dead. This doubling could further imply that Pisanio functions as an allegorical substitute for his master, a possibility also suggested by Posthumus's meta-dramatic instruction to his servant ('That part, thou, Pisanio, must act for me'; 3.4.25). The textual proximity of 'My husband's hand?' (14) to 'Let thine own hand take away her life' (27) is another hint as to Pisanio's status as a projected facet of his master's mind. This reading comports with Landry's contention that the pastoral sequence takes place in a kind of dream-world marked by 'displacement of the self [...], doublings, disguises, misnamings and mistaken identities'.[35] Though Landry is arguing for Fidele (the cross-dressed Imogen), Cloten and Iachimo as allegorical stand-ins for Posthumus, the convention of the allegorical servant suggests a similar role for Pisanio. By this standard, Pisanio's action of throwing away the sword might be taken as an allegorical rendition of the first stirrings of penitence and returning tenderness taking shape in the depths of Posthumus's mind.

The above example shows how metaphors and polysemy may signal the status of a staged gesture as the expression of something unacknowledged or not yet ripe in the mind, of a deeper level of consciousness than what is openly expressed in words, or even in explicitly signifying gestures. In some cases, the intimacy of touch may be an added tip-off that a gesture reflects deep-seated inner motions. This is illustrated in the grotesque scene of Imogen's discovery of Cloten's headless body, which she takes for her husband's:

> The dream's here still. Even when I wake it is
> Without me as within me, not imagined, felt.
> A headless man? The garments of Posthumus?
> I know the shape of's leg; this is his hand,
> His foot Mercurial, his Martial thigh,
> The brawns of Hercules, but his Jovial face –
> Murder in heaven? How? Tis gone. Pisanio,
> All curses madded Hecuba gave the Greeks
> And mine to boot, be darted on thee! Thou,
> Conspired with that irregulous devil, Cloten,
> Hath here cut off my Lord. To write and read
> Be henceforth treacherous. Damned Pisanio
> Hath with his forged letters – damned Pisano –
> From this most bravest vessel of the world
> Struck the main-top! O, Posthumus, alas,
> Where is thy head? [...]
> The drug [Pisanio] gave me, which he said was precious
> And cordial to me, have I not found it
> Mur'drous to th' senses? That confirms it home.
>
> (4.2.306–28)

The passage lends itself to many allegorical readings. If we follow Walter Benjamin in reading the staged corpse of Jacobean drama as an emblem of human frailty and loss, then Imogen's 'feeling up' of Cloten is what Benjamin sees as the ultimate human experience, the mourning of man's humble, fallen, God-forsaken state. More specific psycho-allegorical readings of the scene have been offered. According to Maurice Hunt, for example, Cloten's headless body is an emblematic representation of Posthumus's madness: 'Cloten literally loses what Posthumus has figuratively lost.'[36] *Pace* Vickers, I think this is correct, especially as the passage is crammed with hints that an allegorical reading is in order. These include Imogen's suggestion that she is still dreaming, her reference to mythological figures, her use of a ship metaphor, and her address to her supposedly dead husband, the last two of which contribute to a scattered, dislocated representation of Posthumus, turning him into a site of imaginative projection and fantasy. And yet I would suggest that reading the dead Cloten as a caricature of Posthumus does not exhaust the allegorical potential of this odd moment in the play. What seems to me essential is that the projection allegory whereby Cloten stands for Posthumus is literally sculpted by Imogen's feeling hands.

As Wayne observes in a footnote, 'felt' refers to Imogen's 'tactile sense of the body'.[37] Other indications that Imogen is not just looking at the body but actually running her hands over it are her prone position, the emphasis on shape (which, contrary to size, required touch in order to be truly experienced), the use of deixis in 'this is his hand', which codes for the actor to take hold of it, and possibly Arviragus's earlier reference to 'midnight flowers' (4.2.282) which may give the impression that it is night and therefore too dark to see clearly. The phrase 'this is his hand' also takes up the earlier 'My husband's hand?' (3.4.14), where 'hand' referred to 'handwriting' and by extension, 'character'. Allegorically, then, Imogen is probing her husband's character through a different sense than her eyesight and discovering the hidden monster lurking beneath the surface. Yet I believe that in order to get to the bottom of what is being shown here, it is necessary to keep in mind both the idea of the moving hand as an allegorical rendering of thought (as in Bright), and the play's constant elevating of gesture itself above the object being gestured at or with. In *Cymbeline*, the allegorical focus is often on the gesture, seldom on the object. Thus, if Cloten's headless body can be taken as a projection of Posthumus 'losing his head', the more vivid, grounded allegory is that of Imogen's mind processing that information and coming to terms with what she has learnt about her husband. Imogen's surface horror at her husband's death, expressed verbally, is thus doubled by her deeper, 'felt', realisation of his deeply flawed nature. This is consistent with her anger at Pisanio, and her accusation that he has given her poison. The 'poison' is that new knowledge of her husband she would have been happier without, which has come close to 'killing' her love for him.

Turning to the play's controlling allegory of 'experience', which in early modern English also meant 'experiment',[38] this visual of Imogen inwardly exploring the darkness of her husband's soul (and possibly the depths of her own) ties in with the play's network of forbidden female experimentation and the emblematic gestures that go with it. These include the Queen's experiments with poison, crystallised in her dropping of the box and then handing it over to Pisanio (1.5.59) – a psychological experiment in and of itself – and Imogen's experiment of living like a man (3.6.1–20), and later of drinking poison and taking stock of its effects on her body (4.2.325–7). Echoes of Genesis are naturally also present in the equation of forbidden female knowledge with poison. These echoes are amplified by the tactile component of these experimental gestures. As Karim-Cooper reminds us, 'The enduring image of what prompted the Fall of mankind is not only one of a woman tasting and consuming, but of a female hand reaching and touching the forbidden.'[39] In the case of Imogen's inner exploration of her husband's dark soul, the 'reaching and touching' is also allegorical and, from our enlightened perspective, seems to point to Shakespeare's proto-Freudian awareness of an unconscious or 'Id' where forbidden thoughts and desires are entertained.[40]

Shakespeare's fascination with the meaning of dreams and his creation of characters who are perplexed at their own actions, thoughts and feelings (most famously, Hamlet) tends to support the notion that he was aware of hidden forces directing human thought. This, however, need not imply an anachronistic Freudian subject. Beyond the previously discussed applicability of Freudian categories, there are in fact several objections to reading *Cymbeline*'s gestures entirely along Freudian lines. One is the eventual resolution of the tensions emblematised by the 'groping' scene. In Freudian theory, the Id may eventually be controlled by the Ego, but it is only suppressed, not extinguished. The comedic arc of romance, however, requires healing, regeneration and resolution. In the last act, violence is crystallised and purged through Posthumus's striking of Imogen, followed by their recognition of each other and reconciliation. The final image of Imogen in her husband's arms, now his 'soul', 'hang[ing] like fruit' substitutes for and resolves the groping scene's echoes of Genesis, with Imogen's metaphorical tasting of the fruit of forbidden knowledge. Fittingly, resolution is also achieved through the merging of the various acceptations of 'tender'. The soothsayer's (etymologically fanciful) interpretation of 'tender air' as *mollis aer* or 'woman', joined with the image of the reunited family as a tree throwing out ('tendering') branches, even as Posthumus holds out ('tenders') a hand to Iachimo (5.5.417) and Cymbeline agrees to pay ('tender') tribute, all contribute to collapsing all gestures into a hand held out in love and acceptance. Similarly, apostrophes, in which words are 'tendered' to the self or the void, are replaced by vocative addresses to present people: 'My boys' (259), 'my soul' (263), 'my lord' (270), 'my gentle brothers' (374).

Another objection to ascribing a proto-Freudian intuition to Shakespeare is the Galenic understanding that the body may be endowed with cognitive faculties. Shakespeare wrote before the Cartesian separation of body and thought, and the possibility that thinking could occur through the body would not have been considered unreasonable.[41] In the context of early modern debates around the mind's relation to the body, the choice of gesture as allegorical vehicle raises the question of whether the allegory is based on metaphor (the mind thinking is like a hand reaching out) or metonymy (the hand reaching out is an extension of the body's ability to think).

The question of the body's agency is only hinted at in *Cymbeline*, but it is explicitly raised elsewhere in early modern literature. For example, John Donne writes of a blushing maiden that

> [h]er pure and eloquent blood
> Spoke in her cheeks, and so distinctly wrought
> That one might almost say, her body thought.[42]

The 'almost' in Donne's poem pinpoints the ambiguities of grounded allegory, with its uneasy mixture of denotative (literal) and connotative (metaphorical) forms of reference. On the stage, the paradox of blushing, with its implication of bodily thought, is foregrounded by the un-performability of a blush. While *Cymbeline*'s voluntary gestures sketch out a hidden layer of thought, blushing involves a lack of control over the body, and a sense of split agency. Unlike performable hand gestures, staged blushes must be signified by substitutes, such as descriptive words, hands covering the face, or masks. Shakespeare's blushing men and maidens are scattered throughout the corpus, appearing in *Titus Andronicus*, *Much Ado About Nothing* and *Love's Labour's Lost*, among others, but my next chapter will focus on *Troilus and Cressida*, where the imbrication of blushing, veils and curtains will bring out the allegorical potential of face-concealing stage properties.

Notes

1 Emma Rice, programme notes to *Cymbeline*, dir. Emma Rice, Kneehigh Theatre in association with the Royal Shakespeare Company, Bristol Old Vic, Bristol, 2006.

2 Kennan Tynan, quoted in William Shakespeare, *Cymbeline*, ed. Jonathan Bate and Eric Rasmussen, The RSC Shakespeare, Basingstoke: Macmillan, 2011, p. 164.

3 Catherine Belsey, *Why Shakespeare?*, Basingstoke: Palgrave Macmillan, 2007, pp. ix–x, 81. See also Ciara Rawnsley, 'Behind the "Happily-Ever-After": Shakespeare's Use of Fairytales and *All's Well That Ends Well*', *Journal of Early Modern Studies*, no. 2 (2013), pp. 141–58, https://oajournals.fupress.net/index.php/bsfm -jems/article/view/6991/6989, last accessed 1 June 2021.

4 See Bruno Bettelheim, *The Meaning and Importance of Fairy Tales*, New York: Alfred A. Knopf, 1976.

5 See, for example, Michael Murrin on Pico della Mirandola's commentary on Genesis. 'Renaissance Allegory from Petrarch to Spenser', in Rita Copeland and Peter T. Struck (eds), *The Cambridge Companion to Allegory* (2010), Cambridge: Cambridge University Press, 2011, pp. 162–76 (p. 171).

6 George Puttenham, *The Arte of English Poesie*, ed. Gladys Doidge Willcock and Alice Walker, Cambridge: Cambridge University Press, 1936, p. 154.

7 For facial expression as a sub-category of gesture, see John H. Astington, 'Actors and the Body: Meta-theatrical Rhetoric in Shakespeare', *Gesture*, vol. 6, no. 2 (2006), pp. 241–59 (pp. 248–54).

8 Melly Still's 2016 RSC production had Posthumus throttling Fidele/ Imogen in the reconciliation scene, which brought down the house the night I saw it played at the Barbican.

9 On the evolution of dumb shows, see Dieter Mehl, *The Elizabethan Dumb Show*, London: Methuen, 1965; and Jeremy Lopez, 'Dumb Show', in Henry S. Turner (ed.), *Early Modern Theatricality*, Oxford: Oxford University Press, 2013, pp. 291–305.

10 Andrew Gurr, *Playgoing in Shakespeare's London* (1987), Cambridge: Cambridge University Press, 1996, p. 22.

11   Cicero, *De Oratore*, trans. E. W. Sutton and H. Rackham, 2 vols, Cambridge, MA: Harvard University Press, vol. 2, p. 173.

12   Quintilian, *Institutio Oratoria*, trans. H. E. Butler, 4 vols, Loeb Classical Library, Cambridge, MA: Harvard University Press, 1920, vol. 4, book XI, p. 245.

13   Thomas Heywood, 'A Defence of Drama (*c*.1608)', in Brian Vickers (ed.), *English Renaissance Literary Criticism* (1999), Oxford: Clarendon Press, 2003, pp. 474–501 (p. 490).

14   Farah Karim-Cooper, *The Hand on the Shakespearean Stage: Gesture, Touch, and the Spectacle of Dismemberment*, London: Bloomsbury, 2016, pp. 17, 21.

15   Sir Thomas Elyot, *The Boke Named the Governour* (1531), London, 1580, EEBO, The Huntington Library, fol. 82.

16   Karim-Cooper, *Hand on the Shakespearean Stage*, p. 12.

17   John Bulwer, *Chirologia or the Natural Language of the Hand, Composed of the Speaking Motions and Discoursing Gestures Thereof: Whereunto is Added Chironomia, or the Art of Manual Rhetoricke*, London, 1644, EEBO, Yale University Library. Though Bulwer's treatise postdates *Cymbeline* by decades, John Wesley argues for its relevance, based on its reliance on earlier works and on its similarities with Henry Peacham's 1594/5 sketch of a scene from *Titus Andronicus* in which Aaron the Moor is shown pointing at a kneeling Tamora (Longleat Manuscript). John Wesley, 'Original Gesture: Hand Eloquence on the Early Modern Stage', *Shakespeare Bulletin*, vol. 35, no. 1 (2017), pp. 65–96.

18   John Bulwer, quoted in Evelyn B. Tribble, *Cognition in the Globe: Attention and Memory in Shakespeare's Theatre*, New York: Palgrave Macmillan, 2011, p. 99.

19   Wesley, 'Original Gesture', p. 66.

20   Ibid.

21   Stephanie Gibbs Kamath and Rita Copeland, 'Medieval Secular Allegory: French and English', in Rita Copeland and Peter T. Struck (eds), *The Cambridge Companion to Allegory* (2010), Cambridge: Cambridge University Press, 2011, pp. 136–47 (p. 142).

22   Karim-Cooper, *Hand on the Shakespearean Stage*, p. 87 (original emphasis).

23   Aristotle, *De Anima* ('On the Soul'), quoted in Bruce R. Smith, *Phenomenal Shakespeare*, Chichester: Wiley-Blackwell, 2010, p. 175.

24   Timothy Bright, *A Treatise of Melancholy*, London, 1586, EEBO, The Huntington Library, p. 62. Bright's metaphorical system is flexible. A few pages later, he writes that 'the spirit is the very hand of the soul' (p. 63), making the hand a tool rather than the giver of instructions.

25 See Freud, Sigmund, 'Lecture XI: The Dream-Work', in *Introductory Lectures on Psycho-Analysis*, trans. and ed. James Strachey, intro. Peter Gay, New York and London: W.W. Norton, 1989, pp. 209–26.

26 Meredith Skura, 'Interpreting Posthumus' Dream from Above and Below: Families, Psychoanalysts, and Literary Critics', in Murray M. Schwartz and Coppélia Kahn (eds), *Representing Shakespeare: New Psychoanalytic Essays*, Baltimore, MD: Johns Hopkins University Press, 1980, pp. 203–16 (p. 209).

27 See Arthur Kirsch, *Shakespeare and the Experience of Love*, Cambridge: Cambridge University Press, 1981, pp. 144–73; and D. E. Landry, 'Dreams as History: The Strange Unity of *Cymbeline*', *Shakespeare Quarterly*, vol. 33, no. 1 (Spring 1982), pp. 68–79.

28 Valerie Wayne, in William Shakespeare, *Cymbeline*, ed. Valerie Wayne, The Arden Shakespeare, London: Bloomsbury, 2017, p. 87.

29 Ruth Nevo, *Shakespeare's Other Language*, New York: Routledge, 1987, p. 82.

30 Brian Vickers, *Appropriating Shakespeare: Contemporary Critical Quarrels*, New Haven, CT, and London: Yale University Press, 1993, p. 290.

31 Ibid. p. 292.

32 Ibid. p. 293.

33 On the historically contingent nature of subjectivity, see, for example, Bridget Escolme, *Talking to the Audience: Shakespeare, Performance, Self*, Abingdon: Routledge, 2005, pp. 1–23.

34 Skura, 'Interpreting Posthumus' Dream', p. 204.

35 Landry, 'Dreams as History', p. 70.

36 Maurice Hunt, 'Dismemberment, Corporal Reconstitution and the Body Politic in *Cymbeline*', *Studies in Philology*, vol. 99, 2002, pp. 404–31 (p. 417).

37 Wayne, in Shakespeare, *Cymbeline*, p. 306n.

38 See *OED*, 1b.

39 Karim-Cooper, *Hand on the Shakespearean Stage*, p. 168.

40 The problem with psycho-allegorical readings is knowing where to stop. The 'groping' scene also lends itself perfectly well to Ruth Nevo's reading of Imogen as a repressed prude. Taking Imogen's mistaken recognition of Posthumus in Cloten's body as evidence of her lack of experience of running her hands over her husband's body in a prone position, and considering Posthumus's complaint about his wife's sexual unavailability, one could also read the whole scene as registering Imogen's disgust with sexuality. Though the multiplicity of possible Freudian readings of the scene tends to substantiate Vickers's 'anything goes' objection, it also demonstrates the rich evocative power of gestures as a means to offer enticing glimpses into the dark corners of a character's mind.

41 For a discussion of the mind–body issue, see Nicholas Crawford, 'Language, Duality and Bastardy in Renaissance Drama', *English Literary Renaissance*, vol. 34, no. 2 (Spring 2004), pp. 243–62.
42 John Donne, 'Elegy on Miss Elizabeth Drury', in Ralph Waldo Emerson (ed.), *Parnassus: An Anthology of Poetry*, Boston: Houghton, 1880, ll. 4–6.

Chapter 4

Crimson Veils in
Troilus and Cressida

Consistent with its epic theme, *Troilus and Cressida* begins *in medias res*. Instead of immediately identifying the cause of the Trojan war – the rape of Helen by Paris – the 'Speaker of the Prologue' opens with a description of the Greek princes' angry reaction:

> In Troy there lies the scene. From isles of Greece,
> The princes orgulous, their high blood chafed,
> Have to the port of Athens sent their ships
> Fraught with the ministers and instruments
> Of cruel war.
>
> (Prologue, 1–5)

The antiquated 'orgulous' primes the audience to pay special attention to the second half of line 2, which identifies the 'chaf[ing]' of 'high blood' as the trigger of the war. The explanation is a socio-humoral one: 'high blood' means aristocratic blood, which in proud warriors is quick to react to a provocation. The 'chafed blood' image is allegorically amplified in the second half of the sentence, as the 'fraught' ships gathering around Athens recall Galen's description of anger as blood boiling around the heart.[1] Allegorical echoes may also be detected in the reference to 'the ministers and instruments' of war, terms that in Galenic treatises often refer to the brain's faculties.[2] With these opening lines, the Prologue is not only setting the stage for the upcoming action but also establishing the Trojan War as a reservoir of metaphors for characters' emotions and states of mind in the play about to unfold. This reservoir is tapped into a mere thirty lines later, when Troilus sighs over the 'cruel battle' (1.1.3) between his heart and his will. On a more heroic scale, Hector describes Achilles's 'hot blood' (2.3.173) as the grounds of a battle between 'his mental and active parts' (174), in which the Greek hero 'batters down himself' (176).

The use of war as a metaphor for the struggle between the passions and reason is a commonplace of both classical and medieval thought.[3] In Shakespeare's own time, it was a staple of both neo-Petrarchan love poetry and body politic imagery. It is thus not surprising to find *Troilus and Cressida*, a play about love, politics and war, making use of the convention. What is perhaps more striking is the way the Prologue's opening lines also set the stage for a more theatrically grounded way of allegorising the confrontation between blood and mind, one that is to be found in the play's many occurrences of blushing characters. The operative word here is 'chafed', which David Bevington glosses as 'warmed to valour' or 'irritated'.[4] From the Prologue, the word makes its way to an episode of rather forced banter reported by Pandarus: 'But there was such laughing, and Helen so blushed, and Paris so chafed, and all the rest so laughed, that it passed' (1.2.166–7). Here, as in much of the play, the motif of 'chafed' blood connects manly anger with feminine modesty, with the warrior's boiling blood functioning as a counterpart to the blushing lady's blood rising to her cheeks. The similarity, however, breaks down in performance. If anger is relatively easy to mimic onstage (through shouting, gesturing and striking), blushing is more problematic, being mostly acknowledged as a spontaneous – and thus unperformable – phenomenon. The play's various perspectives on this problem, I will argue, offer performance-based alternatives to the verbal allegories of blood and mind discussed above. These 'scenic' allegories help establish personal agency as a major stake of the Trojan war.

Unperformed Blushes

The episode of Helen's blush is not theatrically problematic: like the 'chafing' of the orgulous princes' blood, it is reported, not dramatised. The play's second reference to blushing is similarly unproblematic, for the blushing is only hypothetical. I am referring to Aeneas's visit to the Greek camp, where he has been sent to issue a challenge. In the presence of Agamemnon, whom he claims not to recognise, the wily Trojan offers the following speech:

Aene. Is this great Agamemnon's tent, I pray you?
[...]   How may
A stranger to those most imperial looks
Know them from eyes of other mortals?
Agam.   How?
Aene.   Ay.
I ask, that I might waken reverence,
And bid the cheek be ready with a blush
Modest as morning when she coldly eyes
The youthful Phoebus.
Which is that god in office, guiding men?
Which is the high and mighty Agamemnon?
Agam. This Trojan scorns us, or the men of Troy
Are ceremonious courtiers.

(1.3.216–34)

The player performing Aeneas need not be seen to blush, as
Aeneas is only offering to blush, not actually doing so. Yet the
episode takes us one step further towards performance, as the
mocking tone rightly suspected by Agamemnon is premised on the
un-performability of the blush. Aeneas's offer to 'bid the cheek be
ready with a blush' archly signifies that any show of deference to
Agamemnon would be a put-on performance, not a spontaneous
expression of awe. Agamemnon's puzzlement stems from uncertainty at Aeneas's tone, but given his obvious ignorance of Trojan
mores, he may also be wondering whether Trojans are indeed
capable of blushing at will.

The performability of the blush was a subject of great interest
to early modern playwrights. In addition to the evidence of their
own practice, they would have been aware of classical writings
positing the impossibility of faking a blush, including on the
stage. An example appears in Stoic philosopher Seneca's eleventh
epistle to Lucilius:

> Actors in the theatre, who imitate the emotions, who portray
> fear and nervousness, who depict sorrow, imitate bashfulness by
> hanging their heads, lowering their voices and keeping their eyes
> fixed and rooted upon the ground. They cannot, however, muster
> a blush, for the blush cannot be prevented or acquired.[5]

The understanding that a blush is an involuntary expression
of emotion is present in earlier Shakespearean plays. In *Love's
Labour's Lost*, for example, Armado, the braggart soldier, blushes
in the presence of his beloved, saying, 'I do betray myself with

blushing' (1.2.107). The point is made more subtly in *Much Ado About Nothing*, in which the slandered Hero is spurned at the altar by the gullible Claudio. In Claudio's rejection of the blushing Hero, theatrical tropes are an index of the young groom's bad faith:

> She's but the sign and semblance of her honor.
> Behold how like a maid she blushes here.
> O, what authority and show of truth
> Can cunning sin cover itself withal!
> Comes not that blood as modest evidence
> To witness simple virtue? Would you not swear –
> All you that see her – that she were a maid,
> By these exterior shows? But she is none.
> She knows the heat of a luxurious bed.
> Her blush is guiltiness, not modesty.
>
> (4.1.33–42)

Discussing this speech, Andrew Fleck notices a shift in the blush's status. Though the relation between the blush and the sin starts out as metonymic (the blush is an index of the sin), it then becomes essentialised as the sin itself (the blush 'is' guiltiness).[6] This, I believe, tracks with Claudio's mid-speech realisation that a blush cannot be faked. After suggesting that Hero is faking a blush ('cover[s] itself', 'exterior shows') to make herself look modest, Claudio suddenly changes tack, accepting that the blush is real, in the sense of spontaneous, but assigning a new meaning to it: 'guiltiness, not modesty'.

The possibility of performing a blush was not entirely ruled out, however. Shakespeare's contemporary, the Italian physician Annibale Pocaterra, wrote that some actors could, indeed, change colour at will, in a feat of the imagination that is vaguely suggestive of method acting:

> It is true that some excellent actors perform this trick [blushing] on stage when, during a performance, they alter their countenance as readily as a chameleon changes colour, yet they can only do so through great artifice. Their art is such that when they wish to alter their colouring and feign some feeling, they first invest the imagined virtue with some terrible, disdainful or merry form so that their reason can better control their feelings.[7]

Whether Elizabethan actors could apply such a method is doubtful. As Sujata Iyengar points out, '[e]ven if Elizabethan actors could flush at will, their blushes would have been invisible under the chalk-white fucus that probably "makes up" whiteness on the

Renaissance stage'.[8] There has been some debate as to whether Elizabethan actors were heavily made up or whether they wore masks.[9] Whatever the case, Iyengar's point holds: even with an 'excellent' method actor, a blush could not have been authentically produced on the Elizabethan stage.

In *Troilus and Cressida*, Aeneas's claimed ability to blush at will, and the puzzlement it generates, foregrounds the un-performability of the blush. More than this, though, the poetics and visuals of the scene hint at possible stage substitutes for a blush. The conventional personification of dawn ('morning'; 1.3.229), for example, might direct the audience's gaze to the prop or piece of drapery used for Agamemnon's tent. If, as Michael Hattaway has conjectured, the 'wooden canopie' mentioned in Henslowe's inventory was meant as scaffolding for a 'stage tent or *scena*',[10] then a tent might have been set up on the stage. Alternatively, for a less cluttered stage, the tent could simply have been suggested by curtains over the discovery space.[11] If the tent or drapes were red, the backdrop might have offered a fitting illustration of the allegory of 'modest [...] morning'. Another technique is suggested by the possibility that the Greek host are wearing concealing helmets. This could explain why Aeneas fails to recognise Agamemnon, or as Bevington argues, provide him with 'a nominal excuse' for the failure.[12] If Agamemnon is helmeted, a spectator might also notice that the helmet's visor or beaver is useful in concealing the absence of an angry flush on his face when he realises that he is being mocked. This suggests that a mask or veil over a player's face might be a similarly apt way to cover for an un-performable blush. This foregrounding of the unstageable blush, and preliminary exploration of possible substitutes, lays the groundwork for the play's only actual dramatisation of blushing, when Cressida is brought before Troilus.

Staging a Blush: Enter the Modest Maiden

The love encounter between Troilus and Cressida begins with Pandarus describing a blushing Cressida to Troilus as the two men stand before her house:

> *Pan.* She's making her ready; she'll come straight. You must be witty now. She does so blush, and fetches her wind so short, as if she were frayed with a sprite. I'll fetch her. It is the prettiest villain! She fetches her breath as short as a new ta'en sparrow. (3.2.30–4)

Pandarus then exits, leaving Troilus alone, and later re-enters with Cressida:

> *Pan.* Come, come, what need you blush? Shame's a baby. Here she is now, swear the oaths now to her that you have to me. [*Cressida draws backward.*] What, are you gone again? You must be watched ere you be made tame, must you? Come your ways, come your ways; and you draw backward, we'll put you i'th'thills. Why do you not speak to her? Come, draw this curtain, and let's see your picture. (3.2.40–7)

In the ensuing action, Troilus and Cressida, left alone while Pandarus builds a fire inside the house, confess their love for each other and kiss. Cressida then repeatedly invites Troilus inside ('Will you walk in, my lord?'; 60). Eventually, Pandarus re-enters and urges the lovers on ('What, blushing still? Have you not done talking yet?'; 100–1).

Modern editors, taking their cue from Pandarus's mention of a curtain concealing Cressida's face (47), add a footnote or stage directions, indicating that Cressida is veiled. Bevington's Arden edition, for example, inserts stage directions to the effect that Cressida enters '[*veiled*]', and that '[*she is unveiled*]' after 'picture' (47). These editorial additions make sense, but they tend to obscure the problematic nature of this scene, as far as staging Cressida's blush is concerned. Pandarus's reference to a curtain suggests quite a few possibilities for performing Cressida's blush. Curiously, however, none of these quite works.

Does Cressida enter veiled? As with Agamemnon's helmet, a veil over the Cressida player's face would be a convenient way to hide the absence of a blush, and by this means to suggest its presence. But this immediately raises the question of how Pandarus can tell that Cressida is blushing as she enters (40). A possible answer is that she is only thinly veiled, allowing the blush to be visible. This was the choice made in Shakespeare's Globe's 2009 production, in which Laura Pyper appeared wearing a sheer veil. The University of California at Santa Cruz's 2021 virtual production also featured a sheer veil, which was given extra prominence thanks to the Zoom box framing the actor's face. However, a gossamer-thin veil, though technically obtainable in the early seventeenth century,[13] does not comport with Pandarus's request that Cressida remove the 'curtain' in order to reveal her 'picture'. With this reference to the contemporary practice of covering paintings with (opaque) curtains, Pandarus is indicating that whatever Cressida is wearing over her face is thick enough to conceal her features. Seeing and unseen, Cressida would possibly have been masked rather than veiled, as is suggested by her earlier remark that she wears a 'mask to defend [her] beauty' (1.2.262). A masked Cressida would have been unsurprising to a Shakespearean audience, given English gentlewomen's custom of wearing masks outside the home. In his *Anatomie of Abuses*, Philip Stubbes describes what these masks would have looked like: 'when they use to ride abrode, they have invisories or visors made of velvet, wherewith they cover all their faces, having holes made in them against their eyes, whereout they look'.[14] As Andrew Gurr observes, 'masks were an efficient form of concealment'.[15]

Leaving aside masks and veils, another possibility is that the 'curtain' Pandarus mentions refers to hair or hands obscuring the face. However, this would leave whole the problem of how Pandarus knows that Cressida is blushing. Alternatively, '[*Cressida draws backward.*]' could be the cue for a skittish Cressida to retreat behind the entrance to her house, as materialised by the actual curtain over the tiring house's discovery space. This implies that Cressida came out bare faced, her blush being theatrically constructed by Pandarus's words (like Hero's by Claudio's in *Much Ado About Nothing*). This is quite possible but would imply that Cressida runs off promptly upon entering, which might seem an excessive reaction to the sight of Troilus, thus edging the scene towards farce.

If we do stick to the idea of a veil or mask, yet another possibility emerges. In *The Woman-Hater* (1607), by Francis Beaumont and John Fletcher, the Duke compares morning to a 'shame-faced maiden [...] hiding her chaste cheeks, like a modest bride / With a red veil of blushes' (1.1.4–7). The 'red veil of blushes' suggests that a stage veil or mask could stand for a blush, as opposed to concealing it.[16] Though gentlewomen's masks were usually black, a satirical poem by Stephen Gosson indicates that by the end of the sixteenth century, a greater array of colours was available:

> Weare masks for vailes to hide and holde
> As Christians did and Turks do use,
> To hide the face from Wantons bolde,
> Small cause then were at them to muse;
> But barring only wind and sun,
> Of verie pride they were begun.

But on each wight now are they seene,
The tallow-pale, the browning-bay,
The swarthy-black, the grassie-greene,
The pudding red, the dapple graie;
So might we judge them toyes aright,
To keep sweet beautie still in plight.[17]

Thus, the Cressida boy player, emerging from the discovery space with a red veil or 'pudding red' mask over his face, could be understood to be visibly blushing. And yet this does not quite work either. For if the mask materialises the blush, how can Cressida be blushing 'still' (line 100), when the mask has necessarily been removed for the kiss? Either Cressida has put the mask back on – in which case one would expect Pandarus to say 'again' rather than 'still' – or the mask has lost its iconic function mid-scene and the capacity of signifying a blush has been transferred to Pandarus's words. Finally, 'blushing' could simply be Pandarus's byword for 'acting coy', but this does not quite jibe with the physicality of his description of Cressida's symptoms in 3.2.30–2.

My point is not that this scene is unplayable – clearly it is not[18] – but that there is no entirely consistent way of playing it. This brings out the irreducible artfulness of the staged blush, and its inherent ambiguity. Fundamental to the semiotics of stage blushing is the fact that a blush is normally not performable, which allows it to code for authentic, spontaneous emotion. Yet by virtue of that very un-performability, a blush must be signified by artificial means, such as a verbal cue, a face turned away, or a hand, mask or veil held before the face. These substitutes invest the staged blush with the artificiality of theatrical performance, thus undermining its validity as a badge of authentic irrepressible emotion. This artificiality remains even if we reduce the complexities of the scene by assuming, as I will do now, that Cressida does, indeed 'enter veiled' – or masked. Yet what is at stake in this foregrounding of theatrical artifice? Though the scene is often discussed in terms of Cressida's assumed or authentic coyness,[19] I will argue that act 3, scene 2 associates the veiled Cressida with cultural representations of self-affirming feminine artistry, thanks to the symbolic force of that most common of stage props, the piece of cloth.

Cloth as a Symbol of Artistry

In her doctoral thesis and subsequent publications, Nathalie Rivère de Carles has demonstrated how essential textile props were to early modern scenography. A piece of drapery could be hung over the tiring house's walls or discovery space, or stretched across the stage pillars, thus creating an onstage 'booth' – a convenient way of suggesting a house or tent. Nailed to a four-poster bed, it created an intimate space of love or murder. Draped around a player's shoulders, it became a concealing cloak. Thrown over a prone body, it became a shroud, or a murdered character's bloody clothing. Worn over the head, it concealed a character's identity, or established that she was in mourning.[20] One of the central points developed in Rivère de Carles's doctoral thesis is that these many uses of cloth might foster a sense of continuity between stage hangings, drapes, veils, masks and the human face or body: '[t]he curtain acts as a visual extension of the actor's body.'[21]

This continuity is in evidence in Cressida's blushing scene, where the veil or mask acts as an echo of the stage hangings through which the blushing maiden enters. The mask then becomes endowed with the self-referential theatricality of the stage curtain, and the blush takes on the character of a performance. Dramatically, this prepares for the accusations of duplicity levelled against Cressida later in the play. The meta-theatricality built into the discovery-space curtains is reinforced by Pandarus's statement that Cressida is 'making her ready' (3.2.30), which takes up Aeneas's earlier statement about 'bid[ding] the cheek be ready with a blush' (1.3.228). Blushing becomes backstage business, akin to a player applying make-up before making his entrance. As in *Much Ado About Nothing*, then, Cressida's blush carries hints of deception. Yet deception is not the full story, as appears when the veil is mentioned in connection with crafts other than theatrical performance, mainly painting and weaving. Pandarus's comparison of Cressida's mask to a curtain drawn over a painted portrait (3.2.47) disrupts the veil's theatrical valence by turning Cressida into the artist of her own face. Though this hints at the use of cosmetics, also decried as a marker of feminine hypocrisy in early modern culture,[22] the reference nevertheless helps establish the blush as a signifier of female creativity and self-fashioning. The effect is amplified by the later reference to Arachne, the girl-turned-spider of Classical mythology.

After his perceived betrayal by Cressida, Troilus uses a spider metaphor to describe the girl's duplicity:

> This is, and is not, Cressid!
> Within my soul there doth conduce a fight
> Of this strange nature, that a thing inseparate
> Divides more wider than the sky and earth,
> And yet the spacious breadth of this division
> Admits no orifex for a point as subtle
> As Ariachne's broken woof to enter.

> (5.2.146–52)

The image is an odd one, but it seems to imply that unlike the mythological Arachne's torn tapestry, the fine partition between Cressida's two identities offers no point of entry. In the image of the spider's web, there is also an implied allusion to feminine wiles and craftiness. Yet this value is tempered, and even inflected with heroism thanks to the Ovidian intertext. Though Troilus mangles the name, the speech nods towards the Arachne tale in Ovid's *Metamorphoses*. In Book 6, Arachne, a Lydian maid famous for her skill at the loom, challenges Minerva, goddess of art and weaving, to a match. The goddess comes in disguise:

> Then said the Goddess: here she is. And therewithal she cast
> Hir oldwives riveled shape away, and shewde hir selfe at last
> Minerva like. The Nymphes did straight adore hir Majestie,
> So did the yong newmaried wives that were of Migdonie.
> The maiden only vnabasht would nought at all relent
> But yet she blusht and sodenly a ruddiness besprent
> Hir cheeks which wanzed away again, even like as doth the Skie
> Look sanguine at the break of day, and turneth by and by
> To white at rising of the Sunne.[23]

The story continues with Arachne weaving into her tapestry various tales of the gods' misdeeds, including several rape scenes, whereupon Minerva, furious at the disrespect, strikes Arachne with a weaver's comb and tears up her work. Arachne hangs herself in shame but is saved from death by Pallas (Athena's other name), who turns her into a spider. In this episode, the maiden's natural blush stands in opposition to the many forms of artificial colouring previously mentioned in the poem, including the purple dye manufactured by her father, the grey tincture that the goddess applies to her hair to make herself look like an old woman, and the purple, gold and white threads of the tapestries that the goddess and girl are weaving. The art/nature opposition is further emphasised by the description of Arachne's activity as 'vnabasht', in contrast with the bashfulness implied by the blush. Crucially, though, Arachne's bashful blush recedes as she weaves. By artistically transferring the colour in her cheeks to the cloth, Arachne turns humility into a source of creative self-assertion. It is significant that Arachne does not use the cloth she is weaving to conceal her blush, but instead turns the blush into an artistic performance. Weaving allows Arachne to evade submission to the goddess and assert narrative control over her destiny through an authorial reappropriation of tales of young girls being victimised by male gods. That this ends badly is a measure of the hubris involved in humans co-opting signs of humility to flaunt their narrative control of meaning. The destruction of Arachne's work by a female god shows that the gods stand together, whatever gender wars they may wage amongst themselves. Yet even as Arachne is vanquished, she controls her destiny by hanging herself with the yarn she had been using for her tapestry.

In *Troilus*, Shakespeare emphasises weaving as a means of self-assertion by playing on the Lydian maiden's name. In the long notes to his edition, Bevington remarks on the unusual spelling of the weaver's name and suggests that 'Ariachne' may be a conflation of 'Arachne' and 'Ariadne'.[24] This would align the web with Ariadne's thread, thanks to which Theseus was guided through the Minotaur's maze. Ariadne's thread, like that of the Parcae, works as a metaphor for destiny.

The power dynamics of the Ovidian episode are reflected at several points in the play. Beyond Troilus's reference to 'Ariachne', we find echoes of a blushing human challenging a disguised deity in Aeneas's encounter with Agamemnon, whom he calls 'a god in office' (1.3.231). The use of cloth as a metaphor for destiny also appears – with a meta-theatrical twist – when Achilles prepares to shed Hector's blood:

> Even with the vail and darkn'ing of the sun
> To close the day up, Hector's life is done
>
> (5.9.7–8)

Bevington notes that 'vail', which meant 'lowering', could be heard as 'veil' by the audience.[25] In the context of a theatrical performance drawing to a close, the line meta-dramatically conflates veils and curtains, strengthening the symbolic force of cloth. As in the Ovidian tale, handling cloth appears as a way for humans to wrest control from the gods, and to appropriate the destiny-shaping forces associated with blood. For in *Troilus and Cressida*, the blush is a recurring reminder of how little agency the characters enjoy, and how powerfully blood dictates their fates.

Blood and Agency

The spontaneous nature of blushing makes it convenient short-hand for the many uncontrollable forces that shape individual destinies. In the early modern period, the controlling nature of blood was rooted both in Galenic humoral theory[26] and in the Christian equation of God's presence with Christ's blood, as evidenced in the debate over transubstantiation. As Ariane M. Balizet has discussed, the medical and theological traditions came together in the writings of several Reformation theologians, who described blood as the spirit of God moving through the body. For Reformation martyr Michael Servetus, for example, blood was 'the substance of the soul'.[27] To this should be added blood as a byword for social class, as when, in *Henry V*, King Harry urges his nobles to 'be copy to men of grosser blood' (3.1.24). Blood, then, curtails individual agency.

Scholarly discussion of *Troilus and Cressida* has often centred on the characters' agency and, more often, on their lack thereof. Margery Garber and Linda Charnes, for example, have shown how characters' awareness of their fictional afterlives seems to condition their behaviour. Charnes refers to the 'proleptic awareness' of Troilus, Cressida and Pandarus,[28] who in the wooing scene speak of themselves as future archetypes of faithfulness, treachery and procuring (3.2.166–99). For Garber, 'characters give voice to their own myth' and 'become personifications'.[29] The idea that all the characters are walking clichés is meta-dramatically conveyed by Achilles and Patroclus's grotesque imitations of the Greek generals (1.3.142–84), which involve reducing each of them to their most comical feature, in the fashion of a Jonsonian humour. Beyond their meta-fictional reflexivity, characters' actions are constricted by the contingencies of their situations, as demonstrated by Hector's agreement to fight a war he does not believe in (2.2.163–93), and which, in fact, nobody wants.

Though the constraints weighing on *Troilus and Cressida*'s characters are of very different types, the play consolidates them by grounding them in blood. Honour, which drives the heroes' actions, is spoken of as 'high blood' in the Prologue. Hector refuses to fight Ajax because of the blood they share (4.5.83–6). Cressida angrily disavows her 'consanguinity' (4.2.97) to her father, which makes it her duty to join him on the Greek side in exchange for Antenor – but goes anyway. Even personifications are rooted in blood, as when Helen is allegorised as 'the heart-blood of beauty' (3.1.32) in the Petrarch-minded servant's overblown Platonic description. The play in fact seems to provide a run-through of all the ways in which blood may play the role of fate, including through humoral control of the affects. Ulysses explains Achilles's pride as an effect of his 'hot blood' (2.3.173), in a straightforward application of Galenic humour theory. In Hector's plea against continuing the fight, the Trojan War exemplifies the way 'the hot passion of distempered blood' (2.2.169) always prevails over 'a free determination of right and wrong' (170–1). The Galenic/Stoic opposition of 'blood' and 'free[dom]' neatly establishes blood as the force driving human action. In this context, any act of self-determination involves finding a way to control, contain or redefine the action of blood.

Throughout the play, controlling the blood flowing to one's face becomes a way of asserting power over one's destiny. Thus, Aeneas's 'deliberate' blush is Troy's expression of defiance before the Greek invader. Facial ruddiness is also how Cressida hopes to evade being handed over to the Greeks. While the Greek Diomedes attempts to exert control over her by praising the 'heaven in her cheek' (4.4.118), Cressida threatens to 'scratch her praised cheek' (4.2.107) as a means of achieving her 'will' (109).

Blood and textile, then, belong to networks of imagery that crystallise in Cressida's blushing scene, where the veil/mask signals both helplessness and active resistance. It is not just, as Thomas Merriam puts it, that Cressida's masked face 'is more art than nature',[30] but that it may stand for performative agency against the determinism of blood. Still, we may wonder what good any of this posturing does. After all, Aeneas's showmanship does not prevent the Greeks from destroying Troy. Cressida's playing with veils and nails does not prevent her from going to the Greeks. These facts suggest a Stoic reading of the blushing dynamics, in which resistance is framed as an internal phenomenon, and the veil/mask functions as an allegory of the mind's self-affirming action. This reading is encouraged by the echoes of the medical literature on blushing that resonate throughout the play.

The Mind's Crimson Veil

With a slight shift of perspective, it is possible to read Aeneas's speech about performing a blush not as a boast but as a medical allegory. Instead of claiming superhuman control over his features, Aeneas could simply be describing how a blush works. With its allegorical language, and clinical use of the definite article in 'the cheek' (1.3.228), the speech reads a bit like the lively accounts of blushing found in early modern Galenic treatises. These stylistic features are in evidence in Timothy Bright's *Treatise of Melancholy*, where blushing is described as the 'discontented' heart's intake and subsequent release of blood:

> Shame [...] forceth redness into the ears and cheeks. [It] procureth that rednesse in the face which we call blushing. The tincture of red ariseth on this sort: the heart, discontented with the opennesse of the offence, maketh a retraction of blood and spirit [at the first] [...] then the blood and spirit break forth againe more vehemently, and fill the parts about the face more than before.[31]

Bright's treatise was published in 1586. By the turn of the century, a very different explanation was making its way through the literature, possibly under the impulse of Annibale Pocaterra's 1592 *Due Dialoghi de la Vergogna*, which followed fifth-century Roman author Macrobius in comparing a blush to a veil or mask drawn over the face.[32] Pocaterra explains:

> Nature [...] covers her face with a crimson veil of blood intending to cover the sinning soul as well. This is no wonder, because hiding and covering are some of the natural properties of shame. We have proof of this when we observe those who, feeling shame and being unable to hide themselves otherwise, cover their face with their hands and lower their eyes as though they wanted their whole face to disappear under their brows.[33]

Lodowick Bryskett's *A Discourse of Civil Life* (1606), published between *Troilus and Cressida*'s 1603 registration and 1609 publication, gives a similar account, but replaces 'nature' with 'the minde', and the veil with 'a maske':

> The minde finding that what is to be reprimanded in us, commeth from abroad, it seeketh to hide the fault committed, and to avoid the reproach thereof, by setting the colour on our face as a maske to defend us withal.[34]

In Robert Burton's 1621 version, the veil/mask image is a bit more 'subtle': 'The face labours and is troubled at his presence that sees our defects; and nature, wishing to help, sends tither heat; heat draws the subtilest blood; and so we blush.'[35] The operative word here is 'subtilest'. Etymologically, 'subtle' comes from the Latin *sub-tela*, with *tela* meaning 'web' or 'fabric'.[36] Bevington notes that *subtilis* is Latin for 'fine-spun'.[37] The implication is that blushing occurs beneath the fabric of the skin, or, since it is 'draw[n]', that the blood itself forms a kind of curtain. Though Burton's *Anatomy of Melancholy* post-dates *Troilus and Cressida*, it seems, based on the sheer number of occurrences, that the 'blush as veil' metaphor had gained currency by the time *Troilus and Cressida* was published, and perhaps even by the time it was registered. As seen above, Beaumont and Fletcher used it in *The Woman-Hater* in 1607.

Thinking of a blush as a gesture of concealment, rather than as a giveaway, is counter-intuitive from our twenty-first-century perspective. To us, the above explanations beg the question of what, exactly, the blush is supposed to conceal. Thomas Wright, in his *Passions of the Minde in Generall* (1601) sheds some light on the issue. In the following passage, Wright begins with examples of masters detecting servants' guilt by reading their facial expressions, then moves on to an explanation of blushing:

> By this example, superiors may learne to conjecture the affections of their subjectes mindes, by a silent speech pronounced in their very countenances [...] Hereby we may also perceyve the cause of blushing, for that those that have committed a fault, & are therein deprehended, [...] if they be [...] of an honest behaviour, they blush, because nature being afrayd lest in the face the fault should be discovered, sendeth the purest blood, to be a defence and succour, the which effect, commonly, is iudjed to proceede from a good and vertuous nature, because no man can but allowe, that it is good to be ashamed of a fault.[38]

A blush is a mask, then, either because it obscures the subject's guilty facial expression or because it redirects the viewer's attention from the blusher's look of guilt to his or her look of virtuous shame.

These accounts of blushing, it should be noted, are couched in the language of allegory and romance. In Bryskett, 'the minde' is like a knight in shining armour, coming from 'abroade' to save the shamed person, which in Wright is expressed as lending 'defence and succour'. Though the mind, in these accounts, is not

explicitly gendered, the knight in shining armour image tends
to masculinise it. The chivalric image is particularly relevant to
Troilus and Cressida, throughout which the beleaguered heroine
is in sore need of a champion. In its evocation of masculine valour,
the knight allegory functions as the counterpart to Cressida's
derogatory, feminised description of her flustered 'thoughts' as
'unbridled children, grown / Too headstrong for their mother'
(3.2.122–3). Here, the mother is a personification of a helpless
mind, unable to corral the thoughts issuing from it. The image of
wilful children – the blood of a mother's blood – running wild is
in fact quite analogous to that of blood spreading uncontrollably.
This bears out Gail Kern Paster's contention that female blushing,
like blood shedding, was a token of helplessness in early modern
culture.[39] These clashing allegories come together in the staged
figure of a blushing Cressida, whose veil or mask can now be read
as the chivalric mind's protective shield, even as it continues to
serve as a theatrical token of uncontrollable emotion.

Transferring these Galenic allegories to the stage shows that
the same veiled or masked figure can be read in two ways, as in an
anamorphosis.[40] Mimetically, the veil signals a helpless Cressida's
effort to conceal an irrepressible blush. Allegorically, the veil stands
for Cressida's mind deploying a protective blush over her face. But
how can Cressida and her mind be engaged in two contradictory
actions at the same time? Is Cressida's mind not Cressida herself?
In a sense, 'this is, and is not, Cressid!' (5.2.146) indeed. What
the superimposed images question, then, is the relation of the
mind to the self, and thus the location of the individual's centre of
command. With its layered blush, the play delivers Cressida – and
her fellow characters – over to the audience's anatomising gaze.

Anatomising the Blush

The twinned motifs of cloth and blushing associate Cressida's
blush with some of the play's other moments of psychological
and anatomical inquiry. One example is Ulysses drawing Achilles
out of his tent with the boast that he has 'unveiled' Achilles's
'thoughts' (3.3.200), to wit, the true reason why he does not wish
to fight, this being his love for Polyxena, a Trojan maid. Achilles's
response to being suddenly and unexpectedly confronted with
his most intimate feelings ('Ha? Known?'; 194) suggests that a
violent blush would not be out of place. Hector's inquisitive gaze

pierces both the cloth of Achilles's tent and the skin of his face as he draws a picture of Achilles's inner self, evoking a war between his 'mental and his active parts' (2.3.174). In this example, as in Cressida's, the layering of blood, skin, cloth, and possibly other protective facial gear recalls the iconography of Renaissance anatomical investigations.

As Jonathan Sawday has shown, early modern plays display an awareness of – and fascination with – theatres of dissection and anatomical plates. These engraved plates would often show a human figure holding his or her flayed skin open in a display of flesh, bone and inner organs. Both the term 'theatre of dissection' and the flayed figure's gesture imply a homology between the codes of theatrical display and the anatomising gaze. In particular, the skin is likened to a curtain whose removal offers a glimpse into the mysterious space beyond. A further similarity is that the anatomised figure is an animated being, presented against a backdrop resembling a stage set:

> A feature of Renaissance anatomic illustration is the intrusion of the cadaver into a landscape, or even an ornately decorated private chamber [...] So, knowledge of the body, in these texts, was presented as knowledge of a living rather than dead body.[41]

Troilus and Cressida's only direct reference to flaying is when Cressida threatens to 'scratch [her] praised cheek' (4.2.106), but it is a telling one if taken together with its layered construction of blushing and its characters' various musings about the location of mental processes.

'Where is my wit?' (3.2.151) Cressida asks after rambling on to Troilus about her divided self. The question is not just a rhetorical one. It is part of a string of statements in which characters wonder about the anatomical location of such agents of thought as the mind, the wit and the spirit. One such moment is when Thersites mockingly locates Ajax's 'wit [...] in his belly' (2.1.73) and Achilles's 'in [his] sinews' (98–9). Similarly, Achilles wonders aloud where he should pierce Hector's body for quickest access to his 'spirit':

> Tell me, you heavens, in which part of his body
> Shall I destroy him? Whether there, or there, or there?
> That I may give the local wound a name
> And make distinct the very breach whereout
> Hector's great spirit flew. Answer me, heavens!
>
> (4.5.242–6)

Achilles's epanaleptic invocation to the heavens is both heroic and proto-scientific, reflecting a spirit of hubristic epistemological inquiry. The play's investigative sequence culminates with Troilus's disgusted and grotesque 'her foot speaks' (4.5.56) as he interprets Cressida's movements in the scene with Diomedes. Here too, the 'spirit' is difficult to locate, as it 'looks out / At every joint or motive of her body' (4.5.56–7).

Coupled with the general question of location, characters more specifically question the depth at which the mind resides or operates. Counterpointing the servant's statement that he knows Pandarus 'superficially' (3.1.10), Achilles looks for himself at the 'bottom' of his 'troubled' mind, which he compares to a 'fountain stirred' (3.3.308–9). This image of the mind's depth is materialised in Cressida's blushing scene by the many layers involved in the theatrical simulation of a blushing face: the tiring house curtains, the veil or mask, the make-up over the boy player's face, the player's skin, the blood beneath the skin. Paradoxically, the veil may even signify depth on its own, if we refer to Sir John Davies's *Nosce teipsum*, a mostly Neoplatonic treatise published in 1599, which Bevington argues is behind the play's many anatomical images. In *Nosce teipsum*, we find a new incarnation of Arachne in the inward-gazing movement of the natural philosopher: 'As Spiders touch'd, seek their web's inmost part [...] teach us to know our Selves.'[42] The web-like veil, then, also stands for the kind of exploration Davies conducts in his treatise, which mainly concerns the workings of the mind.

Davies's relevance to the play is noticeable beyond the spider image. Bevington argues that Hector's reference to the allegorical war between Achilles's 'mental and his active parts' (2.3.174) as well as Ulysses's earlier statement about the superiority of the 'still and mental parts' (1.3.200) over the performing body are consistent with Davies's model of the body and mind. The 'mental and active parts', Bevington suggests, may refer to Davies's division of the upper brain into a passive (mental) part that receives the sense impressions sent by the lower brain and an active part that processes them by abstracting form.[43] Yet, Bevington adds, the 'mental and active parts' could also simply refer to 'his mind and body'.[44] There is uncertainty, then, as to whether decision-making takes place entirely in the brain, or whether it involves both the brain and the body. In Davies, the indeterminacy is compounded by the author's acknowledged doubts about the relationship between brain and mind. After a very specific description of the location of the components of the brain, he confesses:

> But now I have a will, yet want a wit,
> To express the working of the wit and will.
> Which though their root be to the body knit,
> Use not their body, when they use their skill.[45]

In the Aristotelian model of the mind, 'wit and will', along with memory, are the powers, or faculties, of the rational soul. Davies's puzzlement reflects the shifting definition of the soul in Aristotle's *De Anima*. While in some places Aristotle describes the soul as an extended substance merged with the body (the hylomorphic model), in others he speaks of it as a fully immaterial entity.[46] In the play, the problem of locating the 'soul' (1.3.56) is introduced through a body politic metaphor, when Ulysses deplores that 'the general is not like the [bee]hive' (81), glossed by Bevington as meaning that Agamemnon is no longer the 'command centre'.[47] In his famous 'degree' speech, Ulysses goes on to complain that 'Degree being vizarded, / Th'unworthiest shows as worthy in the mask' (84), meaning that a disregard for the outward signs of social status leads to a breakdown in hierarchy. The metaphor of the vizard or mask is literalised by Aeneas when he claims not to recognise the helmeted Agamemnon. This paves the way for Cressida's crimson mask – her blush – to be read as effecting a similar obfuscation, albeit on the microcosmic level of the individual organism. Yet Ulysses's body politic allegory makes for a confusing model when he addresses Agamemnon in these (flattering) terms:

> Agamemnon
> Thou great commander, nerve and bone of Greece,
> Heart of our numbers, soul and only spirit,
> In whom the tempers and minds of all
> Should be shut up.
>
> (1.3.54–8)

The accumulation of anatomical metaphors may sound like rhetorical overkill, but it also neatly reflects early modern confusion about which of the body's organs is the 'commander' of the whole body, and indeed about whether the body's 'active parts' may not be doing a bit of commanding of their own. The issue is further developed by Hector's discussion of '[t]he law of nature'

(2.2.176–7) as the mediating principle between blood's 'high passion' and the ability of 'great minds' to 'make free determination / 'Twixt right and wrong' (2.2.170–1). This identification of nature as the ultimate referee points back to a slight discrepancy in the Galenic accounts of blushing discussed two sections above.

Though Bryskett mentions 'the minde' as the agent behind the blush, Wright puts 'nature' in charge. Nature, in Galenic theory, was the active principle at work in the body, which Davies referred to as 'God's handmaid'.[48] Arguing that Renaissance ideas about the mind emerged from separate philosophical and medical traditions, Guido Giglioni emphasises the Galenic belief in nature's agency:

> Th[e] principle of 'specific attraction' and the fact that it took place without conscious perception [...] were for Galen the defining traits of nature. Nature [was] 'creative' in every single particle of the body. Indeed, Nature was the original artist, in that the way it built bodies was a paragon of efficacy and ingenuity, clumsily imitated by human beings when they fashioned artefacts working from outside in. [...] What is more, nature seemed to display original forms of pre-mental intentionality in the way in which the natural faculties responded to reality by attracting and rejecting, absorbing and transmitting, selecting and shaping.[49]

This idea of nature as constituting a seat of consciousness and creativity dwelling in the body, as distinct from the mind's own consciousness, sits well with Pocaterra's, Wright's and Burton's allegorising of nature in their accounts of blushing. It is also consistent with the layered consciousness implied by the veiled Cressida and goes a long way towards accounting for the paradox of the blush, involving both conscious awareness of a shameful situation and an irrepressible bodily response.

It is perhaps somewhat perplexing that this thick layering of levels of consciousness should produce characters who, in a commonplace of the play's criticism, are decidedly flat. Here I am using 'flat' in E. M. Forster's sense of the word, referring to characters who are devoid of interiority, like caricatures.[50] And indeed, it is notable that, with the arguable exception of Perdita in *The Winter's Tale*, Shakespeare's blushing characters are usually flat. Armado blushes, Berowne does not. Hero blushes, Beatrice does not. For David Hillman, Cressida devolves into 'pure textuality'[51] at the end of the play. The answer to this conundrum may have something to do with the generic humanity posited by the anatomising gaze. Sawday makes this point when he notes that 'the criminal [dissected] body can have no individual identity save that guaranteed by the anatomist'.[52]

The masked figure of Cressida, then, is at the heart of an intra- and intertextual network – one might say a web – of allegories of nature and the mind, pointing to blushing as a phenomenon involving multiple centres of control, of various degrees of materiality. Some of these allegories remain verbal, including the spider, the knight, the flustered mother and the personification of dawn. The most complex and most powerful allegories, however, involve textile stage properties. When a piece of fabric, used as a curtain, mask or veil, indicates a blush, either by concealing it or standing for it, it shows rather than tells. For it is by displaying the inherent limitations of performance that the veil comes to stand for that double agency that so perplexes Troilus.

This allegorical use of the textile stage prop, as I hope to have shown, moots the issue of Cressida's sincerity, for it tends to deconstruct the opposition between craft and spontaneity, due to an unmoored centre of command. The paradox of blushing can also be understood in terms of spectatorship. As blushing only occurs in the presence of onlookers, it is inherently a performance, even when it is spontaneous. Cressida blushes because Pandarus and Troilus are looking at her. Thanks in part to Pandarus's liminal status as a go-between, the offstage audience is invited to recognise itself in the gawking men, and thus to acknowledge its participation in establishing the veil's allegorical meaning. The role, however, is a 'subtle' one, being mostly limited to the imagined effect of the gaze. The audience's participation in allegorical meaning is more obvious in plays involving crowd scenes, such as *Coriolanus*, in which a restive audience is encouraged to project itself onto the Roman crowd, and it is to this that we now turn our attention.

Notes

1 Galen's theory is glossed in Timothy Bright, *A Treatise of Melancholy*, London, 1586, EEBO, The Huntington Library, p. 87: 'the philosophers [have] defined anger as a boiling of the blood about the heart'.

2 Bright describes the senses as 'the instruments of the brain', and the brain and spirits, as 'the corporal ministers' of the mind. Ibid. pp. 104, 105.

3 The *locus classicus* is Prudentius's *Psychomachia* (fifth century), involving a battle between personified vices and virtues. See Rita Copeland and Peter T. Struck (eds), *The Cambridge Companion to Allegory* (2010), Cambridge: Cambridge University Press, 2011, pp. 6–7.

4 David Bevington, in William Shakespeare, *Troilus and Cressida*, ed. David Bevington (1998), The Arden Shakespeare, London: Thomson Learning, 2001, p. 129n.

5 Seneca, *Epistles*, trans. Richard M. Gummere, Loeb Classical Library, Cambridge, MA: Harvard University Press, 1917, p. 63.

6 Andrew Fleck, 'The Ambivalent Blush: Figural and Structural Metonymy, Modesty, and *Much Ado About Nothing*', *ANQ: A Quarterly Journal of Short Articles, Notes and Reviews*, vol. 19, no. 1 (2010), pp. 16–23 (p. 20).

7 Annibale Pocaterra, *Two Dialogues on Shame* (1592), trans. and ed. Werner Gundersheimer and Donald Nathanson, Göttingen, 2013, https://diglib.hab.de/edoc/ed000237/pocaterra.pdf, last accessed 2 April 2022, p. 45.

8 Sujata Iyengar, *Shades of Difference: Mythologies of Skin Color in Early Modern England*, Philadelphia: University of Pennsylvania Press, 2005, p. 127.

9 See Farah Karim-Cooper, *Cosmetics in Shakespearean and Renaissance Drama*, Edinburgh: Edinburgh University Press, 2006. Karim-Cooper objects to Andrew Gurr's claim 'that actors wore masks or vizards as opposed to cosmetics' (p. 136).

10 Michael Hattaway, *Elizabethan Popular Theatre: Plays in Performance* (1982), London: Routledge and Kegan Paul, 2013, p. 38.

11 On the use of curtains on the early modern stage, see Frederick Kiefer, 'Curtains on the Shakespearean Stage', *Medieval and Renaissance Drama in England*, vol. 20 (2007), pp. 151–86; and Nathalie Rivère de Carles, 'Performing Materiality: Curtains on the Early Modern Stage', in Farah Karim-Cooper and Tiffany Stern (eds), *Shakespeare's Theatres and the Effects of Performance* (2013), The Arden Shakespeare, London: Bloomsbury, 2016, pp. 51–69. See also Andrew Gurr and Mariko Ichikawa, *Staging in Shakespeare's Theatres* (2000), Oxford: Oxford University Press, 2013, pp. 6–7.

12 Bevington, in Shakespeare, *Troilus and Cressida*, p. 171n.

13 But expensive: such fine cloth might have to be imported from Venice. See Katherine Bond, 'Fashioned with Marvellous Skill: Veils and the Costume Books of Sixteenth-century Europe', in S. Burghartz, L. Burkart, C. Göttler and U. Rublack (eds), *Materialized Identities in Early Modern Culture, 1450–1750: Objects, Affects, Effects*, Amsterdam: Amsterdam University Press, 2021, pp. 325–68. Items

of clothing could, however, have been received as a legacy or bought second hand. See Ann Rosalind Jones and Peter Stallybrass, *Renaissance Clothing and the Materials of Memory*, Cambridge: Cambridge University Press, 2000, pp. 175–206.

14 Philip Stubbes, *The Anatomie of Abuses*, 1583, EEBO, The Huntington Library, sig. G2, p. 52.

15 Andrew Gurr, '*Measure for Measure*'s Hoods and Masks: The Duke, Isabella, and Liberty', *English Literary Renaissance*, vol. 27, no. 1 (1997), pp. 89–105 (p. 100).

16 Or alternatively, that the 'curtain' Pandarus is referring to is the blush itself, in which case no props at all are needed. This, however, would seem like a bit of a missed opportunity, given the rich array of textiles at the King's Men's disposal.

17 Stephen Gosson, *Pleasant Quippes for Upstart Newfangled Gentlewomen* (1595), London: T. Richards, 1841, pp. 6–7; 'in plight', here, is roughly synonymous with 'on offer'.

18 Though there is no record of its ever having been performed in Shakespeare's time. See Bevington, in Shakespeare, *Troilus and Cressida*, p. 3.

19 See, for example, Thomas Merriam, 'The Old Lady, or All is Not True', in Peter Holland (ed.), *Shakespeare Survey: An Annual Survey of Shakespeare Studies and Production. Volume 54: Shakespeare and Religions*, Cambridge: Cambridge University Press, 2001, pp. 234–45 (p. 237).

20 Rivère de Carles, 'Performing Materiality', p. 53.

21 'Le rideau agit comme un relai visuel du corps de l'actrice', Nathalie Rivère de Carles, 'Entre texte et scénographie: théâtralité de la toile à la Renaissance', PhD dissertation, Montpellier, 2005, p. 395 (my translation).

22 See Farah Karim-Cooper, *Cosmetics in Shakespearean and Renaissance Drama*, Edinburgh: Edinburgh University Press, 2022, pp. 37–42.

23 Ovid, *Metamorphoses*, Book 6, trans. Arthur Golding, London, 1567, EEBO, The Huntington Library, pp. 69–70.

24 Bevington, in Shakespeare, *Troilus and Cressida*, p. 372n.

25 Ibid. p. 347n.

26 In Galenic theory, though blood was only one of the four humours, it ranked above the others: phlegm, yellow bile and black bile could be turned into blood, but not the other way round. See Gail Kern Paster, *The Body Embarrassed: Drama and the Disciplines of Shame in Early Modern England*, Ithaca, NY: Cornell University Press, 1993, p. 69.

27 Ariane M. Balizet, *Blood and Home in Early Modern Drama: Domestic Identity on the Renaissance Stage*, Abingdon and New York: Routledge, 2014, p. 12.

28 Linda Charnes, '"So Unsecret to Ourselves": Notorious Identity and the Material Subject in Shakespeare's *Troilus and Cressida*', *Shakespeare Quarterly*, vol. 40, no. 4 (Winter 1989), pp. 413–40 (p. 422).

29 Margery Garber, Harvard Lecture, ENGL – E21, 2007, https://www.youtube.com/watch?v=5Xb0V0kN_Z4, last accessed 3 April 2022, 20'04".

30 Merriam, 'The Old Lady, or All is not True', p. 237.

31 Bright, *Treatise of Melancholy*, pp. 163–4.

32 Macrobius explained that '[p]hysical scientists also say that when one's nature has been touched by shame, it holds the blood out before itself like a veil, as we see someone who blushes often holding a hand up in front of his face.' *Saturnalia, Volume III: Books 6–7*, ed. and trans. Robert A. Kaster, Loeb Classical Library, Cambridge, MA: Harvard University Press, 2011, p. 243.

33 Pocaterra, *Two Dialogues on Shame*, p. 43.

34 Lodowick Bryskett, *A Discourse of Civil Life*, London, 1606, EEBO, The British Library, p. 218.

35 Robert Burton, *The Anatomy of Melancholy* (1621), London: Longman, 1827, p. 310.

36 See Rivère de Carles, 'Entre texte et scénographie', p. 279.

37 Bevington, in Shakespeare, *Troilus and Cressida*, p. 324n.

38 Thomas Wright, *The Passions of the Minde in Generall* (1601), London, 1604, EEBO, Yale University Library, pp. 29–30.

39 Kern Paster, *Body Embarrassed*, pp. 92–9.

40 Anamorphosis, quite the rage in the Renaissance, refers to a picture that offers two very different viewing experiences when seen from different angles. A famous example is Holbein's *The Ambassadors* (1533).

41 Jonathan Sawday, *The Body Emblazoned* (1995), London and New York: Routledge, 2013, p. 114.

42 Sir John Davies, *Nosce teipsum*, London, 1599, EEBO, Harvard University Library, p. 7.

43 Bevington, in Shakespeare, *Troilus and Cressida*, p. 360n.

44 Ibid. p. 363n.

45 Davies, *Nosce teipsum*, p. 49.

46 See Philip J. van der Eijk, 'Aristotle's Psycho-physiological Account of the Soul–Body Relationship', in John P. Wright and Paul Potter (eds), *Psyche and Soma: Physicians and Metaphysicians on the Mind–Body Problem from Antiquity to Enlightenment* (2000), Oxford: Clarendon Press, 2002, pp. 57–77 (p. 70).

47 Bevington, in Shakespeare, *Troilus and Cressida*, p. 162n.

48 Davies, *Nosce teipsum*, p. 27.

49 Guido Giglioni, 'Medical Approaches to the Mind in the Late Middle Ages and the Renaissance', in Stephan Schmid (ed.),

Philosophy of Mind in the Late Middle Ages and Renaissance: The History of the Philosophy of Mind, Volume 3, London: Routledge, 2019, pp. 41–61 (pp. 41–2). On the body's agency, see also Charis Charalampous, *Rethinking the Mind–Body Relationship in Early Modern Literature, Philosophy and Medicine* (2016), Abingdon: Routledge, 2019.

50 E. M. Forster, quoted in David Lodge (ed.), *20th Century Literary Criticism: A Reader* (1972), London and New York: Longman, 1995, p. 137.

51 David Hillman, 'The Gastric Epic: *Troilus and Cressida*', *Shakespeare Quarterly*, vol. 48, no. 3 (Autumn 1997), pp. 295–313 (p. 318).

52 Jonathan Sawday, 'The Fate of Marysas: Dissecting the Renaissance Body', in Lucy Gent and Nigel Llewellyn (eds), *Renaissance Bodies: The Human Figure, English Culture, c. 1540–1660* (1990), London: Reaktion Books, 1997, pp. 111–35 (p. 116).

Chapter 5

'A River Runs Through It':
The Shape of Hydra in *Coriolanus*

The river Tiber runs through Shakespeare's Roman plays as it runs through Rome, and as the Thames runs through London.[1] Both symbolising and dividing the city, the river is a rich source of allegory for Rome's historical internal conflicts, such as that between Caius Martius and the hungry plebs in *Coriolanus*. Beyond its evocation of division, the river's allegorical potential stems from a tradition of describing crowds as unruly bodies of water requiring management. Though this commonplace is illustrated in several of Shakespeare's plays, as in *Hamlet*, when Claudius describes Laertes as leading an 'ocean' (4.5.100) of followers, it is particularly salient in *Coriolanus*, where controlling the plebeian crowd is often spoken of as a water-engineering problem. As Paul Menzer and others have discussed, such imagery was also applied to playgoing audiences.[2] In this chapter, I will argue that the structural similarities between *Coriolanus*'s plebeians and London's playgoing crowds amplify the play's water-engineering metaphors and help turn them into allegories of thought. The leap from water as a crowd allegory to water as a mind allegory is facilitated by the Hydra figure, this chapter's master metaphor.

Much of this chapter's discussion will involve making educated assumptions about how an early seventeenth-century London audience would react to various stimuli. To reduce the speculative character of this approach, I will place it within the conceptual frameworks of Cognitive Metaphor Theory, which, as seen in Chapter 2, holds that metaphors grow out of embodied experience,[3] and Jungian archetype theory, which holds that literary works strike the imagination by activating shared internalised symbols.[4] Both theories will be modified by historical and contextual considerations. Building on these frameworks, I will submit that *Coriolanus*'s water-based allegories of thought come into being when imagery is 'plugged into' a sensing and moving audience, with memory and imagination at the ready.

The Context: Hungry Plebs and Thirsty Londoners

Coriolanus's entire plot is powered by plebeian hunger, which triggers the showdown between the people and Caius Martius, later Coriolanus. The topicality of the hunger theme, in the context of the 1607–8 Midland corn riots, has long been noted in the play's critical history. R. B. Parker, for example, draws attention to the parallels between *Coriolanus*'s hungry plebeians and the rioting English peasants.[5] More recently, the ecocritical and hydrological turn in Shakespeare scholarship has brought the play's possible allusions to London's strained water distribution system and nascent New River plan under scrutiny.[6] In the years when Shakespeare was writing *Coriolanus*, access to water was a divisive issue, and one that might lead commoners to riot against aristocratic privilege. Though ordinary townspeople had to go and fill tankards at the city's public fountains or conduits, London's elites had water carried to their houses by 'quills', narrow pipes connected to the city's main pipes and necessarily diverting water from the public supply. This dearth occasionally led to rioting. In 1608, the year *Coriolanus* was first performed, the mayor discontinued the Earl of Suffolk's private quill, which the nobleman had been using so wastefully as to endanger the supply to the city conduits and thereby to compromise civil peace. The mayor, in a letter to the Earl, explained his action as designed to prevent mob violence:

> [I am sorry] to give your honour any occasion of mislike but the water so scarce unto the conduittes. And the clamour of the poore is such this tyme of Dearth and scarcity that there could noe other course be taken for their satisfaction, but by cutting of some of the Quiles, which drewe awai soe much water.[7]

One may infer from the letter's deferential tone that only the threat of 'the clamour of the poore' erupting into a riot could have induced the mayor to take such a drastic step and risk infuriating a nobleman. The mayor's fears were not unfounded. Mark Jenner also reports that 'in 1561, the aldermen only just averted a planned water riot in which young men and waterbearers were going to tear up the private quill of Lord Paget, which had caused the Fleet Street Conduit to dry up'.[8] A more lasting solution to such water crises was Sir Hugh Myddleton's New River project, designed to ease the pressure on the city's resources caused by a growing population of Londoners. The project, which involved bringing water to London from Hertfordshire via a 38-mile canal, was introduced in 1605 and adopted by the City of London in 1609.[9]

Disconnecting a nobleman's quill is the water equivalent of distributing the patrician's hoarded corn to the people, one of the responses to hunger rioting in *Coriolanus* (3.1.115–17). However, the London audience watching *Coriolanus* would have recognised its own predicament much earlier in the play, in the famous episode of the fable of the belly.

In the opening scene, Menenius, a patrician, attempts to counter the plebeian crowd's complaints about patrician grain hoarding by giving them his own version of Aesop's fable of the body's hungry members rioting against the greedy belly. In the belly's answer, food courses through the body in a notably aqueous manner:

> I am the storehouse and the shop
> Of the whole body. But if you do remember
> I sent it through the rivers of your blood
> Even to the court, the heart, to th'seat of the brain
> And through the cranks and offices of man
> The strongest nerves and small inferior veins
> From me receive that natural competency
> Whereby they live.
>
> (1.1.133–40)

Shakespeare's main sources for this speech were Plutarch's *Lives*, Livy's *Ab Urbe Condita* and Camden's *Remains*.[10] None of the sources, however, presents the fable with as many topographical details. Most significantly, none refers to blood as 'rivers', and none emphasises the elaborate network of veins through which the blood flows. The 'shops', 'courts' and 'storehouses' are also Shakespeare's invention. To thirsty Londoners, the 'river' metaphor might have come across as a nod to London's water problems. Along with this recognition, the audience might have been reminded of their own city authorities' reliance on water's powerful symbolism to keep crowds in check.

Water Symbolism and Crowd Control in Early Modern London

London's water landmarks featured prominently in the City of London's crowd management strategies. Civic pageants, including coronations, routinely included stops at the city conduit heads or fountains, and annual inspections of the conduit heads were an occasion for public celebration.[11] Celebration could give way to violence. London's growing population frequently resulted in unruly behaviour at the city's crowded public conduits, where long lines led to frayed nerves and angry confrontations. Sites of water distribution then became sites of crowd control and punishment, where whipping and pillorying were carried out.[12] Commenting on the 1531 Statute of Sewers, which provided for the maintenance of sewers and ditches, and mandated penalties for those who soiled them, Jonathan Gil Harris claims that '[t]he imperative to control water was [...] already inseparable from a process of social control'.[13]

Control could also take the gentler form of rhetorical persuasion, in which case fountains and conduits provided a store of imagery. For example, Puritan pastor Richard Greenham urged his audience to think of God's word as 'a conduit or waterpipe, whereby the Lord conveying his mercies unto us, will have them runne through unto us'.[14] William Fisher used similar imagery in a 1591 sermon designed to convince his congregation to open their purses to preachers:

> And you have store of faire and sweete Conduits, wherebye you spare not for any coste, to convey water into every place almost of this populous city. Yea there cannot be a fountaine heard of, or a devise thought of, to yield store of water, but lyke good and careful governers, your hands are in your purse to laye out what so ever it will cost. And will you bestow nothing upon the blessed Pypes, and sugred Conduites which bring you the water of lyfe?[15]

Here, water is a symbol of life, but also a metaphor for God's grace. There is also a hint of the liquidity of money, with the preacher hoping to ease the flow of coins out of the audience's pockets. Rhetorical appropriation of fountain symbolism makes for a powerful dramatic moment in Shakespeare's *2 Henry VI*, written the same year as Fisher's exhortation, where a rabble of Kentish tradesmen are driven to a murderous frenzy by a cheerfully bloodthirsty leader, Jack Cade. Cade promises the thirsty crowd that in the first year of his reign, the 'pissing-conduit will run nothing but claret wine' (4.6.3–4).

The effectiveness of water symbolism in the physical and rhetorical strategies of control outlined above suggests an underlying analogy. Harris has called attention to how a crowd-as-water analogy underpinned both medieval and early modern crowd-control policies:

> The twin tasks of containing 'incontinent' water and 'incontinent'[16] citizens were constantly identified with each other: John Stow notes that the conduit at Cornehill was originally built in 1282 as a prison to contain 'night walkers and suspicious persons', as well as those 'suspected of incontinence'. He tells us also that water reservoirs were built at Newgate and Ludgate prisons.[17]

The analogy between crowds and water is a symbolically powerful one. In *Crowds and Power*, Elias Canetti lists the sea, rivers and rain as archetypal 'crowd symbols', defined as 'collective units which do not consist of men, but are still felt to be crowds'.[18] Consistent with this analysis, early modern authors routinely relied on water metaphors when evoking the dangerous power of crowds, and more specifically audiences. An example is Nathan Field's 1608 description of a crowd attending an entertainment as a 'monster' who 'clapped his thousand hands / And drowned the scene with / His confused cry'.[19] In *Coriolanus*, performed at the Globe the same year, monster and water imagery also combine, in a way that establishes continuity between the onstage Roman plebs and offstage London audience.

Water Metaphors in *Coriolanus*: Staging the Roman Crowd

Coriolanus's noble patricians frequently dismiss the plebeians' concerns by resorting to water metaphors. This begins in a low key, when Menenius describes one of the tribunes' routine peacekeeping duties as dealing with an unruly faucet-seller (2.1.68). The metaphorical leaky faucet swells into a stream in Sicinius's reference to 'the stream o'th'people' (2.3.257), soon to become a river when Coriolanus states that the plebeians' tribunes want to turn '[the patricians'] current in a ditch / and make [their] channel [theirs]' (3.1.97). Tidal wave status is reached when Cominius, the Roman general, refers to the retreating crowd of citizens as 'interrupted waters' (3.1.250) threatening to return with a vengeance.

Water imagery serves several dramatic purposes in these speeches. One is to convey the speaker's contempt for the Roman people. Another is to encourage the Globe audience to visualise the Roman plebeians as a crowd rather than as the mere sprinkling of actors physically present onstage. Staging a 'streaming' crowd at the Globe would have been difficult, due to obvious limitations of space and manpower, but water metaphors would have stimulated the audience's imagination. This imaginative amplification might have been helped along by the playgoers' immediate memory of the river they had just crossed on their way to the bankside playhouse. What is more, the crowd-as-water metaphor could have encouraged the London audience to see itself as an extension of the onstage plebeians by implying a natural tendency for groups of people to flow into each other. It is of course difficult to establish with any certainty how a seventeenth-century audience's imagination would have worked, but Shakespeare's Globe, the 1997 replica of the Globe theatre, has offered opportunities for experimentation. In Dominic Drumgoole's 2006 production of *Coriolanus*, the audience's readiness to extend the onstage crowd was noticeable, as testified to by lead actor Jonathan Cake:

> It's such a gift for a director and an actor to play *Coriolanus* at the Globe because there is a ready-made mob there. [...] In every show, there was an obvious and immediate connection. You could tell the audience understood how coming to see this play was particularly special, that it wasn't like going to see *Othello* or *Hamlet*. There was a natural interaction between the characters onstage and the characters in the audience which included them. You could feel that there was not just a physical proximity to the play but they suddenly realized they could become characters in the play.[20]

Identification was further promoted through forced or suggested movement. Audience members were frequently jostled aside as actors cut through the crowd on their way to or from the stage. At the performance I attended, an amusing moment came after the repeal of Coriolanus's election, when the tribunes tell the citizens to stand by in preparation for Coriolanus's banishment. That afternoon, the actor playing Brutus[21] addressed the line 'go not home' (3.1.328) to a couple of groundlings, who promptly assured him that they would not. By establishing an analogy between the audience's movements to and from the playhouse and the citizens' movement to and from the Capitol, this short exchange encouraged the playgoers to imaginatively supplement the space and movement missing from the performance with their memorised experience of travelling through London's crowded streets.

By activating playgoers' immediate memory, then, *Coriolanus*'s water imagery may have helped the 1608 Globe audience project its own experiences of fluidity onto the Roman crowd. More than this, though, familiarity with audience-management techniques would have primed the London audience to recognise the strategies of control being used on the Roman crowd. For both the play's onstage plebeians and offstage audience, containing, channelling, dividing and rerouting would have been powerful principles of crowd control.

Channelling the Crowd

Andrew Gurr, Kai Wiegandt and Paul Menzer have all produced evidence that contrary to previously held beliefs, early modern audiences were reasonably well behaved.[22] This has prompted them to investigate how such a desirable result was achieved. For Wiegandt, the ritual dimension of the theatre is the operative principle.[23] Just as intriguing is Menzer's theory of the playhouse as a miniature of the city. The round, galleried architecture of the outdoor theatre, Menzer argues, allowed part of the London crowd to be siphoned off into a smaller, neater, self-contained replica of the city itself. This reduction of London's crowds to a manageable size conditioned audiences to inhabit both playhouse and city in an orderly manner.[24] Key moments, in this conditioning, are entrances and exits, when the crowd's watery quality becomes manifest. Menzer mentions Thomas Dekker's use of the word 'torrent' to describe an audience pouring in and out of the playhouse,[25] an image that makes theatrical crowd-control analogous to wild waters being channelled off and contained in a retention basin.

Water-engineering features prominently in the techniques used by *Coriolanus*'s nobles in their attempts to contain the plebeian crowds. Of course, Menenius's exasperated 'I would they were in Tiber' (3.1.264) is no more than wishful thinking. No one seriously considers throwing the plebeians into the river as an answer to Rome's political problems. However, Menenius is also aware of more subtle ways of using the crowd/water analogy. Even before Coriolanus rails at the tribunes for appropriating the patricians' 'channel' (3.1.97), Menenius uses a channelling technique when he verbally isolates the crowd's ringleader from the group, comically calling him the 'great toe' of the assembly:

> *Men.*   What do you think,
>   You, the great toe of this assembly?
> *[1] Cit.* I the great toe? Why the great toe?
> *Men.* For that, being one o'th'lowest, basest, poorest
>   Of this most wise rebellion, thou goest foremost.
>
>   (1.1.154–8)

Peeling the leader of a group away from the bulk is a time-tried method of disabling it and can be seen as metaphorically equivalent to digging a diversion canal. A similar method is applied when the citizens are instructed to approach Coriolanus in groups of two or three (2.3.40), rather than en masse, like a river splitting into rivulets. Wiegandt notes the ritual dimension of this procedure, pointing out that 'it serves to control the crowd'.[26] A more properly psychological form of channelling is the storytelling itself. Menenius's tale of the belly works through a form of diversion or re-routing, as it involves redirecting the focus of the crowd's attention. Menenius's parable momentarily turns the hungry plebeians away from their predicament as they become interested in the narrative for its own sake: 'What answer made the belly?' (1.1.103). This, however, only works for a little while. 'How apply you this?' (144) signals a return to more immediate concerns. A more powerful strategy, which I will illustrate with a quick detour by way of *Julius Caesar*, involves channelling the crowd's collective imagination, so that it will identify with flowing water.

In *Julius Caesar*, Mark Antony's funeral oration in praise of the assassinated Julius Caesar turns the formerly pro-Brutus crowd around and sends it rampaging through the city. Antony begins his speech by replaying the assassination before the bereaved citizens whom Brutus has just managed to pacify. Very gradually, he weaves into his description of Caesar's bleeding body an image of swelling waters.

> If you have tears, prepare to shed them now.
> You all do know this mantle. I do remember

The first time ever Caesar put it on.
'Twas on a summer evening in his tent,
That day he overcame the Nervii.
Look, in this place ran Caesar's blood through.
See what a rent the envious Casca made.
Through this, the well-beloved Brutus stabbed,
And as he plucked his cursed steel away,
Mark how the blood of Caesar followed it,
And rushing out of doors to be resolved
If Brutus so unkindly knocked or no.

(3.2.169–80)

Here, Antony is describing tears and blood rather than water *per se*. In the next few lines, however, blood and water combine in an accumulation of images of fluids escaping their containers. After urging his listeners to weep and describing Caesar's blood gushing out, Antony goes on to describe the Roman hero's 'mighty heart bursting', Pompey's statue 'running blood' and his listeners 'weeping gracious drops'. He then protests that he does not wish to 'stir [their] blood' into 'a flood of mutiny' before evoking Caesar's gift of orchards by the Tiber (186–249). The cumulative effect of these images of rebellious fluids is to cast Antony in the position of lock keeper, opening sluices, valves and floodgates, and thus releasing the pent-up force of the crowd turned mob.[27] Antony's success in turning the crowd into a rampaging mob testifies to his ability to appeal to his listeners' imagination in such a way as to shape their self-representation. Antony rouses his listeners into action by subliminally impressing their minds with images of liquids bursting through pipes and breaking down dams, so that they have no other choice than to become what is being described. Mental and social barriers are then broken down in a flood of unleashed madness.

There is no such scene in *Coriolanus*, yet a similar technique is employed by the tribunes of the people when they convince the plebeian citizens to rescind their votes in favour of Coriolanus's consulship. In this speech, Brutus, one of the tribunes, urges the citizens to justify their change of heart by claiming that they were manipulated by the tribunes themselves:

Bru. Ay, spare us not. Say we read lectures to you,
How youngly he began to serve his country,
How long he continued, and what stock he springs of,
The noble house of Martius, from whence he came

> That Ancus Martius, Numa's daughter's son,
> Who after great Hostilius here was king;
> Of the same house Publius and Quintus were,
> That our best water brought by conduits hither;
>
> (2.3.235–42)

The literal 'conduits' resonates with the metaphorical 'spring', creating a smooth rhetoric wherein the hero's lineage, the city's pipes, and perhaps the tribune's own flow of words are tightly bound together. As a means of persuasion, however, Brutus's praise of Coriolanus's water-engineering ancestors is a bit puzzling, as it is likely to work the way Brutus encourages the citizens to claim it worked, by convincing them to support Coriolanus. Brutus's strategy only becomes clear a few lines later, when Sicinius describes the citizens' progression to the Capitol, where Coriolanus's fate will be decided:

> *Sic.* To th'Capitol, come.
> We will be there before the stream o'th'people,
> And this shall seem, as partly 'tis, their own,
> Which we have goaded onward.
>
> (2.3.260–3)

The word 'stream' suggests that the people have internalised the water-engineering imagery developed by Brutus and are prepared to be channelled in a smooth flow. While *Julius Caesar*'s Antony unleashed a flood, *Coriolanus*'s Brutus organises a shapeless crowd into a purposeful group.

There is a clear meta-dramatic dimension to the tribune's speech. Brutus is telling the Roman people a historical tale, and *Coriolanus* is a historical play. The plebs' fascination with Brutus's 'best water' history may thus be taken as a *mise en abyme* of the London audience's fascination with Shakespeare's historical play. But Brutus's speech is part of that play, which means that the audience is being encouraged to see an image of itself in the Roman crowd's fascination with water systems. Possibly, Shakespeare is tapping into his audience's excitement about the New River plan, relying on the London crowd to project its emotions onto the Roman plebs. It is, of course, quite natural that a people should celebrate the water that sustains life. But, given that the plebeians' response is to vote against rather than for the water bringer, the episode raises the question of why Brutus's imagery has such a hypnotic effect, a question best tackled through the figure of the Hydra.

The Hydra as a Figure of Fascination

The Hydra figure is first introduced as 'the many-headed multitude' (2.3.16–17), which later becomes 'the beast with many heads' (4.1.1–2). Though these monster images contain no explicit water association, they affect the crowd's imagination in the same way as the previously discussed water imagery. Comparing Coriolanus's beast metaphor to Iago's description of Othello as an 'old black ram', Wiegandt argues for a similar effect on the listener of the two images:

> Iago and Coriolanus cause and reinforce an internalization of the animal images they project onto Othello and the Roman people respectively. Othello finally becomes 'the old black ram' (OTH, 1.1.88) as Iago labels him at the beginning of the play, and the Roman people become 'the beast with many heads' (COR 4.1.1–2), which Coriolanus invokes throughout the play.[28]

The idea here is that the monster figure works on the imagination through the power of suggestion. Such appeals to the imagination have been discussed by Todd Butler, who sees the seventeenth century as the time when authors and political figures came to appreciate the power of the image, divorced from *logos*, to move the individual and the masses to action. As Butler describes it, the imagination was 'the faculty that, as [Francis] Bacon theorized, was charged with bringing the future into the present by creating images so attractive to human passion that their existence in the present secured the very future they promised'.[29] In this view, images are a powerful tool because they mobilise the passions. However, this affect-based understanding of the imagination existed alongside a more rational one. For philosophers of the Aristotelian school, the imagination was the faculty that processed sense impressions, or as Deanna Smid puts it, 'the mediator between sense and reason'.[30] The imagination, in this view, is an instrument of the intellect, allowing the mind to abstract orderly form from sense-images. This distinction appears when the term 'many-headed multitude' gives way to 'Hydra'.

Responding to a tribune's perceived presumption, Coriolanus refers to the plebeian multitude as 'Hydra', the mythological many-headed beast slain by Hercules as his second labour:

O good but unwise patricians, why,
You grave but reckless senators, have you thus
Given Hydra here to choose an officer
That, with his peremptory 'shall', being but
The horn and noise o'th'monster's, wants not spirit
To say he'll turn your current in a ditch
And make your channel his?

(3.1.91–7)

The shift from 'many-headed multitude' to the mythologically specific 'Hydra' is significant for several reasons. One is that the mythological many-headed Hydra's fate is to be slain by Hercules, so that the above speech also reads as a threat. The other is that Hydra is etymologically and mythologically a water monster, sometimes referred to as a water snake. The connection with water lies both in the monster's dwelling-place and in its generation. In *The Historie of Serpents*, Edward Topsell mentions that the Hydra's abode is 'the Fountaine *Amymona*', in the marshland of Lerna, and that, at least in Egypt, all serpents are 'engendered by showers of raine'.[31] The watery composition of serpents is also emphasised in Shakespeare's *Antony and Cleopatra*, when Lepidus states that Egyptian serpents are 'bred of [Nile] mud' (2.7.26–7). More generally, Topsell, following Pliny and Galen, explains that serpents are 'of the water' because they are 'cold and moist'.[32] When he deplores 'Hydra' appropriating the patricians' 'channel', *Coriolanus*'s Roman hero is thus playing on the monster's watery nature and origin. In addition to this, he is hinting at the similar shape of the Hydra and the city's network of channels, ducts and pipes. The Hydra's shape, I will argue, is key to its imaginative appeal for *Coriolanus*'s characters and audiences.

Shakespeare's exact source for the Hydra figure is unknown, but Charlotte Coffin argues that the labours of Hercules were known to Shakespeare through a combination of oral transmission, Ovid's *Metamorphoses* (Book 9), and pictorial representations such as Alciato's emblems, Antonio del Pollaiolo's 1475 *Hercules and the Hydra* and Hans Sebald Beham's 1545 *Hercules Slaying the Hydra*.[33] These depictions are worth a pause, as their careful composition sheds light on the way the Hydra's shape conditions its reception in *Coriolanus*.

In the Pollaiolo painting, the beast is decentred, while Hercules, wearing the skin of the Nemean lion he slew as his first labour,

Figure 5.1 Antonio del Pollaiolo, *Hercules and the Hydra* (1475).
Source: Galleria degli Uffizi, Florence.

takes up the centre (Figure 5.1). The beast is somewhat under-whelming, with its dark body merging into the background and only two or three of its heads visible. However, its presence is amplified by the twisting river in the background, whose bends replicate the curvature of the beast's necks. The shape of the Hydra's necks is also echoed by the lion's tail, turning the slaying of the Hydra into an allegory of man's power over nature. The image's impact is based on human fascination with monsters, on the dangerous situation being depicted, but also on the neat com-position, with its repeated pattern.

A different pattern is noticeable in Beham's engraving (Figure 5.2). Here, Hercules, also wearing the lion skin, has teamed up with his nephew Iolaus, who cauterises the stumps as soon as Hercules cuts off the heads, preventing them from growing back. The monster occupies the centre of the frame, with Hercules and Iolaus on either side of it. The river lies far off in the distance, barely visible. Instead of the river, the Hydra's shape is projected onto the trees, whose reticulated branches are isomorphic with

HERCVLES VNA CVM IOLAO HYDRAM OCCIDIT.   1 5 ʙʙ 45

Figure 5.2 Hans Sebald Beham, *Hercules Slaying the Hydra* (1545).
Source: Rijksmuseum, Amsterdam.

the beast's many necks. The trees bring out what Ian Munro has described as the Hydra's 'arborescent' shape.[34] The trees' arborescence, however, is of a higher order than the beast's, with two tiers rather than just one. The trees' fractal pattern thus functions as a reminder of how the beast would grow two new heads for each severed one before Hercules hit on the right solution. The trees may also point forward to Hercules's final labour in the Garden of Hesperides. The trees thus bring in the element of narrative time. Historical time is also present in the introduction of technology. While Hercules's wooden staff symbolises his mastery over both the trees and the beast, Iolaus's incandescent pike symbolises technology. Technology, here, is powered by ingenuity and mathematics. The symmetrical layout emphasises the methodical division of labour between Hercules and Iolaus: as in the Hydra's regenerative mechanism, two heads are better than one. Not only are the trees in the background reminders of Hercules's previous difficulties with the Hydra, but the regularity of their reticulated pattern suggests a broader technological application. These trees, for example, might be chopped down, with the kind of gesture Hercules is displaying, and turned into water ducts for the river in the background, to create a network of irrigation canals or aqueducts. The shape this network would take is illustrated by the Hydra and the trees. Given that this is an engraving, there is possibly also a nod at the artist's own medium in Iolaus's careful application of pressure in the right places. By extension, Iolaus's action stands for the artist's ability to impress a powerful image on the viewer's imagination, also making the point that such an impression requires hard work.

The Hydra's association with mathematics, work and memory is also present in *Coriolanus*. These elements come together when the hero, invoking Hercules, rebukes his mother, Volumnia, for uncharacteristically giving way to despair and bewailing his banishment:

> Resume that spirit when you were wont to say,
> If you had been the wife of Hercules,
> Six of his labours you'd have done, and saved
> Your husband so much sweat.
>
> (4.1.16–19)

Though Hydra is not explicitly mentioned, the water element is present in the reference to 'sweat', as is the division of labour illustrated in Beham's engraving. A hint of the Hydra may also appear in the fantasised two-headed marriage Volumnia is quoted as describing. Also hinted at is the process of impressing an image on the mind. Clearly, Volumnia has carved an indelible image of herself as Hercules's helpmeet in her son's memory. There is no mystery as to how she has managed to make such an impression. Endless repetition over the years, associated with a pleasing image and a neat mathematical pattern, meant she could not miss her mark. The appeal is both to the affects and to the intellect: while the canonisation of Coriolanus's dead father works on Coriolanus's emotions, the mathematical sum pleases his mind. What is pleasing about the Hydra's shape, as appears from these examples, is that it adds structure to a tale by drawing several elements together in a neat pattern. The effect is of a unifying monad or Jungian archetype. For Coriolanus, the Hydra also appears as a proto-Freudian dream-image, one that is rooted in childhood trauma and reactivated in times of crisis.[35]

How would this work for a crowd, though? While the play cannot easily show what is going on in the plebeians' minds as they listen to water-logged patrician speeches, or as they subsequently stream through the streets of the city, the London audience, here again, might fill this lack by projecting the images that were being activated in their own minds. Though, like Coriolanus, audience members might have their own childhood water monsters in mind, they would also share a common image, a civic archetype of sorts, provided by the monstrous network of water pipes spreading across the city.

Water Networks

Late sixteenth-century descriptions of London's water distribution system clearly lay out its reticulated, arborescent organisation. This is the case in John Stow's description of the action of Dutch engineer Peter Morris's pump, which used tidal power to draw water from the Thames and convey it through the city:

> [In the year 1582], a certain German, named Peter Morris, having made an artificial forcier for that purpose, conveyed Thames water in pipes of lead over the steeples of St. Magnus Church, at the north end of London Bridge, and from thence into divers men's houses in Thames street, New Fish street, and Grasse street, up to the north-west corner of Leaden Hall, the highest ground of all the city, where the waste of the main pipe rising into this standard, provided at the charges of the city, with four spouts did at every tide run (according to covenant) four ways, plentifully serving to the commodity of the inhabitants near adjoining in their houses, and also cleansed the channels of the street towards Bishopsgate, Aldgate, the bridge, and the Stockes' market.[36]

By 1608, the year *Coriolanus* was first performed, the system had taken on an even more densely reticulated form. According to Jenner, 'the piped water supplies' of the private water companies that emerged in the early seventeenth century were 'the first network technologies, binding thousands of households into a common system'.[37] Reading Stow's survey, one is likewise struck by the connectedness such networks imply. As water from the river or one of the springs outside the city found its way to the city's conduit heads, and then via water bearers to private homes, or was pumped to the homes of wealthy citizens via quills attached to greater conduits, the city's households became part of a broad network, a great beast that lived and breathed with the tides.

With their own water monsters in mind, the London audience would have supplied the mental dynamics by which Hydra and water distribution imagery reinforce each other in the plebeians' minds, yielding a pattern that has the force of an archetype. Awareness of their own Hydra-shaped water network might also have led the London audience to recognise a water image in the third citizen's reaction to Coriolanus describing the people as the 'many-headed multitude':

> We have been called so of many, not that our heads are some brown, some black, some abram, some bald, but that our wits are so diversly coloured; and truly I think if all our wits were to issue out of one skull, they would fly east, west, north, south, and their consent of one direct way should be at once to all the points of the compass. (2.3.18–24)

The third citizen misunderstands 'many' as meaning 'diverse' rather than 'numerous'. This leads him to develop his own version of the Hydra image. No longer an ugly monster, the 'many-headed multitude' is now a graceful 'four-spout[ed]' fountain, sending off sprays in the cardinal directions. The Hydra-shaped fountain, in turn, becomes an image of thought: one head sending its 'wits' off in every direction can be read as a spatialised rendition of the exploratory nature of thought. In the process, the crowd has been reduced to one individual. The many heads of the crowd are now the many wits of one head. Here, the third citizen is demonstrating how the Hydra image can be repurposed by extracting form from matter. It is through this process of abstraction that the water monster goes from being an image impressed on the mind to an image of the mind in action.

The Hydra as a Structure of Thought

As in the painting and engraving discussed above, the Hydra's arborescent or fractal motif is scattered all over the play-text. In places, the pattern is described in detail, as with Menenius's evocation of the body's 'strongest nerves and small inferior veins' (1.1.138). Elsewhere, it is evoked in passing, as when characters mention 'rakes' (1.1.23), Neptune's 'trident' (3.1.255), or the 'viper's' (263) forked tongue. In yet other instances, the pattern is only implied, as in Brutus's above-discussed reference to Rome's water system, or in Menenius addressing a citizen as a 'big toe'. In all these examples, a single stem divides into narrower branches, in an arborescent pattern.

The pattern is not just in the imagery: it carries over to characters' actions, worldviews and speech. As Wiegandt has noticed, Coriolanus speaks and thinks in oppositional patterns, his whole worldview being structured by binary oppositions.[38] In the Roman hero's mind, the world is subdivided into Rome and Antium, Rome itself into patricians and plebeians, and the plebeians into tribunes and the people. As for the patricians, they are subdivided into Coriolanus himself and everybody else. Similarly, Coriolanus sees action as involving a choice between two opposite courses, as testified to by the frequency of the 'either/or' and the 'rather/than' markers in his speech (as illustrated below). In fact, it sometimes sounds as if the eponymous hero's main quarrel with the people is that they do not think as he does. When the first citizen complains about Coriolanus's insults, the Roman hero expresses disgust at the people's inability to make choices:

> What would you have, you curs
> That like not peace nor war? The one affrights you,
> The other makes you proud. [...] Trust ye? Hang ye!
> With every minute you do change a mind,
> And call him noble that was now your hate,
> Him vile that was your garland.
>
> (1.1.168–84)

Though Coriolanus presents the inability to choose as a typically plebeian problem, it is not. Menenius shares such sloppy thinking, as when, indulging in a decidedly un-martial Petrarchan cliché, he rejoices in feeling 'light and heavy' (2.1.180). To Coriolanus's horror, even his mother starts urging compromise when she advises him to reconcile his Roman and Volscian loyalties. When he eventually gives in to such thinking, Coriolanus's speech is appropriately full of images of shapeless water, as 'icicle' (5.3.65) and 'snow' (66) give way to 'melt[ing]' (5.3.27), 'sea' (75) and tears (197).[39] Not only do patricians lapse into compromise, but the plebeians are perfectly capable of structuring their thoughts along neat fractal lines. This appears when they organise the repeal of their previous votes in favour of Coriolanus. Though Coriolanus later characterises the repeal as another example of the people's muddled thinking, they go about it in a very organised fashion:

3. Cit. He's not confirmed, we may deny him yet.
2. Cit. And will deny him.
   I'll have five hundred voices of that sound.
1. Cit. I twice five hundred, and their friends to piece'em.

(2.3.209–12)

The citizens are using a Hydra pattern as the template for their canvassing: the flow of information from the second and first citizens, the two 'heads' of the operation, will subdivide into five hundred sub-heads as it reaches a second tier of citizens, then branch out again when it reaches the third tier. As this episode comes shortly after Coriolanus has called the people the 'many-headed multitude' (16–17), their neat thinking might be seen as resulting from an internalisation of Coriolanus's Hydra speech. Conversely, it could be seen as an inherent pattern of thought, something ingrained in every human. The latter interpretation is in keeping with a late humanist pedagogical movement that swept through Europe and was spearheaded by Peter Ramus.

Ramist Arborescences

Pierre de la Ramée, known as Peter Ramus, was a French reformer who taught philosophy, mathematics and rhetoric, all of which he grounded in logic. A Protestant and something of an iconoclast, Ramus was suspicious of a Neoplatonic trend that encouraged using striking images as stimulants for memory. Instead, he promoted dialectical thinking, a means of arriving at the truth by working through alternatives. This grew into his famed 'method' and can be summed up by the disjunctive syllogism, a unit of reasoning that involved a choice between two options. In his *Dialecticae*, Ramus gives the following example:

   It is day or night
   But it is day
   It is therefore not night[40]

Though this is textbook Socratic logic, Ramus turned the disjunctive syllogism into a method of investigation and classification of ideas, from 'the most general proposition to the most specific'.[41] In the Ramist method, thought moves forward through a series of disjunctive syllogisms, each more narrowly targeted than the previous one. Mapping out all the alternatives relating to a topic

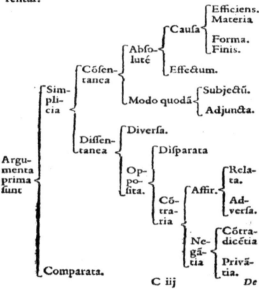

DIALECTICAE LIB. I.   37
CAP. XVIII.
De Paribus.

HActenus de argumentis fimplicibus ftrictim dif-
feruimus : quæ idcirco fic appellantur,quód ab-
foluté abfque ulla omnino comparatione confide-
rentur.

Figure 5.3 Ramus, Petrus, *Dialectica*, Cambridge: Ex Officina Thomae Thomasij (1584), p. 37.
Source: The Huntington Library, San Marino, California. Image published with permission of ProQuest. Further reproduction is prohibited without permission.

resulted in a tree-like formation, which is now referred to as a 'Ramus tree'. An example of a Ramus tree, leading from the general idea of 'argument' to narrower sub-categories of argument, is given in Figure 5.3.

Tree-like diagrams, the aptly named Ramus insisted, were the only way of organising data or thoughts, because it was the natural way, reflecting the design of both the world and the human mind.[42] As Robert Goulding puts it:

> In the case of dialectic, the methodized art is not just a useful way to arrange the precepts of logic, but a representation of the deep structure of discourse, and hence of the human mind, the instrument of discourse and hence the source of dialectic.[43]

This, as Goulding also points out, is not specific to the educated mind. Instead, Ramus insisted that binary patterns of thought were most noticeable in ordinary labourers, whose minds had not been spoiled by exposure to rhetorical excess. Cutting through social boundaries, the pattern also cut through national ones. Ramus's arborescent 'method' was influential in England, having been swiftly taken up by satirist Thomas Nashe and lawyer–rhetorician Abraham Fraunce.[44]

The seemingly universal validity of the arborescent pattern is related to its abstraction. Though the figure retains a tree-like shape, the tree has been reduced to its starkest, purest form. The abstractness of Ramus's dialectic was poignantly noted by Frances Yates:

> gone in the Ramist system are the images, the emotionally strik-ing and stimulating images the use of which had come down through the centuries from the art of the classical rhetor. The 'natural stimulus for memory' is now not the emotionally excit-ing memory image; it is the abstract order of dialectical analy-sis which is yet, for Ramus, 'natural', since dialectical order is natural to the mind.[45]

Lars Engle sees this move towards abstraction as part of a late sixteenth-century paradigm shift. Speaking of the pragmatic turn instituted by the shift to a market economy, he writes that Shakespeare 'lived at a moment when serious intellectual culture was about to take up the abstraction of fixed structures from the flux of experience as its major project', and that 'the move towards decontextualized generalization or abstraction by way of dialectic – Plato's philosophical path toward truth – is a rhetorical one which aims at persuasion'.[46]

In *Coriolanus*, the Platonic abstraction of thought from 'the flux of experience' has tragic consequences.

Mathematical Abstraction vs Embodied Thought

Much of the play's exploration of the relation of thought to the body is developed in Menenius's water and Hydra imagery. Near the end of the play, when Coriolanus is menacing Rome, Menenius takes up his former 'fable of the belly' imagery and offers a Galenic explanation for the hero's persistent truculence. After Cominius's plea fails to sway the vengeful hero, Menenius offers to try his hand:

I'll undertak'd
I think he'll hear me. [...]

He was not taken well, he had not dined.
The veins unfilled, our blood is cold, and then
We pout upon the morning, are unapt
To give or to forgive; but when we have stuffed
These pipes and these conveyances of our blood
With wine and feeding, we have suppler souls
Than in our priest-like fasts. Therefore I'll watch him
Till he be dieted to my request,
And then I'll set upon him

(5.1.47–58)

Persuasion is comically reduced to a matter of hydraulics, in a way that is not inconsistent with the Galenic understanding of the way the body affects the mind. Here, 'pipes and conveyances' are just barely metaphorical; water-engineering imagery is based not so much on similarity as on quasi-identity, as veins are indeed the body's pipes. In this speech, 'pipes' and 'veins' mobilise the audience's awareness of both London's conduits and Menenius's earlier reference to 'the rivers of [the] blood' and the body's 'strongest nerves and small inferior veins'. The network that supports thought is not abstract but identical with the body's own irrigation system, through which the Galenic subject thinks.

Yet the same Menenius, together with Volumnia, develops a very different model when jubilantly tallying the war scars on Coriolanus's body:

Vol. He received in the repulse of Tarquin seven hurts i'th'body.
Men. One i'th'neck and two i'th'thigh – there's nine that I know.
Vol. He had before this last expedition twenty-five wounds upon him.
Men. Now it's twenty-seven. Every gash was an enemy's grave.

(2.1.149–56)

Twenty-seven is a significant number because it can be diagrammed as a three-tiered arborescent system, being the number 3 raised to the third power. The Hydra analogy applies if we allow for a three-headed instead of two-headed growth pattern, as in some versions of the Hydra.[47] The Hydra here is a purely mathematical construct and has no geometrical affinity with the body. In their enthusiastic totalling up, Volumnia and Menenius forget that every gash was not just 'an enemy's grave' but also an occasion of pain and danger to Coriolanus's own flesh. The blood has been drained out of this sanitised reconstruction of the Roman hero's body.

Coriolanus himself, of course, embraces this kind of disembodied thinking, as when he rails at the people whose ignorance 'finds not till it feels' (3.3.129). Yet abstract Hydra imagery leads him to make fatal errors. When, after Coriolanus's defection to the Volscian side, the two generals agree on a two-headed army, half of it being led by Aufidius and the other half by Coriolanus, the idea looks good on paper. However, the emotional complications of such an arrangement are not factored in. When rivalry, jealousy and resentment rear their ugly heads, the 'twin[ned]' (4.4.15) friends are unprepared.

Such abstract representations of thought are reflected in some of the mind-as-water allegories of early modern treatises. Perhaps because the brain does not resemble water in any of its shapes – it was sometimes compared to a walnut – water-based allegories of thought worked best when the mind was considered as quite distinct from the body. Thus, John Donne described the mind as a 'whirlpool',[48] and Timothy Bright described it as a wind-driven water-pump. Bright's mechanistic description was meant as an illustration of the mind's perfection, whatever the frailty of the body, as demonstrated by its ability to conduct several operations at once:

> In water works I have seen a mill driven by the wind, which hath both served for grist, and avoiding of rivers of water out of drowned fens & marshes, which to an American ignorant of the device would seem to be wrought by a lively action of every part, and not by such a general mover as the wind is.[49]

Coriolanus, however, falls short of the cold, unemotional thinking he aspires to. He is in fact highly passionate, as his various outbursts demonstrate. Eventually, when '[h]e holds her by the hand, silent' (5.3.182–3), it is the feeling of his mother's hand in his that motivates his decision to spare Rome. In the playhouse, the fallacy of Coriolanus's claim to abstract thought would have been exacerbated by the audience's own embodied experience. With strong visual stimuli on the stage and bodies pressing all around, any thinking going on in a spectator's mind would have been affected by his or her immediate environment, and by the group movements he or she was caught up in. This interpenetration of thought and environment would have started before the play proper, as the audience filed into the Globe's yard and galleries.

The Audience as Hydra

Dekker's description of an exiting audience as a 'torrent' implies a similar watery analogy for an entering audience. Given the Globe's architecture, the process would have looked something like a river splitting into streams as the spectators entered from two doors, then split at each door into groundlings and gallery spectators, then again between cushioned booths in the galleries near the stage and un-cushioned rows in the galleries further away. Because early modern spectators did not book their tickets in advance, they would have had to make decisions as they moved along with the crowd. Basing his description on the report of Thomas Platter, a Swiss visitor attending a 1599 performance at the Curtain, Andrew Gurr gives the following impression of an early modern spectator choosing a place in the playhouse:

> You went in by the entrance door directly to the yard, as you would entering a coaching innyard through its great double gates. Once in the yard you could choose to enter the galleries for a seat, and if you wanted more privacy and a cushion you could pay once again for a room in the galleries closest to the stage. This arrangement [was] a sequence of choices.[50]

Though the choices may have been determined by the playgoer's purse, and thus worked out in the mind ahead of time, they could also, as Gurr suggests, have been influenced by factors such as how comfortable the seats looked, how crowded the yard was, how companiable or attractive potential neighbours appeared, and other contingencies. In this case, a Hydra-patterned sequence of choices would mark the body's physical progression through the playhouse, mind and body working in tandem.

True, Gurr points out that the organisation was slightly different for the Globe, with a more socially segregated admission system:

> Access to the gallery in these playhouses did not entail passing through the yard. Once in one of the two entrance-ways you chose either to enter the yard or to mount the stairs which rose in towers above the entrance-ways directly into the galleries.[51]

The 'sequence of choices', then, remained. Though this embodied Hydra-thinking – whereby every path taken generated two more to choose from – must have mostly taken place before the play started, other physical processes would have contributed to giving body to the play's aqueous allegories of thought. Platter also mentions that 'food and drink'[52] were on offer at the Curtain throughout the performance. This must have also been the case at the Globe, as testified to by a 1613 incident in which a man was doused with beer after his breeches caught fire.[53] In 1608, an audience member could thus have been taking a gulp of beer while listening to Menenius's speeches about 'stuf[fing]' the body's 'pipes' (5.1.53) and about grain travelling through the body's' 'rivers of [...] blood' (1.1.132). The Hydra would then have been felt from within, giving flesh to the image.

Conclusion

Ultimately, theatrical allegories come into being in the spectator's mind. To some degree, this is true of any allegory in any play. *Coriolanus*, however, is unique in the way it mobilises the audience's memories, imagination, senses and environment to flesh out and animate the Hydra, allowing it to become an allegory of rational, yet embodied, thought. By tapping into the energies of a live audience, the Hydra allegory is removed from the ambit of Platonic abstraction and takes on flesh.

In this chapter, I have discussed audience response mainly in terms of the embodied imagination, which has led me to argue for a representation of thought as both mechanistic and embodied. This is fitting for a Roman play that is mostly devoid of transcendence. Yet *Coriolanus* is not without an elusive sense of the mind's mystery, as when '[he] holds her by the hand, silent'. Silence combines with stillness for a moment of solemnity and suspended action, during which the audience is left to speculate about what is going on in the Roman hero's mind. *The Merchant of Venice*, my next case study, exploits this effect more extensively, resulting in a more spiritual model of mind. In Chapter 6, I will approach the semiotics of stillness in *The Merchant of Venice* through the conjoined issues of performance style and audience empathy.

Notes

1   The chapter title is taken from Norman MacLean, *A River Runs Through It and Other Stories*, Chicago: University of Chicago Press, 1976.

2   Paul Menzer, 'Crowd Control', in Jennifer Low and Nova Myhill (eds), *Imagining the Audience in Early Modern Drama, 1558–1642*, New York: Palgrave Macmillan, 2011, pp. 19–36 (p. 27).

3   See George Lakoff and Mark Johnson, *Metaphors We Live By*, Chicago: University of Chicago Press, 1980.

4   See Carl Jung, 'Psychology and Literature' (1930), in David Lodge (ed.), *20th Century Literary Criticism: A Reader* (1972), London and New York: Longman, 1995, pp. 174–88 (p. 184).

5   R. B. Parker, in William Shakespeare, *Coriolanus*, ed. R. B. Parker (1994), The Oxford Shakespeare, Oxford and New York: Oxford University Press, 1998, p. 34.

6   See, for example, Randall Martin, 'Ecocritical Studies', in Evelyn Gajowski (ed.), *The Arden Research Handbook of Contemporary Criticism*, London: Bloomsbury, 2020, pp. 189–203 (pp. 192–200). Martin relates Coriolanus's talk of 'channelling' to the disputed ownership of the River Lea water that was to be diverted to London as part of the New River plan.

7   Mayor of London, quoted in Mark S. R. Jenner, 'From Conduit Community to Commercial Network? Water in London 1500–1725', in Paul Griffiths and Mark S. R. Jenner (eds), *Londinopolis: Essays in the Cultural and Social History of Early Modern London*, Manchester and New York: Manchester University Press, 2000, pp. 250–72 (pp. 253–4).

8   Ibid. p. 254.

9   Ibid. p. 257.

10   See Parker, in Shakespeare, *Coriolanus*, p. 18.

11   William Matthews, *Hydraulia: A Historical and Descriptive Account of the Waterworks of London*, London: Simpkin, Marshall, 1835, p. 16.

12   Jenner, 'From Conduit Community', p. 254.

13   Jonathan Gil Harris, '"This is not a pipe": Water Supply, Incontinent Sources, and the Leaky Body Politic', in Richard Burt and John Michael Archer (eds), *Enclosure Acts: Sexuality, Property, and Culture in Early Modern England*, Ithaca, NY: Cornell University Press, 1994, pp. 203–28 (p. 210).

14   Richard Greenham, *Workes*, 1612, EEBO, University of Chicago Library, p. 490.

15   William Fisher, 'A godly sermon preached at Paul's Cross the 31. Day of October 1591', London, 1592, EEBO, Cambridge University Library.

16   Meaning 'unruly'.

17   Harris, '"This is not a pipe"', p. 210, quoting John Stow, *A Survey of London*, Oxford: Clarendon Press, 1908.

18   Elias Canetti, *Crowds and Power* (1960), trans. Carol Stewart, London: Penguin, 1992, p. 87.

19   Nathan Field, quoted in Menzer, 'Crowd Control', p. 26.
20   Jonathan Cake, in Guillaume Winter, 'An Interview with Jonathan Cake, Starring as Coriolanus at Shakespeare's Globe Theatre in 2006', in Delphine Lemonnier-Texier and Guillaume Winter (eds), *Lectures de* Coriolan *de William Shakespeare*, Rennes: Presses Universitaires de Rennes, 2006, pp. 171–80 (p. 177).
21   John Dougall.
22   See, for example, Menzer, 'Crowd Control', pp. 25–6.
23   Kai Wiegandt, *Crowd and Rumour in Shakespeare*, London: Routledge, 2012, p. 57.
24   Menzer, 'Crowd Control', p. 27.
25   Thomas Dekker, *Strange Horse Race* (1613), in *The Non-Dramatic Works of Thomas Dekker*, ed. A. B. Grossart, London, 1885, quoted in Menzer, 'Crowd Control', p. 27.
26   Wiegandt, *Crowd and Rumour*, p. 85.
27   The word 'floodgate', which had acquired its literal and metaphorical meanings by 1548 (*OED*, 1b), even appears subliminally in the text, in the conjunction of the people's 'flood of mutiny' (3.2.211) and the reference to Brutus and Cassius riding 'like madmen through the gates of Rome' (269). An isomorphic connection is thus established between the vengeful crowd, the city's waterworks and Caesar's blood, so that the mob's pursuit of the conspirators becomes an enactment of Antony's description of Caesar's blood 'rushing out' in pursuit of Brutus.
28   Wiegandt, *Crowd and Rumour*, p. 82.
29   Todd Butler, *Imagination and Politics in Seventeenth-century England*, Aldershot: Ashgate, 2008, p. 59.
30   Deanna Smid, *The Imagination in Early Modern English Literature*, Leiden and Boston: Brill, 2017, p. 14.
31   Edward Topsell, *The Historie of Serpents*, London, 1608, EEBO, University of Michigan Library, pp. 201, 6.
32   Ibid. p. 6.
33   Charlotte Coffin, 'Hercules', in Yves Peyré (ed.), *A Dictionary of Shakespeare's Classical Mythology*, 2009, http://www.shakmyth .org/myth/111/hercules, last accessed 6 April 2022. Shakespeare would also have been reminded of Hercules on a daily basis, given that the Globe's sign featured Hercules carrying the world on his back.
34   Ian Munro, *The Figure of the Crowd in Early Modern London*, New York: Palgrave Macmillan, 2005, p. 110.
35   For the origin of archetypes in dreams, see Northrop Frye, 'The Archetypes of Literature', in David Lodge (ed.), *20th Century Literary Criticism: A Reader* (1972), London and New York: Longman, 1995, pp. 422–33; reprinted from *Fables of Identity: Studies in Poetic Mythology*, New York: Harcourt, Brace & World, 1963 (p. 431).

36 John Stow, *Stow's Survey of London* (1603, 2nd edn), London: J.M. Dent and Sons; New York: E.P. Dutton, 1956, p. 169.

37 Jenner, 'From Conduit Community', p. 264.

38 On Coriolanus's 'antithetical syntax', see Wiegandt, *Crowd and Rumour*, p. 75.

39 Just as appropriately, he has previously described begging for votes as squeezing his booming voice through a narrow pipe, like water through a badly designed water duct (3.2.115).

40 Pierre Ramée (Petrus Ramus), *Dialectique*, Paris, 1555, p. 110 (my translation).

41 Robert Goulding, 'Method and Mathematics: Peter Ramus's Histories of the Sciences', *Journal of the History of Ideas*, vol. 67, no. 1 (January 2006), pp. 63–85 (p. 65).

42 *Ramus* is the Latin for 'branch', as noted by Eliza Wright.

43 Goulding, 'Method and Mathematics', p. 66.

44 See Laetitia Sansonetti, '"A flat dichotomist": critique marlovienne de la méthode ramiste', *Revue LISA/LISA e-journal*, vol. 12, no. 5 (2014), published online 14 October 2014, http://journals.openedition.org/lisa/6261, last accessed 8 April 2022, § 2.

45 Frances Yates, *The Art of Memory* (1966), London: Pimlico, 1992, p. 230.

46 Lars Engle, *Shakespearean Pragmatism: Market of His Time*, Chicago and London: University of Chicago Press, 1993, pp. 10, 16.

47 See, for example, Topsell, *Historie of Serpents*, p. 201: 'while *Hercules* strucke off one of these heads, there euer arose two or three more in the roome thereof'.

48 John Donne, 'Sermon 70, preached at Whitehall April 8th, 1621', in *The Works of John Donne, D.D., Dean of Saint Paul's, 1621–1631*, ed. Henry Alford, London: John. W. Parker, 1839, pp. 245–61 (p. 256).

49 Timothy Bright, *A Treatise of Melancholy*, London, 1586, EEBO, The Huntington Library, pp. 66–7. The 'ignorant' American Bright refers to would be a Native American.

50 Andrew Gurr, *Playgoing in Shakespeare's London* (1987), Cambridge: Cambridge University Press, 1996, p. 16.

51 Ibid. pp. 17–18.

52 Thomas Platter, quoted in Andrew Gurr, *The Shakespearean Stage 1574–1642*, Cambridge: Cambridge University Press, 1970, p. 142.

53 This took place during the 1613 fire that destroyed the Globe theatre. Mentioned in Barry Day, *This Wooden 'O': Shakespeare's Globe Reborn* (1996), London: Oberon Books, 1997, p. 15.

Chapter 6

Histrionics, Restraint and Empathy in *The Merchant of Venice*

Because there is frustratingly scant evidence about early modern performance styles, scholars have looked for clues in the plays' own meta-theatrical commentaries, such as Hamlet's diatribe against ham actors who 'tear a passion to totters' (3.2.9–10), or in rare contemporary illustrations of early modern performances, such as Henry Peacham's *Titus Andronicus* sketch in the Longleat manuscript.[1] The 1997 Shakespeare's Globe and the attending Original Practices project has also offered scholars the opportunity to test various hypotheses about early modern acting, at least to the extent that performance style is conditioned by a playhouse's architecture. These approaches have led to diverging conclusions, which John Wesley summed up in his 2017 article on gesture.[2] Andrew Gurr, for example, believes that the turn of the seventeenth century marked a shift from 'academic' or 'formal' acting to a more 'naturalistic' style. For others, including Peter Thomson and Farah Karim-Cooper, there is evidence of 'formal and natural styles'[3] coexisting. Wesley himself, pointing to a rhetorical tradition of envisaging conventional gestures as stabilised versions of naturally occurring ones, resists the distinction between 'formal' and 'natural'.[4]

The limits of the 'formal/natural' opposition are hinted at in Karim-Cooper's discussion of Dominic Drumgoole's 2010 production of *1 Henry IV* at Shakespeare's Globe. In *The Hand on the Shakespearean Stage*, Karim-Cooper infers from Roger Allam's performance as Falstaff that despite its size and open-air plan, the original Globe did not require excessive gesturing for purposes of clarity. Instead, she writes, '[a]ctors in the reconstructed Globe [...] deploy a broad range of "gestural arts", stillness being as effective in there as immoderate movement; formality as effective as instinctive or what we consider to be "natural" movement.'[5]

The insight is extremely valuable, but the inverted commas and caveats around the word 'natural' are telling. One of the problems with the concept of 'natural' appears in early modern attempts to reconcile the 'decorous' and the 'natural', as in this *locus classicus* of performance theory, Hamlet's advice to the players:

> Speak the speech, I pray you, as I pronounced it to you, trippingly on the tongue. But if you mouth it, as many of your players do, I had as lief the town-crier had spoke my lines. Nor do not saw the air too much with your hand, thus, but use all gently; for in the very torrent, tempest, and, as I may say, the whirlwind of your passion, you must acquire and beget a temperance that may give it smoothness. O, it offends me to the soul to hear a robustius periwig-pated fellow tear a passion to totters, to very rags, to split the ears of the groundlings, who, for the most part, are capable of nothing but inexplicable dumb-show and noise. [...] Be not too tame, either, but let your own discretion be your tutor. Suit the action to the word, the word to the action, with this special observance, that you o'erstep not the modesty of nature. For anything so o'erdone is from the purpose of playing, whose end, both at the first and now, was and is to hold as 'twere the mirror up to nature; to show virtue her feature, scorn her own image, and the very age and body of the time his form and pressure. (3.2.1–24)

Hamlet's speech reflects a classical and Renaissance concern with reconciling appropriateness – suiting the word to the action – and restraint. This, however, leaves open the question of why shouting and thrashing about should not be the 'natural' way of representing a violent passion. Paul Menzer has addressed this issue by proposing a performative aesthetic grounded in convention rather than verisimilitude, with the necessarily subjective 'natural' vs 'artificial' opposition being jettisoned in favour of the more objective 'stillness' vs 'motion' one.[6] Drawing on Renaissance treatises on rhetoric and on meta-dramatic parodies of histrionic behaviour in early modern plays, Menzer argues that by the late Elizabethan period, histrionics had come to denote madness or insincerity, while restrained, understated performances could code for authentic emotion. In this equation, the argument goes, suppression of passion paradoxically denotes strong emotion:

> To act well is to perform a scripted stasis, a particular algebra where the absence of x equals y. If real and feigned behav-

iours are ultimately indistinguishable, then to stage the body's suppression of passion may ultimately be the only way to reveal it.[7]

In Menzer's reading, decorous restraint is reconciled with natural behaviour by the character's sense of dignity. By explicitly refusing to kick and scream, the character not only reveals his strong passion but also comes across as a self-respecting figure deserving of the respect of the other characters and the audience. In this dynamic, allegory dwells only partly in the performative stylistic figure whereby the still body codes for emotion. Only partly, for if the character's restraint elicits respect from the audience, then a new layer of meaning accrues, one rooted in fellow-feeling and communal response. This response is what I propose to explore in *The Merchant of Venice*, a play that pits the group against the individual in often meta-dramatically significant ways. My starting point is the vexed question of how Shylock should be played.

How to Play Shylock?

How should Shylock be performed? The answer to this question depends on how one perceives the character, and Harold Bloom, for one, has argued that the present-day perception of Shylock as a pathetic victim of Venetian oppression is probably poles apart from the way he would have been seen in Shakespeare's own time.[8] Performances well received by the public nowadays are those that emphasise the character's dignity, and thus downplay the histrionics. For example, David Suchet's restrained performance in John Barton's 1981 Royal Shakespeare Company (RSC) production was much acclaimed. This preference for restraint is also expressed in Dominic Cavendish's negative review of Ian McDiarmid's 'camp' 2014 performance of Shylock at the Almeida in London, which he compared unfavourably with Patrick Stewart's more sober rendition in the 2011 RSC production: 'Gone is the gravitas Patrick Stewart brought to the role. Instead, we get a stylish, camp, petulant man whose accent gargles (and even Germanises) some of his lines.'[9] Stewart's 'gravitas' in the part, however, was the product of bitter experience. In a 2016 interview with the *Guardian*, he reminisced about a disastrous earlier performance at the Bristol Old Vic, in which he 'raged like a tempest', opining that he 'should have been arrested for overacting'.[10] Reviewing Michael Radford's 2004 screen version of the play, Peter Bradshaw praised Al Pacino for tamping down his usual 'croaky shouting and preening' and presenting a 'cool, considered Shylock'.[11] As for Adrian Schiller's Shylock in Abigail Graham's 2022 production at the Sam Wanamaker Playhouse, *Time Out* critic Andrzej Lukowski approvingly describes him as 'dignified' and 'impassive', albeit 'slightly neurodivergent'.[12]

These calls for a dignified Shylock run on the assumption that *The Merchant of Venice* is not an anti-Semitic play, or at least that Shakespeare expected his audience to experience some degree of sympathy for the maligned Jew. Against this consensus, Harold Bloom, somewhat provocatively, holds that *The Merchant of Venice* is 'a profoundly anti-Semitic work' and that Shylock is a comic villain, to be acted 'like a hallucinatory bogeyman, a walking nightmare flamboyant with a big false nose and a bright red wig'.[13] It is of course no mystery that present-day audiences, in the Western world at least, come to this most problematic of Shakespeare's 'problem plays' with a historical perspective radically different from that of Shakespeare's original audiences, to whom a Venetian Jew would have been as exotic a creature as the Indians that New World explorers described in their journals and sometimes exhibited at fairs. Clues to original performance style and audience response need thus be sought in the text itself.

The play-text contains quite a few stylistic clues to the way Shylock would have been performed in its original production. As Paul Yachnin has observed, Shylock's lines are characterised by distinct speech patterns, most noticeably repetition of short fragments, denoting excitement and nervous tension. Shylock is repeatedly and insultingly compared to a dog in the play,[14] and Yachnin notes that his speech patterns are indeed reminiscent of canine yapping.[15] If the principle of 'suit[ing] the word to the action, the action to the word'[16] expressed in *Hamlet* held for real-life performances, then one would expect sharp, feverish gestures along with the words, possibly modelled on the aggressive head-thrusts of a barking dog warning an intruder away, or alternately on the erratic to-and-fro of a frisky canine eager for a walk or titbit. Apart from this de-humanising evocation of a dog, cues for a histrionic performance are embedded in the text, both in Shylock's own lines and in those spoken about him. For example, Solanio's mocking narration of Shylock's despair at the flight of his daughter and ducats conjures up a comic, gesticulating figure, whose disjointed cries of 'My daughter, O my ducats, O my daughter' (2.8.15) are the grotesque expression of his 'passion so confus'd / So strange, outrageous and variable' (2.8.12–13). This Shylock has all the characteristics of the *senex iratus* of Roman Comedy, popularised in both Italy and England as the *commedia dell'arte*'s *pantalone*.[17] More immediately, though, he is also, as Nicole M. Coonradt has pointed out, an example of the 'Jew as Clown' of early modern drama.[18] The boys following and imitating him in a *charivari* which is a parody of the festive masking Shylock so despises are part of this depiction of a clownish figure of fun. Another immediate source, according to Harold Bloom, is of course Marlowe's prancing and gloating Barabas, from *The Jew of Malta*.[19]

Even less obviously outrageous moments seem to call for a bit of hamming. Let us look, for example, at Shylock's famous 'do we not bleed?' speech, which contains quite a few implicit stage-directions. This is Shylock's answer to Salerio's question as to what use Antonio's pound of flesh will be to him:

> To bait fish withal, – if it will feed nothing else, it will feed my revenge; he hath disgrac'd me, and hind'red me half a million; laughed at my losses, mock'd at my gains, scorned my nation, thwarted my bargains, cooled my friends, heated my enemies, – and what's his reason? I am a Jew. Hath not a Jew eyes? Hath not a Jew hands, organs, dimensions, senses, affections, passions? Fed with the same food, hurt with the same weapons, subject to the same diseases, healed by the same means, warmed and cooled by the same winter and summer as a Christian is? – if you prick us do we not bleed? If you tickle us do we not laugh? If you poison us do we not die? And if you wrong us shall we not revenge? – if we are like you in the rest, we will resemble you in that. If a Jew wrong a Christian, what is his humility? Revenge! If a Christian wrong a Jew, what should his sufferance be by Christian example? – why revenge! The villainy you teach me I will execute, and it shall go hard but I will better the instruction. (3.1.53–73)

Beyond what can be inferred from the repetitions, harsh sounds and minatory tone, the speech's syntax codes for certain gestures. The speech begins with a string of enumerations, which seems to call for gestural punctuation, such as pointing in an accusatory way or ticking items off on one's fingers, as in Thomas Wright's description of angry women.[20] We may also note an insistent use of pronouns. In particular, the recurrent second person 'you' might be driven home with a pointing finger, chin thrust or a threatening step forward. Finally, the speech's emphasis on parts of the body may prod the actor to either use those body parts or point to them. For example, the question 'hath not a Jew hands [...]?' (59) may cue for an illustrative display of the hands, which is indeed how Al Pacino played the line in Radford's film. The word 'revenge', which is foregrounded through repetition and end-focusing, also seems to call for a strong accompanying gesture. For an indication of what gestures might have been deemed appropriate on the Shakespearean stage, we may refer again to John Bulwer's 1644 *Chirologia/Chironomia*, a repertoire of conventional oratorial and stage gestures. Appropriate gestures in Bulwer's list include '*Explodo*, to clap the right fist on the left palm',[21] which Bulwer identifies as 'a natural expression made by those who mock, chide, brawl and insult, reproach and rebuke',[22] and '*Minor*, to shew and shake the bended fist at one',[23] which Bulwer identifies as the habit of those 'who are angry, threaten, would strike terrour, menace, revenge, show enmity, despite, contemn, humble, challenge, defy, express hate, and offer injury'.[24] Elsewhere, the inarticulacy of onomatopoeia ('Ha! ha!'; 3.1.107) suggests a display of pure glee, possibly underscored by jubilant hand-rubbing corresponding to Bulwer's '*Lucri apprehensione plaudo*', which involves 'rubbing the palms of the hands together, with a kind of applause, much after the manner as some are wont to do who take pains to heat their hands'.[25] This gesture, Bulwer adds, 'is an itching note of greedy haste, many times used by those who applaud some pleasing thought of deceit, that they have in their heads'.[26] With such gestures, the medieval hobgoblin of the flesh-eating Jew comes alive on the stage.

However, there are also indications that the performance should not be overly histrionic. If we consider the above-mentioned report of Shylock comically wailing through the streets of Venice with mocking boys trailing him, it should be noted that the visual impact of the scene is greatly lessened by being reported rather than staged. Of course, the actor playing Solanio might illustrate his story with extravagant gestures, but those would be only remotely attached to Shylock's character in the spectator's mind. Another tempering factor is Shylock's explicit rejection of histrionics, an attitude which, as Menzer has argued, would have conveyed a sense of dignity and self-control, or 'mastery'.[27] Shylock's disdain for histrionics is first expressed as a refusal to 'bend low' (1.3.123) before his oppressors, then as a refusal to 'shake the head, relent and sigh' (3.3.15). Though by reducing humility and mercy to bad acting Shylock is displaying his lack of Christian kindness, his rejection of histrionic excess also suggests that it would be improper to play him as a clown. At any rate, that slot is taken by Launcelot Gobbo. The issue is further complicated by the fact that like many Shakespearean villains, Shylock grows more subdued as his hour of reckoning comes upon him. His dismay at Portia's devastating ruling against him is registered only as a pause ('Why does the Jew pause?'; 4.1.335), a stillness underscored by Gratiano's gleeful taunting. Shylock's next lines, devoid of his previous repetitions, jerky syntax and exclamations, suppose a flat delivery, and his 'I am not well' (4.1.396) comes across as textbook understatement.

It seems, then, that cues for a mixed performance – somewhat histrionic but not too histrionic and not consistently so – are written into Shylock's part. How would a contemporary audience have been expected to read and respond to those shifts? A clue may reside in what the play itself has to say about restraint and stillness, and how they correlate with powerful emotion.

Stillness, Motion and Emotion

Corroboration of Menzer's paradoxical linking of physical stasis and powerful feeling is explicitly provided in several of Shakespeare's plays. In *The Winter's Tale*, for example, after Perdita stoically withstands the flow of abuse hurled at her by Polixenes, her lover's father, she reveals that she was brimming with anger all the time and about to explode (4.4.441–6). *The Merchant of Venice* provides an even stronger example of the interchangeability of motion and emotion – both etymologically and conceptually linked at the time – with Lorenzo's emblem-like vignette of rambunctious horses stilled by music. After Jessica admits that she is 'sad' (solemn) at the sound of music, Lorenzo offers the following Orphic explanation, appropriately using horse imagery to discourse upon passion:

> *Lor.* The reason is your spirits are attentive:
> For do but note a wild and wanton herd
> Or race of youthful and unhandled colts
> Fetching mad bounds, bellowing and neighing loud,
> Which is the hot condition of their blood, –
> If they but hear perchance a trumpet sound,

Or any air of music touch their ears,
You shall perceive them make a mutual stand,
Their savage eyes turn'd to a modest gaze,
By the sweet power of music: therefore the poet
Did feign that Orpheus drew trees, stones, and floods,
Since naught so stockish, hard and full of rage,
But music for the time doth change his nature, –
The man that hath no music in himself
Nor is not moved by concord of sweet sounds,
Is fit for treason, stratagems and spoils,
The motions of his spirit are dull as night,
And his affections dull as Erebus.
Let no such man be trusted: mark the music.

(5.1.70–88)

In this speech about the soothing effect of music, it is remarkable that the words 'motion' and 'moved' are applied to inner states rather than to the wild movements described in the first few lines. Furthermore, inner 'motion', or emotion, is correlated with the stillness of the suddenly tamed beasts. The horses' stillness is thus paradoxically a sign that they have been 'moved'.

The conjunction of stillness and powerful emotion can be noticed throughout the play, as when Salerio reports 'wish[ing] in silence that [the foundered vessel] were not [Antonio's]' (2.8.32) or when the luckless Prince of Aragon observes 'a long pause' (2.9.53) before reacting to the ugly contents of the silver casket he has just opened. Aragon's pause anticipates Shylock's (4.1.335), in that both serve to register dismay and helplessness at finding their doom inscribed in the place where they hoped to find triumph and riches. The cases are also similar insofar as little sympathy is extended by the onstage audiences to either Aragon or Shylock in their moments of frozen dismay. The matter of how the offstage audience is expected to respond to such moments is not immediately obvious, and perhaps best explored through a broader pattern of restraint, which I will here refer to as 'character-baiting', modelling the term on that of 'bear-baiting'.

Character-baiting

Bear-baiting was a cruel spectator sport, much enjoyed by Elizabethan audiences, in which a bear was tied to a stake and set upon by a pack of angry dogs. The bear's movements were restrained by the chain, thus making it difficult for it to fight back. In the *Merchant of Venice*, it could be argued that Shylock goes from dog to bear. A ferocious attacker throughout most of the action, he is eventually helpless in the trial scene, where a pack of relentless Christians set upon him, shredding his wealth, safety, dignity, faith and integrity. His dog-like speech patterns have been transferred to Gratiano ('A second Daniel, a Daniel, Jew!'; 4.1.333) and his relentlessness to Portia, Antonio and the Duke, who pile humiliation upon humiliation. As in the bear-baiting pit, the attacks are unremitting and come from all directions. Shylock's restraint in this scene reflects the realisation that he is trapped. With this tense moment, *The Merchant* (c. 1597) anticipates a slew of Jacobean plays – both comedies and tragedies – in which the action revolves around a powerful scene of character-baiting.

I will here define a scene of character-baiting as one in which a character is provoked – deliberately or not – to a strong passion which he or she cannot display, because this would cause him or her to betray a secret, reveal a disguise, fail in an endeavour, or lose face. Like a bear chained to a stake, the character is shackled by the situation, and this translates into a necessarily subdued performance of the hidden passion. Such scenes are a favourite comic device in Ben Jonson's plays. Possibly, the most successful one appears in *Volpone*, when the eponymous old miser, pretending to be deaf, dumb and dying, must remain still as his crafty servant Mosca and greedy visitor Corvino hurl abuse at him.

CORV. [...] Art sure he does not hear us?
MOS. Sure, sir! Why, look you, credit your own sense.
                    [*Shouts in Volpone's ear*]
The pox approach, and add to your diseases,
If it would send you hence the sooner, sir,
For your incontinence, it hath deserv'd it. [...]
Throughly and throughly and the plague to boot!
Those filthy eyes of yours, that flow with slime
Like two frog-pits. And those same hanging cheeks,
Cover'd with hide instead of skin – Nay, help, sir! –
That look like frozen dish-clouts set on end!
CORV. Or like an old smoked wall, on which the rain
Ran down in streaks!
MOS.   Excellent, sir, speak out:
You may be louder yet; a culverin
Discharged in his ear would hardly bore it.

CORV. His nose is like a common sewer, still running.
MOS. 'Tis good! And what about his mouth?
COR. A very draught.[28]

The joke is both on Corvino, who is tricked into insulting to his face the man whose heir he hopes to become, and on Volpone himself, who must withstand an onslaught of abuse without letting slip his disguise. In Jonson's play, this double gulling, apart from the immediate comic effect, paves the way for Mosca's eventual betrayal of his master. The comic genius of such scenes is reliant on dramatic irony, on the scaling of levels of awareness. In Shakespeare's Jacobean plays, similar scenes, also premised on dramatic irony, offer moments of more ambiguous comedy.

An example appears in *Measure for Measure*, usually slotted as a tragicomedy, when Isabella, a novice nun, pleads for the life of her brother, whom the pitiless Angelo, substituting for the Duke of Vienna, has condemned to death for fornication. In a soliloquy, the audience has been made aware that Angelo, whose merciless crackdown on sexual misbehaviour is premised on his own unimpeachable virtue, is powerfully attracted to her. The following passage shows us Angelo leading up to a dastardly proposition, involving Isabella's agreeing to sleep with him in exchange for her brother's life:

> *Ang.* Admit [...] that there were
>   No earthly means to save him, but that either
>   You must lay down the treasures of your body
>   To this suppos'd, or else let him suffer;
>   What would you do?
> *Isab.* As much for my poor brother as myself;
>   That is, were I under the terms of death,
>   Th'impression of keen whips I'd wear as rubies,
>   And strip myself to death as to a bed
>   That longing have been sick for, ere I'd yield
>   My body up to shame.
> *Ang.* Then must your brother die.

(2.4.88–104)

The audience cannot help but notice the erotic charge of Isabella's description of the martyrdom she is willing to undergo, even as she refuses Angelo's bargain, and is well aware of the effect it must be having on Angelo, whose desire has already been identified as both strong and involving a measure of sadistic perversity. The audience is also aware that Angelo must keep his excitement in check for the time being if he is to have any chance of sweet-talking Isabella into giving in to him. We can therefore assume that the player cast as Angelo will remain relatively static and expressionless while Isabella speaks. The audience thus imagines Angelo struggling to contain himself, with an inner enjoyment of his predicament given that the deputy is, after all, the villain of the piece.

Dramatically, such shows of restraint are useful in that they display a character's ability to dissemble, and thus allow the audience to take note of how dangerous he is. They also offer a moment of release, as the audience laughs at the villain's discomfiture. Perhaps one of the most interesting things about such scenes of suppressed emotions is that they call for a reconstructive activity on the part of the audience. In order to imagine Volpone's frustration or Angelo's excitement, the audience must extrapolate, using information gleaned from the character's earlier speeches, asides and soliloquies, be they self-directed or addressed to the audience. Simultaneously, the spectator extrapolates the character's feelings from how he or she would feel in the same situation. As stage representation transitions from explicit speech to repressed emotion, the audience is made to enter the character's consciousness and imaginatively recreate his inner life.[29]

The Merchant of Venice displays an obsession with this kind of psychological extrapolation. The play begins with Salerio and Solanio sounding the depths of Antonio's sadness and claiming to know how he feels based on how they themselves would feel in the same situation, that is, if their entire fortunes were riding the waves on the high sea (1.1.8–40). The assumption is that like-minded people all respond similarly to a given stimulus, just as, to use Bassanio's image, a second arrow shot off in the same direction as the first, all other things being equal, will end up in the same place (1.1.140–5).[30] Religious differences do not seem to present a barrier to such extrapolation, and, despite their horror at Shylock's 'Jewish heart' (4.1.80), the Venetian characters routinely claim to be able to guess what he is thinking and feeling, as when Antonio correctly guesses one of the reasons for Shylock's hatred of him (3.3.21–4). Similarly, as Gratiano's taunting demonstrates, it is not difficult for the Venetian characters and English audience to imagine the frustration, anger and defeated despair taking hold of Shylock's being, even as he declares, 'I am content' (4.1.394). As Shylock has made clear in the 'do we not bleed?' speech, hatred, anger and thirst for revenge are feelings instantly understandable by Christian and Jew alike, notwithstanding the prohibition against revenge in both faiths.

The question, then, is whether such understanding is expected to foster derision or compassion. Though one is sometimes tempted to assume that Elizabethan audiences would have reacted with some degree of sympathy for the underdog, Gratiano's taunting clearly demonstrates the difference between understanding someone's feelings and sympathising with that person's predicament. How, then, might Shakespeare have wished to affect his audience with the staging of repressed emotion? Part of the answer may lie in the way Shakespeare and his contemporaries understood and represented the connections between stillness, imagination and empathy.

Stillness, Imagination and Empathy

If we return to Lorenzo's speech about colts standing still at the sound of music, a significant element is that the horses are a herd, or group, which encodes emotion as something that is shared rather than restricted to individual experience. Indeed, the speech inscribes Jessica's impressionistic description of her feelings within a collective experience, shared by all good people and even the animal world. This vision of emotions as intrinsically collective has been identified by Bridget Escolme as an essential difference between modern and early modern understandings of the emotions. In *Emotional Excess on the Shakespearean Stage*, Escolme writes that in early modern England, emotions were 'that which makes one less of an individual',[31] as opposed to the individualising faculty of reason. This collective nature of the passions could make them a vehicle for compassion. Thus Wright, after warning his reader that the passions are 'perturbations [...] inducing (for the most part) to vice',[32] concedes that

> passions are not only, not to be wholy extinguished (as the Stoiks seemed to affirme) but to be moued and stirred vp in the seruice of virtue [...] for mercie and compassion will mooue us often to pittie.[33]

In Wright's account, passion and compassion merge 'in the service of virtue'. In this dynamic, one would expect staged emotions to be a perfect vehicle for empathy, with the represented emotion pointing towards a shared experience and creating a phenomenological link between represented character and audience members.

Such a dynamic of emotion circulating from a static figure to an onlooker is meta-dramatically rendered in *Coriolanus*, when the Roman hero poignantly capitulates to his mother's pleas: '*[Coriolanus] holds her by the hand, silent*' (5.3.182–3). When Coriolanus later appeals to Aufidius, whom he has effectively betrayed by sparing Rome, the Volscian simply answers, 'I was moved withal' (5.3.194). A static tableau expressing powerful emotion has thus caused a spectator to be 'moved' inwardly, that is, to share the emotions implied by the tableau. The thinking behind this process is also made clear in Coriolanus's bid for sympathy:

> Now, good Aufidius,
> Were you in my stead would you have heard
> A mother less, or granted less, Aufidius?
>
> (5.3.191–3)

In this episode, which is structured both as a theatrical performance and a trial scene, Coriolanus seeks empathy by inviting Aufidius, in the position of both spectator and judge, to put himself in his place in order to understand his feelings and thus be compassionate. Stillness, it would seem, is an opportunity for an exercise in mental projection on the part of the audience, leading to an empathetic response.

Recent scholarship, drawing from Renaissance humoral theory and classical rhetoric, has emphasised the imaginative component of empathy in Shakespeare's drama. Leah Wittington, for example, points to the mediated nature of empathy in Shakespeare's *The Tempest*, adducing the scene in which Ariel arouses Prospero's pity by describing the suffering of the three 'men of sin' in their absence (5.1.17–27). Wittington points out that 'Ariel's description of the lords' suffering acts more powerfully than the actual spectacle of them transfixed in the magic circle'.[34] Similarly, Richard Meek identifies a shift in early modern ideas about empathy by tracing a change in the meaning of the word 'sympathy', which first denoted an instinctive and mimetic response, but then evolved to imply a more intellectual one. Like Wittington, Meek points to the role of narrative in arousing compassion, suggesting that 'pity and compassion are complex imaginative processes, rather than simply automatic or humoral phenomena'.[35] Though Wittington and Meek rely on classical rhetorical models, a more convincing source for pity as a process of imaginative reconstruction can be found in Aristotle's *Poetics*, which represents pity as deriving almost entirely from plot. For Aristotle, 'the plot should be so structured that, even without seeing it performed, the person who hears the events that occur experiences horror and pity at what comes about'.[36] In this perspective, whereby spectacle is downplayed and imagination emphasised, a performer's stillness may open up a space for imaginative identification.

Yet, as Wittington reminds us, the humoral/classical approach is only part of the story.[37] In Shakespeare's day, the foremost paradigms of both patient enduring and compassion would have been Christian ones. The Scriptures premise human compassion on God's extension of mercy to sinful man, as in Ephesians 4: 32: 'And be ye kind to one another, tenderhearted, forgiving one another, even as God for Christ's sake hath forgiven you.'[38] This injunction, echoed elsewhere in Shakespeare,[39] roots compassion for others in one's own sinful nature and requires the person extending mercy to think of him- or herself as both human and godlike, in an imitation of Christ. Transposed to a situation of spectatorship, this hybrid state implies a combination of identification and all-knowing detachment, one we can read into many character-baiting scenes, especially those with explicit references to grace, forgiveness and salvation.

Stillness and Grace

In Shakespeare, unlike Jonson, representations of repressed emotion occur in scenes explicitly concerned with issues of divine grace and its worldly counterpart, human mercy. Right before the passage from *Measure for Measure* quoted above, for example, Angelo has briefly considered pardoning Claudio, based on the similarity of their desires. 'O let her brother live!' he cries in a poignant soliloquy, 'Thieves for their robbery have authority, / when judges steal themselves' (2.2.175–6).

Grace is also the subject of a character-baiting moment in *Othello*, when Iago forces drink on Cassio, whom he secretly envies, in order to further his dis-grace. In a soliloquy, Iago, whose rank is ensign, or standard-bearer, has previously expressed anger at being passed over for the lieutenancy in favour of Cassio. Here, a very drunk Cassio rambles on about salvation:

> *Cas.* Well, God's above all, and there be souls must be sav'd and there be souls must not be sav'd.
> *Iago* It's true, good lieutenant.
> *Cas.* For mine own part – no offence to the general, nor any man of quality – I hope to be sav'd.
> *Iago* And so do I too, lieutenant.
> *Cas.* Ay; but, by your leave, not before me; the lieutenant is to be sav'd before the ensign. Let's have no more of this; let's to our affairs. God forgive us our sins!
>
> (2.3.102–12)

Onstage, Iago's reaction to Cassio's claim of precedence – which, we may note in passing, is theological nonsense – may involve a range of explicitness. Cassio's abrupt change of subject seems to allow for some display of anger on Iago's part. However, given that the success of Iago's plan depends on his ability to conceal his envy and hatred of Cassio, restraint is called for. As far as the audience is concerned, no display is necessary for us to understand that Cassio's gaffe has stirred Iago's resentment. If there was any doubt about this, Iago's first line after this exchange, describing a departing Cassio as 'this fellow that is gone before' (2.3.121), shows how much the words have rankled. In this scene, the audience is prodded in two ways. First, Iago's passivity in the face of Cassio's provocation invites us to enter his consciousness and imagine his inner rage. Second, Cassio's drunken appeal for forgiveness, in the name of errant humanity rather than in his own, is an invitation for the audience to consider using this moment of insight as an opportunity to extend compassion towards the villain. This pattern, which is quite common in the late plays, is something Shakespeare seems to be working towards in *The Merchant of Venice*.

Though there may be an implicit association of music and grace in Lorenzo's speech about sensitive horses, *The Merchant of Venice* links restraint and grace more explicitly, and more meta-dramatically, in a comic dialogue between two of the Venetian gentlemen. As Bassanio and his friend Gratiano are about to pay a visit to Portia, Bassanio urges his friend to restrain his 'skipping spirits [and] wild behaviour' (2.2.178) when they are in Belmont, lest his exuberance reflect badly on his friend and compromise his prospects. Gratiano's reply connects performed gravity with grace:

Signior Bassanio, hear me, –
If I do not put on a sober habit,
Talk with respect, and swear but now and then,
Wear prayer-books in my pocket, look demurely,
Nay more, while grace is saying hood mine eyes
Thus with my hat, and sigh and say 'amen':
Use all the observance of civility
Like one well studied in a sad ostent
To please his grandam, never trust me more.

(2.2.189–97)

In this speech, Gratiano constructs restraint as a theatrical performance, as indicated by his emphasis on poses, costumes and
props, and by his awareness of an audience. The speech is of
course a comic one with its twisted logic (a hypocritical performance is presented as proof of trustworthiness) and exaggerated
show of repression. Another comic element is that the context
– Gratiano is helping his penniless friend to acquire a rich wife
– tends to shift the meaning of 'grace' from divine mercy to the
granting of worldly riches. Nevertheless, the residual notion that
receiving grace requires a state of composure and self-control is
present beneath the comic surface, with the meta-dramatic dimension of the scene suggesting that a performer–spectator dynamic
is at stake.

In the examples above, there is always a level of dramatic
irony, involving either the real audience or an onstage audience
or both. In the examples from *Measure for Measure* and *Othello*,
the offstage spectators are aware of the characters' inner turmoil,
but the onstage interlocutors are not. In the passage from *The
Merchant of Venice* discussed above, there is a *mise en abyme* of
dramatic irony, with Bassanio in the position of an ironic onstage
spectator, aware that his friend is putting on an act. In all three
cases, dramatic irony places the audience in an ambiguous position. On the one hand, the spectator is a sinner, like the character
repressing emotion. On the other, he or she is all-knowing, like
God, and in a position to pardon or condemn, be it only in his or
her own mind. The spectator thus simultaneously indulges in two
activities which Portia sees as 'opposite', that is, 'to offend and
judge' (2.9.61). In the case of Bassanio and Gratiano, the onstage
spectator's extension of grace may take a very tangible form, as
we have started to see. If Gratiano's performance is sufficiently
subdued, his audience, Bassanio, will grace him with a share of
the booty – if not directly, then with the lavish entertainment

befitting the friend of a rich man. Such a system of reward for good behaviour follows the logic of Catholic grace. Empathy for villains such as Iago and Angelo, however, seems to call for a type of forgiveness more along the Calvinist lines, prompted not by the sufferer's deservingness but by the paradoxical combination of the spectator's God-like goodness, allied to an awareness of his human sinfulness. And yet the arbitrary nature of Calvinist grace, added to the fact that the villain of *The Merchant of Venice* is a Jew, renders the equation between understanding, empathy and mercy somewhat problematic, as appears through a number of contextual elements.

Ambiguity and Mixed Responses

Interpreting the intended effect of a given scene is complicated by possible differences between our own responses and those of an Elizabethan crowd. Shakespeare's audiences, after all, also enjoyed bear-baiting. Possibly, sadistic pleasure and pity were commingled in the audience's reception of such spectacles, as Shakespeare's characters often hope to elicit pity by comparing themselves to baited bears.[40] Similarly, a measure of pity and 'fellow-feeling' in the scenes of character-baiting we have been discussing may not have precluded a vengeful attitude.

Such ambiguity is on display in the scene from *Coriolanus* mentioned above, in which Aufidius declares himself 'moved' by the tableau of the Roman hero's silent surrender. As Escolme notes, being moved does not prevent Aufidius from going on to kill Coriolanus for betraying the Volsces:

> Aufidius is rarely portrayed as 'moved' in the modern sense of empathetic tearfulness. His response is ambiguous, and in fact he is moved to have Coriolanus killed. Passion is motion/emotion in the early modern drama and often leads to passionate action.[41]

Nevertheless, in the context of Coriolanus's explicit appeal to Aufidius's empathy, it is difficult to take the Volscian's statement as an unequivocal threat. Instead, mixed feelings are suggested.

Whether or not the imaginative reconstruction of a villain's state of mind can be expected to produce sympathy might be considered in relation to two sixteenth-century developments, namely the Calvinist replacement of sacramental confession with private and communal prayer and the growing encroachment of the common law courts on the jurisdiction of the ecclesiastical courts. Along with this expansion, as historians such as Lorna Hutson, Luke Wilson and Charles Spinosa have shown,[42] the common law courts co-opted the Church's concern with the workings of the human soul by displaying a new interest in a defendant's intentions, in matters both criminal and contractual. As a result of these developments, establishing an individual's state of mind became dissociated from the process of confession and absolution, and integrated in a retributive process. Spinosa sees something of the kind in the trial scene, where Portia chooses to read murderous intent into Shylock's bond (4.1.346–62). Spinosa argues that this reflects a shift in late sixteenth-century English law whereby contracts were no longer simply records of a transaction but promises or *assumpsit*, implying an intention on the part of the contractors.[43] For Portia, reconstructing Shylock's state of mind leads not to compassion but to a death sentence, later reduced.

Insight into a culprit's state of mind is thus a double-edged sword, potentially resulting in either – or both – fellowly compassion and righteous ire, in the impulse to forgive and the desire to punish. Such wavering is apparent in *Measure for Measure* where the omniscient Duke's wild veering between extreme severity and a general pardon produces a somewhat incongruous effect. In Angelo's penultimate speech, the Duke's all-knowingness, which is extended to the audience thanks to dramatic irony, is associated with an odd conflation of divine grace and retribution:

> O my dread lord,
> I should be guiltier than my guiltiness
> To think I can be undiscernible,
> When I perceive your grace, like power divine,
> Hath looked upon my passes. Then, good prince,
> No longer session hold upon my shame,
> But let my trial be mine own confession.
> Immediate sentence, then, and sequent death
> Is all the grace I beg.
>
> (5.1.366–74)

As 'confession' is subsumed by 'trial', 'grace' becomes synonymous with power and punishment. In the plays, forgiveness based on 'fellow-feeling', most poignantly dramatised in *The Tempest*, coexists with a more complicated dynamic, involving mixed responses and divided sympathies. Such complexities are in evidence in another part of the *Merchant of Venice*'s trial scene, where a curious variation on the baiting pattern appears.

In the trial scene, Shylock is not the only character holding back his emotions. Portia and her gentlewoman, Nerissa, both in disguise, are forced to stand by (almost) impassively as their newly acquired husbands, Bassanio and Gratiano, make light of their claims to marital loyalty. Portia, in her disguise as the young Doctor of Law, Balthazar, thus hears her husband, in an impassioned plea, protest that he would willingly send her to the devil to save his friend:

> *Bass.* Antonio, I am married to a wife
> Which is as dear to me as life itself,
> But life itself, and my wife, and all the world,
> Are not with me esteem'd above thy life.
> I would lose all, ay sacrifice them all
> Here to this devil, to deliver you.
> *Por.* Your wife would give you little thanks for that
> If she were by to hear you make the offer. [...]
> *Shy.* [*Aside*] These be the Christian husbands!
> I have a daughter–
> Would any of the stock of Barrabas
> Had been her husband, rather than a Christian.
>
> (4.1.282–97)

Hampered by her disguise, Portia is unable to react to her husband's writing-off of her as forcefully as the remark would warrant. Instead, her probable inner indignation is not only registered by the offstage audience but voiced onstage by Shylock, of all people. In this scene in which mercy, though thematically central, is lacking on all parts, a strange undercurrent of sympathy is generated through the proxy of Shylock's runaway daughter, as the play's official villain displays the kind of protective concern that Portia's dead father is no longer able to extend. This undercurrent of sympathy, connecting Portia, Shylock and the audience, runs counter to the main thrust of the scene, which is punitive and vengeful, complicating our response to all the protagonists. An added irony is that in being made to side with the Jew's blanket condemnation of 'Christian husbands', the (Christian) audience is being wrenched from a position of Christian complacency to an awareness of a level of human interconnectedness that has little to do with religion.

Conclusion

In *The Merchant of Venice*, Shakespeare seems to be using the 'otherness' of his Jewish villain to experiment with performative restraint as a means of eliciting spectatorial empathy. I would thus argue against Harold Bloom's contention that any pathos perceptible in Shylock is the result of Shakespeare's getting carried away by his creative genius after setting out to create a stage clown.[44] Instead, Shakespeare seems to have set out very deliberately to see whether he could tap into his audience's belief in Christian grace to elicit sympathy for a Jewish villain, based on an awareness of shared emotions.

The allegorical meaning of the still figure is premised on this production of sympathy. Though the first level of allegory is the correspondence between performed stillness and inner suffering, the collective experience of recognition, disgust and sympathy turns the still figure into an image of the sinning soul in need of grace. Though the dynamic harks back to Catholic ritual and the medieval morality play, it also partakes of more specifically Renaissance forms, such as the dumb show and the emblem. Like Lorenzo's moralised tale of rapt colts, *The Merchant of Venice* follows the semiotic workings of the emblem by encoding allegorical meaning in the interplay between a static icon and its accompanying textual and contextual elements. In addition to creating the conditions of sympathetic communion between audience and character, then, *The Merchant of Venice*'s encrypted subdued acting might have appealed to the early modern taste for puzzles and hidden meanings.

Notes

1 Portland Papers I, fol. 159v (the Longleat manuscript), Longleat House, Warminster, Wiltshire.
2 John Wesley, 'Original Gesture: Hand Eloquence on the Early Modern Stage', *Shakespeare Bulletin*, vol. 35, no. 1 (2017), pp. 65–96.
3 Ibid. p. 67.
4 Ibid.
5 Farah Karim-Cooper, *The Hand on the Shakespearean Stage: Gesture, Touch, and the Spectacle of Dismemberment*, London: Bloomsbury, 2016, p. 90.

6 Paul Menzer, 'The Actor's Inhibition: Early Modern Acting and the Rhetoric of Restraint', in Mary Floyd-Wilson and Garrett A. Sullivan, Jr (eds), *Renaissance Drama 35: Embodiment and Environment in Early Modern Drama and Performance*, Evanston, IL: Northwestern University Press, 2006, pp. 83–111 (p. 84).

7 Ibid. p. 106.

8 Harold Bloom, *Shakespeare and the Invention of the Human*, New York: Riverhead, 1998, p. 172.

9 Dominic Cavendish, 'The Merchant of Venice, Almeida review', *Telegraph*, 16 December 2014.

10 Andrew Dickson, 'Patrick Stewart on Shylock: "I should have been arrested for overacting"', *Guardian*, 22 August 2016.

11 Peter Bradshaw, 'Film: The Merchant of Venice', film review, *Guardian*, 3 December 2004.

12 Andrzej Lukowski, '"The Merchant of Venice": review', *Time Out*, 3 March 2022.

13 Bloom, *Invention of the Human*, p. 172.

14 See, for example, Solanio's reaction to Shylock's insistence on having his bond: 'It is the most impenetrable cur / That ever kept with men' (3.3.19).

15 Paul Yachnin, 'Shakespeare's Public Animals', in Andreas Höfele and Stephan Laqué (eds), *Humankinds: The Renaissance and its Anthropologies*, Berlin and New York: De Gruyter, 2011, pp. 185–98 (p. 196).

16 The same idea, drawn from classical oratory, is expressed in Thomas Heywood, 'A Defence of Drama (*c.*1608)', in Brian Vickers (ed.), *English Renaissance Literary Criticism* (1999), Oxford: Clarendon Press, 2003, pp. 474–501 (p. 490).

17 For Shylock's generic descent from Plautus and the *commedia dell'arte*, see, for example, Christophe Camard, '"Be acquainted with my two zanies here": l'influence du théâtre professionnel italien sur le théâtre élisabéthain', *Les Cahiers de La Licorne – Shakespeare en devenir. No. 8: Le texte-Italie dans l'œuvre de Shakespeare*, published online 24 November 2014, http://shakespeare.edel.univ-poitiers.fr/index.php?id=737, last accessed 17 April 2022.

18 Nicole M. Coonradt, 'Shakespeare's Grand Deception: *The Merchant of Venice* – Antisemitism as "Uncanny Causality" and the Catholic–Protestant Problem', *Religion and the Arts*, vol. 11, no. 1 (2007), pp. 74–97 (p. 76).

19 Bloom, *Invention of the Human*, p. 172.

20 '[T]hey with their fingers number the wrongs offered them.' Thomas Wright, *The Passions of the Minde in Generall* (1601), London, 1604, EEBO, Yale University Library, p. 216.

21 *Chirologia or the Natural Language of the Hand, Composed of the*

Speaking Motions and Discoursing Gestures Thereof: Whereunto is Added Chironomia, or the Art of Manual Rhetoricke, London, 1644, EEBO, Yale University Library, p. 34, image 32.

22 Ibid.
23 Ibid. p. 57, image 43.
24 Ibid.
25 Ibid. pp. 40–1, image 35.
26 Ibid.
27 Menzer, 'Actor's Inhibition', p. 96.
28 Ben Jonson, *Volpone*, in *Volpone and The Alchemist*, Mineola, NY: Dover, 2004, 1.5.55–71. A 'draught' is a cesspool.
29 The real-life counterpart to this, described among others by Baldassare Castiglione in *The Book of the Courtier*, is sitting at a party and hearing a guest unknowingly disparage an attending friend's relatives, situation or sexual preference. At such times we wince, because we know the person, we understand that the remark pains them and feel called upon to react but are held back by the fear of making things worse. *The Book of the Courtier* (1561), trans. Sir Thomas Hoby, London: David Nutt, 1900; Forgotten Books, 2012, p. 189.
30 The point is made in several other places. This principle is what allows Portia (as Balthazar) to say that any wife – if she were not a madwoman – would understand Balthazar's request for the ring (4.1.440–4). More structurally, the doubling of the lovers, Bassanio and Portia on the one hand, Gratiano and Nerissa on the other, is an opportunity to normalise emotional responses and establish them as standard ones. Of course, such claims to read the mind of the other are often manipulative, as when the Duke claims to be able to read 'gentle' intentions in Shylock's mind (4.1.17–34).
31 Bridget Escolme, *Emotional Excess on the Shakespearean Stage: Passion's Slaves*, London, New Delhi, New York and Sidney: Bloomsbury, 2014, p. xiv.
32 Wright, *Passions of the Minde*, p. 14.
33 Ibid. p. 31.
34 Leah Wittington, 'Shakespeare's Virgil: Empathy and *The Tempest*', in John Cox and Patrick Gray (eds), *Shakespeare and Renaissance Ethics*, Cambridge: Cambridge University Press, 2014, pp. 98–120 (p. 115).
35 Richard Meek, '"Rue e'en for Ruth": *Richard II* and the Imitation of Sympathy', in R. Meek and E. Sullivan (eds), *The Renaissance of Emotion: Understanding Affect in Shakespeare and his Contemporaries*, Manchester: Manchester University Press, 2015, pp. 130–52 (p. 132).
36 Aristotle, *Poetics*, trans. Stephen Halliwell, in *Aristotle: Poetics, Longinus: On the Sublime. Demetrius: On Style*, Loeb Classical

Library, Cambridge, MA: Harvard University Press, 1995, pp. 27–141 (pp. 73–5).

37 Wittington, 'Shakespeare's Virgil', p. 98.
38 King James's Bible.
39 See, for example, the wording of Bolingbroke's pardon of Aumerle in *Richard II*: 'I pardon him, as God shall pardon me' (5.3.131).
40 See, for example, Gloucester in *King Lear*: 'I am tied to the stake and must stand the course' (3.7.54).
41 Escolme, *Emotional Excess*, p. xxiii.
42 For a discussion of the foregrounding of *mens rea* and *assumpsit* in common law trials, see Luke Wilson, *Theaters of Intention: Drama and the Law in Early Modern England*, Stanford, CA: Stanford University Press, 2000; and Lorna Hutson, *The Invention of Suspicion: Law and Mimesis in Shakespeare and Renaissance Drama*, Oxford and New York: Oxford University Press, 2007.
43 Charles Spinosa, 'The Transformation of Intentionality: Debt and Contract in *The Merchant of Venice*', *English Literary Renaissance*, vol. 24, no. 2 (Spring 1994), pp. 370–409 (p. 402).
44 Bloom, *Invention of the Human*, p. 181.

Conclusion: Particulars and Universals

Shakespeare's allegories testify to his – and his culture's – infinite curiosity about the human mind: what it is made of, how it works, what controls it, where it resides, how it changes over time. Staging the mind through allegory does not provide definitive answers to these questions, but it does offer a flexible, experimental model, while adding depth or emblematic value to the staged character.

Shakespeare's use of 'grounded' allegory as a tool for characterisation brings with it some of the inherent ambiguities that I discussed in the Introduction. In particular, the issue of whether allegory deals in particulars or universals is brought to the fore. In the first pages of this book, I argued for 'grounded' allegory as being rooted in the material conditions of theatrical performance. To some extent, this implies that Shakespeare's images of the mind will vary along with venue, cast, historical context and other contingencies. For example, the allegorising effects I discussed in the *Macbeth* and *Coriolanus* chapters are venue specific. In other cases, such as the gesture-based allegories of *Cymbeline*, the effect will carry over to different venues. Concerning *Troilus and Cressida*, the choice of textile used for Cressida's veil or mask will affect the degree of deliberateness associated with her blush. Recent productions have displayed great creativity in the use of blush-signifying props, as with Trevor Nunn's use of a red ribbon worn as a choker in his millennial production at the National Theatre. Bridget Escolme notes that in Nunn's production, 'Cressida has various degrees of ownership of the ribbon' implying 'varying degrees of agency'.[1]

In other ways, however, the grounded nature of Shakespeare's staged allegories has a generalising effect. This is especially the case when allegories tap into the audience's collective experience. I made this point explicitly for *Coriolanus* and *The Merchant of Venice*, but it is to some degree valid for all the plays. In contrast to *prosopopoeia*, or explicit personification, staged allegories are not self-evident. Instead, they work by triggering recognition in the audience, based on personal and cultural memory and on an integration of the play's own structuring patterns. This collaborative process adds an emblematic dimension to staged characters' minds, one that is further amplified by the play's resonances with early modern writings on 'the' mind. Of course, as Jennifer Low and Nova Myhill discuss in *Imagining the Audience*, there is a difference between 'the audience', a collective entity, and 'audiences', a group of individuals.[2] The character's degree of representativity will naturally depend on the level of audience integration achieved by the production, or in Jonathan Cake's words, on whether the audience can be made to form 'a collective brain'.[3]

The idea of 'a collective brain' implies transcending barriers of age, class, religion, ethnicity and gender. I have already touched on the way religious differences are undermined in *The Merchant of Venice*, partly thanks to the circulation of empathy. I have also argued for a downplaying of class in *Coriolanus* thanks to a shared archetype of thought. A broader range of processes is at work when it comes to gender. The images of the mind generated by the plays tend to come across as ungendered, partly as a result of meta-theatrical references to cross-dressed boy players, but more generally due to the blurring of gender lines in many of the passages I have identified as involving allegories of mind. These range from Lucius and Portia forming a composite mind in *Julius Caesar*, to Lady Macbeth 'unsexing herself' in *Macbeth*, to Imogen dressing and living as a boy in *Cymbeline*, to the un-blushing Aeneas comparing himself to feminised 'morning' (1.3.229) in *Troilus and Cressida*, to the asexually reproducing Hydra in *Coriolanus*, to the cross-dressed Portia in the *Merchant of Venice*. In these depictions of ambiguously gendered minds, Shakespeare was not going against the grain, at least as far as Galenic treatises were concerned. Though they followed Aristotle and Galen in considering women's bodies to be colder than men's, Bright, Wright, Crooke and Burton more frequently spoke of the mind in generic terms, referring to 'the' mind and 'our' mind. Shakespeare, however, presses the point by foregrounding the ambiguously gendered boy player's body at crucial points in the allegorising process.

To some extent, recent 'gender-blind' or 'cross-gender' casting, at Shakespeare's Globe in particular, may be seen as an extension of Shakespeare's universalising project. If, as Hailey Bachrach argues, gender-blind casting results in gender being presented 'not as invisible, but as something that is performed, not inherently tethered to [...] the person performing it',[4] then it contributes to the representation of the human mind as essentially genderless and plastic. Yet this Butlerian view of gender is complicated by Bachrach's implicit aligning of theatre semiotics and transgender identification. She quotes Robin Craig as writing:

> actors present themselves as female characters and the audience takes them on their word, believing them for the duration of the show. gender in these shows is entirely based on self-expression and identification. you say you're a woman, you're a woman.[5]

The phrasing suggests a semiotic proximity between a cross-dressed actor and a transgender individual, and indeed, Bachrach reports audience members speculating as to whether Rosalind, played by Jack Laskey in Michelle Terry's 2018 production of *As You Like It* at Shakespeare's Globe, was supposed to be transgender. Yet transgender people may not see themselves as 'performing' gender but as expressing their true, biologically determined identity.[6] A twenty-first-century audience, then, may very well take a cross-dressed actor as an allegory of a brain at odds with the body it is encased in, which an early modern audience probably would not. Reception, however, also depends on the individual spectator, as Bachrach herself 'read [Laskey's Rosalind] as a cis woman'.[7] The fascinating question of differentiated audience reception was the object of an as-yet-unpublished survey conducted at the Globe by Penelope Woods, Bridget Escolme and Farah Karim-Cooper, who tested for correlations between audience responses and such factors as venue, culture, language and prior knowledge of the plays.[8] Such approaches promise to open up the field of investigation into Shakespearean allegory by factoring cultural differences into the construction of meaning. And yet, it remains a fact of theatre that a successful performance will, to some degree, transcend these differences and allow its spectators to throb to the same beat.

It seems, then, that despite their 'grounded' quality, Shakespeare's allegories of mind recover something of the

Platonic model, whereby the tenor (or meaning) of the allegorical vehicle (or signifier) is an 'Idea', meaning a universal blueprint or paradigm. And yet the 'Idea' does not dwell in a remote and unchanging realm but depends for its existence on the interplay of text, staging, reception and culture as well as various contingencies attending specific performances. The rich quality of Shakespeare's staged allegories lies in the fact that the processes of producing and interpreting them are partly blended. This is in keeping with Bruce R. Smith's contention that '[p]henomenology does not demonstrate. It *proves*',[9] by which he points to the subjective dimension of the playgoing experience. Where the hermeneutics of the medieval morality play were sturdily undergirded by the eternal values of the Christian Church, Shakespeare's allegories of mind take shape within the time-space of performance, and then, like the 'bubbles [of the] earth' (*Macbeth*, 1.3.79), they burst, only to form again in another place, at another time.

Notes

1   Bridget Escolme, *Talking to the Audience: Shakespeare, Performance, Self*, Abingdon: Routledge, 2005, p. 37.
2   Ibid. pp. 1–17.
3   Jonathan Cake, in Guillaume Winter, 'An Interview with Jonathan Cake, Starring as Coriolanus at Shakespeare's Globe Theatre in 2006', in Delphine Lemonnier-Texier and Guillaume Winter (eds), *Lectures de* Coriolan *de William Shakespeare*, Rennes: Presses Universitaires de Rennes, 2006, pp. 171–80 (p. 173).
4   Hailey Bachrach, '"Gender Blind" Casting: Who and What Goes Unseen?', *King's English*, 23 May 2018, https://blogs.kcl.ac.uk/english/2018/05/23/shakespeare-and-gender/, last accessed 30 November 2022.
5   Robin Craig, (@robin__craig), Twitter post, 15 May 2018, quoted in ibid.
6   According to opinion writer and trans activist Jennifer Finney Boylan, 'gender variance is a fundamental truth of human biology'. 'Coming Out as Trans is Not a Teenage Fad', *New York Times*, 8 January 2019. This is, of course, a disputed and controversial topic.
7   Bachrach, '"Gender Blind" Casting'.
8   See Penelope Woods, 'Globe Audiences: Spectatorship and Reconstruction at Shakespeare's Globe', PhD thesis, Queen Mary,

University of London, 2012; see also Penelope Woods, 'Audiences at the Old Globe and the New', in Bruce R. Smith (ed.), *The Cambridge Guide to the World of Shakespeare*, Cambridge: Cambridge University Press, 2016, pp. 1538–44.

9 Bruce R. Smith, *Phenomenal Shakespeare*, Chichester: Wiley-Blackwell, 2010, p. 180.

Bibliography

Anderson, Judith, *Reading the Allegorical Intertext: Chaucer, Spenser, Shakespeare, Milton*, New York: Fordham University Press, 2008.

Anon., *The lamentable tragedie of Locrine*, London, 1595. EEBO. The Huntington Library.

Aristotle, *On the Soul*, trans. J. A. Smith, in *The Complete Works of Aristotle: The Revised Oxford Translation*, ed. Jonathan Barnes, 2 vols, Bollingen Series, Princeton, NJ: Princeton University Press, 1984, vol. 1, pp. 641–92.

——, *Poetics*, trans. Stephen Halliwell, in *Aristotle: Poetics, Longinus: On the Sublime. Demetrius: On Style*, Loeb Classical Library, Cambridge, MA: Harvard University Press, 1995, pp. 27–141.

—— [attributed name], *Problems of Aristotle*, 1595. EEBO. Bodleian Library.

Ascham, Roger, *The Scholemaster* (1570), in *English Works*, ed. William Aldis Wright, Cambridge: Cambridge University Press, 1904.

Astington, John H., 'Actors and the Body: Meta-theatrical Rhetoric in Shakespeare', *Gesture*, vol. 6, no. 2 (2006), pp. 241–59.

Aurelius, Marcus, *Meditations* (AD 167), trans. Meric Casaubon, London, 1634.

Austin, J. L., *How to Do Things with Words*, The William James Lectures, Cambridge, MA: Harvard University Press, 1962.

Bachrach, Hailey, '"Gender Blind" Casting: Who and What Goes Unseen?', *King's English*, 23 May 2018, https://blogs.kcl.ac.uk/english/2018/05/23/shakespeare-and-gender/, last accessed 11 April 2022.

Balizet, Ariane M., *Blood and Home in Early Modern Drama: Domestic Identity on the Renaissance Stage*, Abingdon and New York: Routledge, 2014.

Beaumont, Francis and John Fletcher, *The Woman-Hater*, 1607. EEBO. The Huntington Library.

Belsey, Catherine, *Why Shakespeare?*, Basingstoke: Palgrave Macmillan, 2007.

Bettelheim, Bruno, *The Meaning and Importance of Fairy Tales*, New York: Alfred A. Knopf, 1976.

Bickley, Pamela and Jenny Stevens, *Shakespeare and Early Modern Drama:*

Text and Performance, The Arden Shakespeare, London: Bloomsbury, 2016.

Bloom, Harold, *Shakespeare and the Invention of the Human*, New York: Riverhead, 1998.

Bond, Katherine, 'Fashioned with Marvellous Skill: Veils and the Costume Books of Sixteenth-century Europe', in S. Burghartz, L. Burkart, C. Göttler and U. Rublack (eds), *Materialized Identities in Early Modern Culture, 1450–1750: Objects, Affects, Effects*, Amsterdam: Amsterdam University Press, 2021, pp. 325–68.

Boughner, Daniel C., 'The Psychology of Memory in Spenser's *Faerie Queene*', *PMLA*, vol. 47, no. 1 (March 1932), pp. 89–96.

Boylan, Jennifer Finney, 'Coming Out as Trans is Not a Teenage Fad', *New York Times*, 8 January 2019.

Bradshaw, Peter, 'Film: The Merchant of Venice', film review, *Guardian*, 3 December 2004.

Brennan, Anthony S., '"That Within Which Passes Show": The Function of the Chorus in *Henry V*', *Philological Quarterly*, vol. 58, no. 1 (Winter 1979), pp. 40–52.

Bright, Timothy, *A Treatise of Melancholy*, London, 1586. EEBO. The Huntington Library.

Brunschwig, Hieronymus, *The noble experyence of the handie warke of surgeri*, London, 1561. Proquest.

Bryskett, Lodowick, *A Discourse of Civil Life*, London, 1606. EEBO. The British Library.

Bullough, Geoffrey (ed.), *Narrative and Dramatic Sources of Shakespeare. Volume V, The Roman Plays: Julius Caesar, Antony and Cleopatra, Coriolanus*, London: Routledge and Kegan Paul, 1964.

——, *Narrative and Dramatic Sources of Shakespeare. Volume VII, Major Tragedies: Hamlet, Othello, King Lear, Macbeth*, London: Routledge and Kegan Paul, 1975.

Bulwer, John, *Chirologia or the Natural Language of the Hand, Composed of the Speaking Motions and Discoursing Gestures Thereof: Whereunto is Added Chironomia, or the Art of Manual Rhetoricke*, London, 1644. EEBO. Yale University Library.

Burton, Robert, *The Anatomy of Melancholy* (1621), London: Longman, 1827.

Butler, Todd, *Imagination and Politics in Seventeenth-century England*, Aldershot: Ashgate, 2008.

Calvin, Jean, *A commentarie of Iohn Caluine, vpon the first booke of Moses called Genesis*, trans. Thomas Tymme, 1578. The Huntington Library.

——, *The Institution of Christian Religion*, trans. Thomas Norton (from the 1536 Latin edn), London, 1634. EEBO. Harvard University Library.

——, *Sermons of M. Iohn Calvin, upon the X Commandementes of the Lawe*, trans. John Harison, London, 1579. EEBO. The Huntington Library.

Camard, Christophe, '"Be acquainted with my two zanies here": l'influence du théâtre professionnel italien sur le théâtre élisabéthain', *Les Cahiers de La Licorne – Shakespeare en devenir. No. 8: Le texte-Italie dans l'œuvre de Shakespeare*, published online 24 November 2014, http://shakespeare.edel.univ-poitiers.fr/index.php?id=737, last accessed 17 April 2022.

Canetti, Elias, *Crowds and Power* (1960), trans. Carol Stewart, London: Penguin, 1992.

Castiglione, Baldassare, *The Book of the Courtier* (1561), trans. Sir Thomas Hoby, London: David Nutt, 1900; Forgotten Books, 2012.

Cavendish, Dominic, 'The Merchant of Venice, Almeida review', *Telegraph*, 16 December 2014.

Charalampous, Charis, *Rethinking the Mind–Body Relationship in Early Modern Literature, Philosophy and Medicine* (2016), Abingdon: Routledge, 2019.

Charnes, Linda, '"So Unsecret to Ourselves": Notorious Identity and the Material Subject in Shakespeare's *Troilus and Cressida*', *Shakespeare Quarterly*, vol. 40, no. 4 (Winter 1989), pp. 413–40.

Cicero, *De Oratore*, trans. E. W. Sutton and H. Rackham, 2 vols, Cambridge, MA: Harvard University Press.

Coffin, Charlotte, 'Hercules', in Yves Peyré (ed.), *A Dictionary of Shakespeare's Classical Mythology*, 2009, http://www.shakmyth.org/myth/111/hercules, last accessed 6 April 2022.

Coonradt, Nicole M., 'Shakespeare's Grand Deception: *The Merchant of Venice* – Antisemitism as "Uncanny Causality" and the Catholic–Protestant Problem', *Religion and the Arts*, vol. 11, no. 1 (2007), pp. 74–97.

Crane, Mary Thomas, *Shakespeare's Brain: Reading with Cognitive Theory*, Princeton, NJ, and Oxford: Princeton University Press, 2001.

Crawford, Nicholas, 'Language, Duality and Bastardy in Renaissance Drama', *English Literary Renaissance*, vol. 34, no. 2 (Spring 2004), pp. 243–62.

Crooke, Helkiah, *Mikrokosmographia*, London, 1615. EEBO. The Huntington Library.

Curtius, Ernst Robert, *European Literature and the Latin Middle Ages*, trans. Willard R. Trask, Princeton, NJ: Princeton University Press, 1953.

Davies, Sir John, *Nosce teipsum*, London, 1599. EEBO. Harvard University Library.

Day, Barry, *This Wooden 'O': Shakespeare's Globe Reborn* (1996), London: Oberon Books, 1997.

Dekker, Thomas, *Strange Horse Race* (1613), in *The Non-Dramatic Works of Thomas Dekker*, ed. A. B. Grossart, London, 1885.

Dickson, Andrew, 'Patrick Stewart on Shylock: "I should have been arrested for overacting"', *Guardian*, 22 August 2016.

Donne, John, 'Elegy on Miss Elizabeth Drury', in Ralph Waldo Emerson (ed.), *Parnassus: An Anthology of Poetry*, Boston: Houghton, 1880.

——, 'Sermon 70, preached at Whitehall April 8th, 1621', in *The Works of John Donne, D.D., Dean of Saint Paul's, 1621–1631*, ed. Henry Alford, London: John. W. Parker, 1839, pp. 245–61.

Elam, Keir, *The Semiotics of Theatre and Drama* (1980), London and New York: Routledge, 2002.

Eliot, T. S., 'Hamlet and His Problems' (1920), reprinted as 'Hamlet', in *Selected Essays*, 3rd edn, London: Faber and Faber, 1951, pp. 141–6.

Elyot, Sir Thomas, *The Boke Named the Governour* (1531), London, 1580. EEBO. The Huntington Library.

Engle, Lars, *Shakespearean Pragmatism: Market of His Time*, Chicago and London: University of Chicago Press, 1993.

Enterline, Lynn, *Shakespeare's Schoolroom: Rhetoric, Discipline, Emotion*, Philadelphia: University of Pennsylvania Press, 2012.

Escolme, Bridget, *Emotional Excess on the Shakespearean Stage: Passion's Slaves*, London, New Delhi, New York and Sidney: Bloomsbury, 2014.

——, *Talking to the Audience: Shakespeare, Performance, Self*, Abingdon: Routledge, 2005.

Ficino, Marsilio, *Platonic Theology, Volume 4: Books XII–XIV*, trans. James Hankins and William R. Bowen, Cambridge, MA: Harvard University Press, 2001.

Fisher, William, 'A godly sermon preached at Paul's Cross the 31. Day of October 1591', London, 1592. EEBO. Cambridge University Library.

Fitzpatrick, Tim, 'Shakespeare's Exploitation of a Two-door Stage: *Macbeth*', *Theatre Research International*, vol. 20, no. 3 (1995), pp. 207–30.

Fleck, Andrew, 'The Ambivalent Blush: Figural and Structural Metonymy, Modesty, and *Much Ado About Nothing*', *ANQ: A Quarterly Journal of Short Articles, Notes and Reviews*, vol. 19, no. 1 (2010), pp. 16–23.

Fletcher, Angus J. S., *Allegory: The Theory of a Symbolic Mode*, Ithaca, NY, and London: Cornell University Press, 1964.

——, 'Allegory Without Ideas', in Brenda Machowsky (ed.), *Thinking Allegory Otherwise*, Stanford, CA: Stanford University Press, 2010, pp. 9–33.

Frampton, Michael, *Embodiments of Will: Anatomical and Physiological Theories of Voluntary Animal Motion from Greek Antiquity to the Latin Middle Ages, 400 B.C.–A.D. 1300*, Saarbrücken: VDM Verlag Dr. Müller, 2008.

Freeman, Donald C., '"Catching the nearest way": *Macbeth* and Cognitive Metaphor', in Jonathan Culpeper, Mick Short and Peter Verdonk (eds), *Exploring the Language of Drama: From Text to Context*, The Interface Series, Abingdon and New York: Routledge, 1998, pp. 96–111.

Freud, Sigmund, 'Lecture XI: The Dream-Work', in *Introductory Lectures on Psycho-Analysis*, trans. and ed. James Strachey, intro. Peter Gay, New York and London: W.W. Norton, 1989, pp. 209–26.

Frye, Northrop, 'The Archetypes of Literature', in David Lodge (ed.), *20th Century Literary Criticism: A Reader* (1972), London and New York: Longman, 1995, pp. 422–33; reprinted from *Fables of Identity: Studies in Poetic Mythology*, New York: Harcourt, Brace & World, 1963.

Garber, Margery, Harvard Lecture, ENGL – E21, 2007, https://www.youtube.com/watch?v=5Xb0V0kN_Z4, last accessed 3 April 2022.

Gibbs Kamath, Stephanie and Rita Copeland, 'Medieval Secular Allegory: French and English', in Rita Copeland and Peter T. Struck (eds), *The Cambridge Companion to Allegory* (2010), Cambridge: Cambridge University Press, 2011, pp. 136–47.

Giglioni, Guido, 'Medical Approaches to the Mind in the Late Middle Ages and the Renaissance', in Stephan Schmid (ed.), *Philosophy of Mind in the Late Middle Ages and Renaissance: The History of the Philosophy of Mind, Volume 3*, London: Routledge, 2019, pp. 41–61.

Gosson, Stephen, *Pleasant Quippes for Upstart Newfangled Gentlewomen* (1595), London: T. Richards, 1841.

Goulding, Robert, 'Method and Mathematics: Peter Ramus's Histories of the Sciences', *Journal of the History of Ideas*, vol. 67, no. 1 (January 2006), pp. 63–85.

Greenham, Richard, *Workes*, 1612. EEBO. University of Chicago Library.

Gurr, Andrew, '*Measure for Measure*'s Hoods and Masks: The Duke, Isabella, and Liberty', *English Literary Renaissance*, vol. 27, no. 1 (1997), pp. 89–105.

——, *Playgoing in Shakespeare's London* (1987), Cambridge: Cambridge University Press, 1996.

——, *The Shakespearean Stage 1574–1642*, Cambridge: Cambridge University Press, 1970.

—— and Mariko Ichikawa, *Staging in Shakespeare's Theatres* (2000), Oxford: Oxford University Press, 2013.

Harris, Jonathan Gil, '"This is not a pipe": Water Supply, Incontinent Sources, and the Leaky Body Politic', in Richard Burt and John Michael Archer (eds), *Enclosure Acts: Sexuality, Property, and Culture in Early Modern England*, Ithaca, NY: Cornell University Press, 1994, pp. 203–28.

Hattaway, Michael, *Elizabethan Popular Theatre: Plays in Performance* (1982), London: Routledge and Kegan Paul, 2013.

Heywood, Thomas, 'A Defence of Drama (*c*.1608)', in Brian Vickers (ed.), *English Renaissance Literary Criticism* (1999), Oxford: Clarendon Press, 2003, pp. 474–501.

Hillman, David, 'The Gastric Epic: *Troilus and Cressida*', *Shakespeare Quarterly*, vol. 48, no. 3 (Autumn 1997), pp. 295–313.

Hunt, Maurice, 'Dismemberment, Corporal Reconstitution and the Body Politic in *Cymbeline*', *Studies in Philology*, vol. 99, 2002, pp. 404–31.

Hutson, Lorna, *The Invention of Suspicion: Law and Mimesis in Shakespeare and Renaissance Drama*, Oxford and New York: Oxford University Press, 2007.

Ivic, Christopher, 'Spenser and Interpellative Memory', in Donald Beecher and Grant Williams (eds), *Ars Reminiscendi: Mind and Memory in Renaissance Culture*, Toronto: Center for Reformation and Renaissance Studies, 2009, pp. 289–310.

Iyengar, Sujata, *Shades of Difference: Mythologies of Skin Color in Early Modern England*, Philadelphia: University of Pennsylvania Press, 2005.

Jenner, Mark S. R., 'From Conduit Community to Commercial Network? Water in London 1500–1725', in Paul Griffiths and Mark S. R. Jenner (eds), *Londinopolis: Essays in the Cultural and Social History of Early Modern London*, Manchester and New York: Manchester University Press, 2000, pp. 250–72.

Jones, Ann Rosalind and Peter Stallybrass, *Renaissance Clothing and the Materials of Memory*, Cambridge: Cambridge University Press, 2000.

Jonson, Ben, *Volpone*, in *Volpone and The Alchemist*, Mineola, NY: Dover, 2004.

Jung, Carl, 'Psychology and Literature' (1930), in David Lodge (ed.), *20th Century Literary Criticism: A Reader* (1972), London and New York: Longman, 1995, pp. 174–88.

Karim-Cooper, Farah, *Cosmetics in Shakespearean and Renaissance Drama*, Edinburgh: Edinburgh University Press, 2006 (1st edn); 2022 (rev. edn).

——, *The Hand on the Shakespearean Stage: Gesture, Touch, and the Spectacle of Dismemberment*, London: Bloomsbury, 2016.

Kelley, D. R. and R. H. Popkin (eds), *The Shapes of Knowledge from the Renaissance to the Enlightenment*, Dordrecht, Boston and London: Kluwer Academic Publishers, 1991.

Kern Paster, Gail, *The Body Embarrassed: Drama and the Disciplines of Shame in Early Modern England*, Ithaca, NY: Cornell University Press, 1993.

Kerrigan, John, 'Shakespeare, Oaths and Vows', *Proceedings of the British Academy*, vol. 167 (2010), pp. 61–89.

——, *Shakespeare's Binding Language*, Oxford: Oxford University Press, 2016.

Kerrigan, William, *Hamlet's Perfection*, Baltimore, MD, and London: Johns Hopkins University Press, 1994.

Kiefer, Frederick, 'Curtains on the Shakespearean Stage', *Medieval and Renaissance Drama in England*, vol. 20 (2007), pp. 151–86.

——, *Shakespeare's Visual Theatre*, Cambridge: Cambridge University Press, 2003.

Kirsch, Arthur, *Shakespeare and the Experience of Love*, Cambridge: Cambridge University Press, 1981.

Lakoff, George and Mark Johnson, *Metaphors We Live By*, Chicago: University of Chicago Press, 1980.

Landry, D. E., 'Dreams as History: The Strange Unity of *Cymbeline*', *Shakespeare Quarterly*, vol. 33, no. 1 (Spring 1982), pp. 68–79.

Lin, Erika, *Shakespeare and the Materiality of Performance*, New York: Palgrave Macmillan, 2012.

Lodge, David (ed.), *20th Century Literary Criticism: A Reader* (1972), London and New York: Longman, 1995.

Lopez, Jeremy, 'Dumb Show', in Henry S. Turner (ed.), *Early Modern Theatricality*, Oxford: Oxford University Press, 2013, pp. 291–305.

Loughnane, Rory, 'Middleton, Gender, and the ur-Macbeth', Paper given at the convention of the Société Française Shakespeare, Paris, 17–19 March 2022.

Lukowski, Andrzej, '"The Merchant of Venice": review', *Time Out*, 3 March 2022.

MacLean, Norman, *A River Runs Through It and Other Stories*, Chicago: University of Chicago Press, 1976.

Macrobius, *Saturnalia, Volume III: Books 6–7*, ed. and trans. Robert A. Kaster, Loeb Classical Library, Cambridge, MA: Harvard University Press, 2011.

Marlowe, Christopher, *Dr Faustus* (A-text, 1594), ed. Roma Gill, London: A&C Black; New York: Norton, 1989.

Marshall, Cynthia, 'Shakespeare, Crossing the Rubicon', in Peter Holland (ed.), *Shakespeare Survey: An Annual Survey of Shakespeare Studies and Production. Volume 53: Shakespeare and Narrative*, Cambridge: Cambridge University Press, 2000, pp. 73–88.

Martin, Randall, 'Ecocritical Studies', in Evelyn Gajowski (ed.), *The Arden Research Handbook of Contemporary Criticism*, London: Bloomsbury, 2020, pp. 189–203.

Matthews, William, *Hydraulia: A Historical and Descriptive Account of the Waterworks of London*, London: Simpkin, Marshall, 1835.

Meek, Richard, '"Rue e'en for Ruth": *Richard II* and the Imitation of Sympathy', in R. Meek and E. Sullivan (eds), *The Renaissance of Emotion: Understanding Affect in Shakespeare and His Contemporaries*, Manchester: Manchester University Press, 2015, pp. 130–52.

Mehl, Dieter, *The Elizabethan Dumb Show*, London: Methuen, 1965.

Menzer, Paul, 'The Actor's Inhibition: Early Modern Acting and the Rhetoric of Restraint', in Mary Floyd-Wilson and Garrett A. Sullivan, Jr (eds), *Renaissance Drama 35: Embodiment and Environment in Early Modern Drama and Performance*, Evanston, IL: Northwestern University Press, 2006, pp. 83–111.

——, 'Crowd Control', in Jennifer Low and Nova Myhill (eds), *Imagining the Audience in Early Modern Drama, 1558–1642*, New York: Palgrave Macmillan, 2011, pp. 19–36.

Merriam, Thomas, 'The Old Lady, or All is Not True', in Peter Holland (ed.), *Shakespeare Survey: An Annual Survey of Shakespeare Studies and Production. Volume 54: Shakespeare and Religions*, Cambridge: Cambridge University Press, 2001, pp. 234–45.

Munro, Ian, *The Figure of the Crowd in Early Modern London*, New York: Palgrave Macmillan, 2005.

Murrin, Michael, 'Renaissance Allegory from Petrarch to Spenser', in Rita Copeland and Peter T. Struck (eds), *The Cambridge Companion to Allegory* (2010), Cambridge: Cambridge University Press, 2011, pp. 162–76.

Nevo, Ruth, *Shakespeare's Other Language*, New York: Routledge, 1987.

Nuttal, A. D., *Two Concepts of Allegory*, London: Routledge and Kegan Paul, 1967.

Ovid, *Metamorphoses*, Book 6, trans. Arthur Golding, London, 1567. EEBO. The Huntington Library.

Parker, Patricia, *Shakespeare from the Margins: Language, Culture, Context*, Chicago and London: University of Chicago Press, 1996.

Plutarch, 'Life of Cato the Younger', in *The Parallel Lives*, vol. 8, trans. Bernadotte Perrin, Loeb Classical Library, Cambridge, MA: Harvard University Press, 1919, pp. 289–91.

Pocaterra, Annibale, *Two Dialogues on Shame* (1592), trans. and ed. Werner Gundersheimer and Donald Nathanson, Göttingen, 2013, https://diglib .hab.de/edoc/ed000237/pocaterra.pdf, last accessed 2 April 2022.

Puttenham, George, *The Arte of English Poesie*, ed. Gladys Doidge Willcock and Alice Walker, Cambridge: Cambridge University Press, 1936.

Quintilian, *Institutio Oratoria*, trans. H. E. Butler, 4 vols, Loeb Classical Library, Cambridge, MA: Harvard University Press, 1920.

Ramée, Pierre (Petrus Ramus), *Dialectica*, Cambridge, 1584. EEBO. The Huntington Library.

——, *Dialectique*, Paris, 1555.

Rawnsley, Ciara, 'Behind the "Happily-Ever-After": Shakespeare's Use of Fairytales and *All's Well That Ends Well*', *Journal of Early Modern Studies*, no. 2 (2013), pp. 141–58, https://oajournals.fupress.net/index .php/bsfm-jems/article/view/6991/6989, last accessed 1 June 2021.

Rivère de Carles, Nathalie, 'Entre texte et scénographie: théâtralité de la toile à la Renaissance', PhD dissertation, Montpellier, 2005.

——, 'Performing Materiality: Curtains on the Early Modern Stage', in Farah Karim-Cooper and Tiffany Stern (eds), *Shakespeare's Theatres and the Effects of Performance* (2013), The Arden Shakespeare, London: Bloomsbury, 2016, pp. 51–69.

Sansonetti, Laetitia, '"A flat dichotomist": critique marlovienne de la méthode ramiste', *Revue LISA/LISA e-journal*, vol. 12, no. 5 (2014), published online 14 October 2014, http://journals.openedition.org/lisa /6261, last accessed 8 April 2022.

Sawday, Jonathan, *The Body Emblazoned* (1995), London and New York: Routledge, 2013.

——, 'The Fate of Marysas: Dissecting the Renaissance Body', in Lucy Gent and Nigel Llewellyn (eds), *Renaissance Bodies: The Human Figure, English Culture, c. 1540–1660* (1990), London: Reaktion Books, 1997, pp. 111–35.

Seneca, *Epistles*, trans. Richard M. Gummere, Loeb Classical Library, Cambridge, MA: Harvard University Press, 1917.

Shakespeare, William, *Coriolanus*, ed. R. B. Parker (1994), The Oxford Shakespeare, Oxford and New York: Oxford University Press, 1998.

——, *Cymbeline*, ed. Jonathan Bate and Eric Rasmussen, The RSC Shakespeare, Basingstoke: Macmillan, 2011.

——, *Cymbeline*, ed. Valerie Wayne, The Arden Shakespeare, London: Bloomsbury, 2017.

——, *Julius Caesar*, ed. David Daniell, The Arden Shakespeare, Walton-on-Thames: Thomas Nelson and Sons, 1998.

——, *Julius Caesar*, ed. John Dover Wilson, The Cambridge Dover Wilson Shakespeare, Cambridge: Cambridge University Press, 1949.

——, *Julius Caesar*, ed. Arthur Humphreys (1984), The Oxford Shakespeare, Oxford and New York: Oxford University Press, 2008.

——, *Macbeth*, ed. Nicholas Brooke (1990), The Oxford Shakespeare, Oxford World's Classics, Oxford and New York: Oxford University Press, 1998.

——, *The Riverside Shakespeare*, 2nd edn, Boston: Houghton Mifflin, 1997.

——, *Troilus and Cressida*, ed. David Bevington (1998), The Arden Shakespeare, London: Thomson Learning, 2001.

Shirley, Frances A., *Swearing and Perjury in Shakespeare's Plays*, London, Boston and Sydney: George Allen & Unwin, 1979.

Skura, Meredith, 'Interpreting Posthumus' Dream from Above and Below: Families, Psychoanalysts, and Literary Critics', in Murray M. Schwartz and Coppélia Kahn (eds), *Representing Shakespeare: New Psychoanalytic Essays*, Baltimore, MD: Johns Hopkins University Press, 1980, pp. 203–16.

Smid, Deanna, *The Imagination in Early Modern English Literature*, Leiden and Boston: Brill, 2017.

Smith, Bruce R., *Phenomenal Shakespeare*, Chichester: Wiley-Blackwell, 2010.

Spenser, Edmund, *The Faerie Queene*, ed. A. C. Hamilton, London and New York: Longman, 1977.

Spinosa, Charles, 'The Transformation of Intentionality: Debt and Contract in *The Merchant of Venice*', *English Literary Renaissance*, vol. 24, no. 2 (Spring 1994), pp. 370–409.

Stow, John, *Stow's Survey of London* (1603, 2nd edn), London: J.M. Dent and Sons; New York: E.P. Dutton, 1956.

Stubbes, Philip, *The Anatomie of Abuses*, 1583. EEBO. The Huntington Library.

Sullivan, Erin, 'The Passions of Thomas Wright: Renaissance Emotion across Body And Soul', in R. Meek and E. Sullivan (eds), *The Renaissance of Emotion: Understanding Affect in Shakespeare and His Contemporaries*, Manchester: Manchester University Press, 2015, pp. 25–44.

Thomas, Miranda Fay, *Shakespeare's Body Language: Shaming Gestures and Gender Politics on the Renaissance Stage*, The Arden Shakespeare, London: Bloomsbury, 2020.

Todd, Obbie Tyler, 'The Preeminence of Knowledge in John Calvin's Doctrine of Conversion and Its Influence Upon His Ministry in Geneva', *Thelemios*, vol. 42, no. 2 (2017), pp. 306–20.

Topsell, Edward, *The Historie of Serpents*, London, 1608. EEBO. University of Michigan Library.

Trevor, Douglas, *The Poetics of Melancholy in Early Modern England*, Cambridge: Cambridge University Press, 2004.

Tribble, Evelyn B., *Cognition in the Globe: Attention and Memory in Shakespeare's Theatre*, New York: Palgrave Macmillan, 2011.

——, '"The Dark Backward Abysm of Time": *The Tempest* and Memory', *College Literature*, vol. 33, no. 1 (Winter 2006), pp. 151–68.

van der Eijk, Philip J., 'Aristotle's Psycho-physiological Account of the Soul–Body Relationship', in John P. Wright and Paul Potter (eds), *Psyche and Soma: Physicians and Metaphysicians on the Mind–Body Problem from Antiquity to Enlightenment* (2000), Oxford: Clarendon Press, 2002, pp. 57–77.

Vaught, Jennifer C., *Architectural Rhetoric in Shakespeare and Spenser*, Berlin and Boston: Walter de Gruyter, 2019.

Vickers, Brian, *Appropriating Shakespeare: Contemporary Critical Quarrels*, New Haven, CT, and London: Yale University Press, 1993.

—— (ed.), *English Renaissance Literary Criticism* (1999), Oxford: Clarendon Press, 2003.

Wehrs, Donald, 'Moral Physiology, Ethical Prototypes and the Denaturing of Sense in Shakespearean Tragedy', *College Literature*, vol. 33, no. 1 (2006), pp. 67–92.

Weimann, Robert and Douglas Bruster, *Shakespeare and the Power of Performance: Stage and Page in the Elizabethan Theatre*, Cambridge: Cambridge University Press, 2008.

Wesley, John, 'Original Gesture: Hand Eloquence on the Early Modern Stage', *Shakespeare Bulletin*, vol. 35, no. 1 (2017), pp. 65–96.

Whitehead, Christiania, *Castles of the Mind: A Study of Medieval Architectural Allegory*, Cardiff: University of Wales Press, 2003.

Wiegandt, Kai, *Crowd and Rumour in Shakespeare*, London: Routledge, 2012.

Wilder, Lina Perkins, *Shakespeare's Memory Theatre: Recollection, Properties, and Character*, Cambridge: Cambridge University Press, 2010.

Wiles, David, 'Place et espace du mal dans *Macbeth*', trans. François Laroque, in Gisèle Venet (ed.), *Le Mal et ses masques: théâtre, imagi-*

naire, société, Lyons: ENS Éditions, 1998, pp. 347–62, http://books
.openedition.org/enseditions/7228, last accessed 24 April 2022.

Wills, Garry, *Witches and Jesuits: Shakespeare's* Macbeth, New York and
Oxford: Oxford University Press, 1995.

Wilson, Jean, *The Shakespeare Legacy: The Material Legacy of Shakespeare's
Theatre*, London: Bramley Books, 1995.

Wilson, Luke, *Theaters of Intention: Drama and the Law in Early Modern
England*, Stanford, CA: Stanford University Press, 2000.

Winter, Guillaume, 'An Interview with Jonathan Cake, Starring as
Coriolanus at Shakespeare's Globe Theatre in 2006', in Delphine
Lemonnier-Texier and Guillaume Winter (eds), *Lectures de* Coriolan *de
William Shakespeare*, Rennes: Presses Universitaires de Rennes, 2006,
pp. 171–80.

Wittington, Leah, 'Shakespeare's Virgil: Empathy and *The Tempest*', in
John Cox and Patrick Gray (eds), *Shakespeare and Renaissance Ethics*,
Cambridge: Cambridge University Press, 2014, pp. 98–120.

Woods, Penelope, 'Audiences at the Old Globe and the New', in Bruce
R. Smith (ed.), *The Cambridge Guide to the World of Shakespeare*,
Cambridge: Cambridge University Press, 2016, pp. 1538–44.

——, 'Globe Audiences: Spectatorship and Reconstruction at Shakespeare's
Globe', PhD thesis, Queen Mary, University of London, 2012.

Wright, John P. and Paul Potter (eds), *Psyche and Soma: Physicians
and Metaphysicians on the Mind–Body Problem from Antiquity to
Enlightenment* (2000), Oxford: Clarendon Press, 2002.

Wright, Thomas, *The Passions of the Minde in Generall* (1601), London,
1604. EEBO. Yale University Library.

Yachnin, Paul, 'Shakespeare's Public Animals', in Andreas Höfele
and Stephan Laqué (eds), *Humankinds: The Renaissance and its
Anthropologies*, Berlin and New York: De Gruyter, 2011, pp. 185–98.

Yates, Frances, *The Art of Memory* (1966), London: Pimlico, 1992.

Productions and Films Cited

Productions

Coriolanus, dir. Dominic Drumgoole, Shakespeare's Globe Theatre, London, 2006.

Cymbeline, dir. Peter Hall, Royal Shakespeare Company, Stratford, 1957.

Cymbeline, dir. Emma Rice, Kneehigh Theatre in association with the Royal Shakespeare Company, Bristol Old Vic, Bristol, 2006.

Cymbeline, dir. Melly Still, Royal Shakespeare Company, first performed at the Royal Shakespeare Theatre, Stratford, 2016.

1 Henry IV, dir. Dominic Drumgoole, Shakespeare's Globe, 2010.

Julius Caesar, dir. Arthur Nauzyciel, first performed at the American Repertory Theater, Cambridge, MA, 2008.

The Merchant of Venice, dir. John Barton, Royal Shakespeare Company, with David Suchet at the Royal Shakespeare Theatre, Stratford, 1981, first performed with Patrick Stewart at The Other Place, London, 1978.

The Merchant of Venice, dir. Rupert Goold, Almeida, London, 2014, first performed at the Royal Shakespeare Theatre, Stratford, 2011.

The Merchant of Venice, dir. Abigail Graham, Sam Wanamaker Playhouse, 2022.

Troilus and Cressida, dir. Matthew Dunster, Shakespeare's Globe, London, 2009.

Troilus and Cressida, dir. Trevor Nunn, National Theatre, London, 1999.

Troilus and Cressida, The Humanities Institute at the University of California Santa Cruz, 'Undiscovered Shakespeare', virtual event, 2021.

Films

Julius Caesar, dir. Joseph Mankiewicz, 1953.

The Merchant of Venice, dir. Michael Radford, 2004.

Index